Think Like an Archipelago

SUNY series: Philosophy and Race

Robert Bernasconi and T. Denean Sharpley-Whiting, editors

Think Like an Archipelago

PARADOX IN THE WORK OF ÉDOUARD GLISSANT

Michael Wiedorn

Published by State University of New York Press, Albany

© 2018 State University of New York

All rights reserved

Printed in the United States of America

No part of this book may be used or reproduced in any manner whatsoever without written permission. No part of this book may be stored in a retrieval system or transmitted in any form or by any means including electronic, electrostatic, magnetic tape, mechanical, photocopying, recording, or otherwise without the prior permission in writing of the publisher.

For information, contact State University of New York Press, Albany, NY
www.sunypress.edu

Production, Ryan Morris
Marketing, Kate R. Seburyamo

Library of Congress Cataloging-in-Publication Data

Names: Wiedorn, Michael, 1977- author.
Title: Think like an archipelago : paradox in the work of Édouard Glissant / Michael Wiedorn.
Description: Albany, NY : State University of New York, 2017. | Series: SUNY series, philosophy and race | Includes bibliographical references and index.
Identifiers: LCCN 2016053167 (print) | LCCN 2017040219 (ebook) | ISBN 9781438467047 (e-book) | ISBN 9781438467030 (hardcover : alk. paper)
Subjects: LCSH: Glissant, Édouard, 1928-2011. | Paradox in literature. | Contradiction in literature.
Classification: LCC PQ3949.2.G53 (ebook) | LCC PQ3949.2.G53 Z95 2017 (print) | DDC 841/.914—dc23
LC record available at https://lccn.loc.gov/2016053167

10 9 8 7 6 5 4 3 2 1

For Nick Hanlon

Contents

Acknowledgments ix

List of Acronyms xi

Introduction xiii

Chapter One 1

A Wholly New Totality:
Glissant's *Tout-monde*

Chapter Two 35

Writing a Caribbean Ethics of Alterity:
Faulkner, Mississippi and *Sartorius:
Le roman des Batoutos*

Chapter Three 67

Teleology Undone:
Tout-monde and *Le quatrième siècle*

Chapter Four 95

Philosophie de la Relation:
Making Sense with Glissantian Philosophy

Conclusion 113

How to Think Like an Archipelago

Notes 135

Works Cited 141

Index 149

Acknowledgments

No work is ever done truly alone, and I owe thanks to a host of people and institutions. The Andrew W. Mellon Foundation and the Fulbright-Hays Program provided generous support in the form of grants. Fond recollections of the institutions that were my academic homes as many of the ideas in the pages to follow came to light in a fledgling form mean that they cannot go unmentioned here: I thank Southwestern University, the Université catholique de l'Ouest, the University of Pennsylvania, the Université Paris Diderot, Tulane University, and St. Edward's University, in chronological order. But most importantly, the Ivan Allen College of Liberal Arts at the Georgia Institute of Technology, where the bulk of this book was conceived and written, made this project possible, as did the encouragement and solidarity of my colleagues there. Many colleagues, friends, and loved ones have offered help of all kinds along the way. In particular, I am grateful to Cecilia Barella, Celia Britton, Ann Coco, Rita Copeland, Alessandro Corio, Joan DeJean, Fayçal Falaky, Kaiama Glover, Nick Hanlon, Louise Hardwick, Christophe Ippolito, Raphaël Lauro, Valérie Loichot, Buata Malela, Helene Meyers, Portia Morales, Lydie Moudileno, Martin Munro, Manuel Norvat, Gerald Prince, Jean-Michel Rabaté, Paulette Richards, Juan-Carlos Rodríguez, Liliane Weissberg, and Shannon Winnubst. A portion of chapter 2 was published in an early form as "Go Slow Now: Saying the Unsayable in Glissant's Reading of Faulkner," in *American Creoles: The Francophone Caribbean and the American South*, *Francophone Postcolonial Studies* (the annual publication of the Society for Francophone Postcolonial Studies), vol. 3 (2012): 183–96. An earlier version of chapter 4 appeared as "Glissant's *Philosophie de la Relation*: 'I Have Spoken the Chaos of Writing in the Ardor of the

Poem,'" in *Callaloo* 36.4 (Fall 2013): 902–15. Both publications gave their kind permission to reprint here. Last but not least, Andrew Kenyon, Ryan Morris, Kate R. Seburyamo, and the rest of the editorial team at SUNY Press, in addition to the Press's anonymous readers, contributed vital feedback and guidance. My heartfelt thanks go out to them.

List of Acronyms for Titles by Glissant

FM	*Faulkner, Mississipi*
IPD	*Introduction à une poétique du Divers*
IL	*L'imaginaire des langues*
IP	*L'intention poétique*
CL	*La cohée du Lamentin*
LL	*La Lézarde*
DA	*Le discours antillais*
LQ	*Le quatrième siècle*
PhR	*Philosophie de la Relation*
PR	*Poétique de la Relation*
SC	*Soleil de la conscience*
TM	*Tout-Monde*
TTM	*Traité du Tout-Monde*
NR	*Une nouvelle région du monde*

Introduction

> The countries that I inhabit spread out like stars, in archipelagoes.
> —Glissant, *Traité du Tout-Monde*

"*Nothing is True, all is living.*" That gnostic proclamation provided the title of Édouard Glissant's last public lecture at his beloved Institut du Tout-Monde in Paris. It also, in something of a ludic gesture, served as the epitaph on his tomb at the Diamant Cemetery in Martinique. Among the last of the long suite of aphorisms that Glissant spent a considerable part of his creative life generating and repeating, that declaration is of course an echo of the classic "liar's paradox": if it is the case that nothing is true, then what are we to make of that proposition itself, or for that matter of the one that immediately follows it? Are they true, or false, or both, or rather something else entirely? Glissant's puzzling, final formulation indicates just how far his thought had come in nearly sixty years of intellectual production. It also creates a dilemma for critical reception of his vast body of work today.

The late twentieth century would hear a near-unanimous chorus of praise for Glissant emanating from academics working in the Anglo-American academy. "A leading French public intellectual," Glissant had, in Charles Forsdick's words, "emerged, beyond the French-speaking world, as an internationally recognizable, some would say 'Nobel-ready,' intellectual" ("Late Glissant" 124). For J. Michael Dash, Glissant was "the major writer and theorist from the French West Indies"; he had, for Françoise Lionnet, "outlined the task of the postcolonial intellectual" (Dash, *Glissant* 5; Lionnet, *Autobiographical Voices* 245). By the time of his passing in 2011 he had become, and rather despite himself, "an ideological founding father, the precursor of a national renaissance" (Dash, "The Poetics of Risk" 104).

In his *Caliban's Reason*: *Introducing Afro-Caribbean Philosophy*, Paget Henry's endorsement of Glissant's "project" of creolization proclaims it to be "the context in which we can envision the reenfranchising of African and Afro-Caribbean philosophies, the reestablishing of their ability to accumulate authority and their capacity for ontological resistance" (88). Nick Nesbitt, in turn, found Glissant to be "the foremost postcolonial thinker in the Francophone world" ("The Postcolonial Event" 103). And Nesbitt would later use Glissant's name as a bookend to mark the end of an episteme, opposite the name of a very different sort of Antillean icon, in his *Caribbean Critique*: *Antillean Critical Theory from Toussaint to Glissant* (2013). There, Nesbitt would hold that "Glissant's corpus is the single most developed and philosophically sophisticated body of work in the tradition of Caribbean Critique" (238).

The argument that binds together the impressive array of ideas in Nesbitt's study bears repeating, however, as it is far from self-evident. Nesbitt shows that there indeed exists a way of theorizing and undertaking critique that can be cogently aligned with the last two hundred years of history in that particular region of the Caribbean basin. There *is*, in short, a Caribbean critique, or Theory, even a Caribbean Philosophy. But Nesbitt's decision to pair Glissant with Toussaint Louverture, the Haitian revolutionary leader who joined philosophical critique with praxis to the utmost degree, is something of a tricky one. What, in the last analysis, do the two really have in common?

Chris Bongie's work on Glissant affords us a possible answer to that question, one that is remarkable for its cynicism. As he breaks from the enraptured masses that make up the majority of Glissant's readers, Bongie sums up the sentiment that has led a small yet vocal group of critics to rethink their estimation of Glissant.

> An increasing number of academic readers of Glissant have, in line with Hallward, understandably registered a certain unease, and even distress, when it comes to his later writings, which, in their espousal of the 'fecund exaltation of the sense of uncertainty' (2005, 219).... clearly align themselves with a non-adversarial 'post-political vision' that has no grounds for 'challenging existing power relations' (Mouffe, 2005, 51). Those who wish to continue representing the writings of Glissant as 'a postcolonial intervention, an insurgent discourse with an alternative sense of nationhood and spatial connection' (Hitchcock, 2003, 43), and to speak

of him as being a 'revolutionary writer[] in situ' (59), certainly have their work cut out for them. (*Friends and Enemies* 339)

If we are to follow Bongie, then, it would seem that by the time of his "later writings" there remained little or nothing at all of Toussaint in Glissant. A turn in Glissant's thought, in other words, would later lead his more scrupulously politicized academic readers to turn away from him. Their disappointment when faced with what Bongie labels Glissant's "indisputably 'highbrow' theory" is to some degree understandable (Bongie, *Friends and Enemies* 340). How, after all, are we to reconcile the youthful Glissant of the 1950s, a hot-blooded partisan of Martinican independence, or the fierce critic of neocolonialism and imperialism in his monumental collection *Le discours antillais* (1981), with the increasingly abstruse and even utopian essayist who could meaningfully, and quite literally *finally*, assert in 2010 that "nothing is true, all is living"?

This book will argue that the increasing prominence of paradox in Glissant's thought from roughly the early 1990s until his passing in 2011 can help to account for that supposed disjunction. Rather than constituting a weakness, paradox proves to play a key role in Glissant's political and aesthetic ambitions. It allows Glissant to pursue his—arguably quite political—goal of using art to breathe new life into thought. In the pages to follow, I will argue that a set of the core ideas in the vast and multifarious corpus of Glissant's writing can best be understood in terms of the author's long-term objective of using paradox to reformulate some of the fundamental categories of Western thought. That undertaking, ambitious enough in itself, was part of a greater goal: Glissant sought to elicit radical change in the world, whether in large-scale political institutions or in human beings' most basic ways of interacting with one another in their daily lives. Plainly put, for Glissant, our world was desperately in need of a colossal transformation, and one that only the philosopher-poet could bring about. As he campaigned for what he called an "enormous insurrection of the imaginary faculties" or for a "new category of literature," his ultimate, utopian aim was to bring about political change, nothing short of the birth of a new world (CL 24–25; NR 96).[1]

The Caribbean was, for Glissant, a wellspring of potential for launching that insurrection. For him, engaging with and coming to understand, if not fully *grasp* (a key distinction in Glissantian parlance), Caribbean cultures and landscapes could elicit change in humankind's ways of imagining and acting. Implicit, then, in Glissant's larger project of *rethinking* basic categories of thought, or of rethinking even thought itself, is the sense that the Caribbean cultural zone can serve as a source of inspiration and at times as an archetype for that enterprise of rethinking. Glissant's reason for according such primacy to the Caribbean lies in what he believed to be that region's unmistakable particularities. A list of them might begin with the geographical form of the archipelago, and move on to cultural and linguistic creolization, or open with Caribbean subjects' search for origins, haunted as it is by the lingering presence-absence of the transatlantic slave trade, going on to the necessarily paradoxical modes of artistic representation engendered by the plantation system's downfall.

In another instance of Caribbean particularity that Glissant cites, the play of rootedness and relation that the tiny countries of the Caribbean have long known so well looks very much like the radical interconnection within difference that is (for him) the hallmark of the (post)modern condition. In other words, Glissant believes that a way of being inherent to the whole of the Caribbean in all of its many linguistic and political forms—a fundamental unity within the context of diversity that is reflected in the title of Van Haesendonck and D'Haen's scholarly collection titled *Caribbeing* (2015)—has much to teach the rest of the world. But if we are to learn from the Caribbean, we must first change our way of imagining (in) the world. If we do not make that change, Glissant repeatedly admonishes, we will no doubt repeat the historical horrors of the twentieth century (cf. IDP 90–91).

Key to Glissant's strategy of bringing about such a cognitive upheaval is an emphasis on ways of thinking that, while they are no strangers to the Western intellectual tradition, have often proved problematic, if not anathema, to that tradition: namely paradox, and in particular paradox grounded in contradiction. As the *Oxford Dictionary of English Etymology* explains, *paradox*, derived from the Greek *parádoxos*, has in modern English come to refer to a "statement or tenet contrary to received opinion; [a] proposition on the face of it . . . [that is] self-contradictory." That bipartite definition communicates two different things, both of which are entirely pertinent to Glissant's thought: a paradox will first and foremost break with preconceived and widely shared ideas, and it may also contradict itself. Contradiction, in turn, likewise proves to be altogether germane to what Glissant has set about doing with a set of his core ideas. From the Latin *contra dicere*, contra-diction quite literally signifies "to speak against." A contradiction is a statement where (at least) two arguments are articulated against one another, or spoken in opposition to one another.

Contradictions lie at the heart of many a paradox, and Glissant's penchant for phrasings such as "saying the unsayable" is impossible to overlook (cf. FM 190, et passim). Furthermore, the modern world has, for Glissant, become a "non-systematic system," one that is most properly understood as an "immobile movement" (TTM 248, 12). But what is it about the Caribbean per se that inclines that region, its cultures, and its peoples, toward paradox? In a number of ways, the Caribbean exemplifies the paradoxical, modern zeitgeist for Glissant: there, subjects are at once rooted and adrift, deeply connected to a place that they inhabit, but also profoundly aware that there is much more to the world than their island. In other words, they are both conscious of the entire world as one, a totality, *and* firmly anchored in the particularity of their own place, which is but one among many. In yet another manifestation of paradox, the Glissantian model of the self truly knows the other precisely through *not* knowing him or her, through acknowledging, even rejoicing in, what Glissant calls the other's opacity. Glissant found that particular mode of relating to the other to be exemplified in the curious intermingling of intimate knowledge and inexorable ignorance that defined William Faulkner's portrayal of his black characters. And Faulkner's literary representations of the postplantation societies of the US Gulf South demonstrated, in Glissant's eyes, that region's fundamental kinship with what he saw as the other creole societies of the Caribbean or Brazil.

Like Faulkner's, Glissant's own novels can offer a staging ground for a paradoxical approach to quest narratives. In a repeated schema, Glissant shows the Caribbean subject's desire for his or her cultural origins, or for a clear and undisputable family tree, to be just as impossible as it is inevitable. The novelistic genre allowed Glissant to present his idea that the *search* for such objects of desire itself holds more creative, aesthetic potential than true attainment ever could. That very process, in other words, proves to be more productive than the product it seeks.[2] Elsewhere, in yet another manipulation of paradox, Glissant's vision of philosophy as manifested in his 2009 book *Philosophie de la Relation* (*Philosophy of Relation*) frames the Mother of all Disciplines as being at its most powerful when it undoes itself, which is to say, when it is non- or other-than-philosophical—in other words, when the philosophical discipline is rewritten from what Glissant frames as a Caribbean perspective.

Those instances of paradox can be crystallized into four ideas that have, to varying degrees, played key roles in the Western philosophical tradition: totality, alterity, teleology, and philosophy itself. Those categories are reflected in the four thematic axes of this book, with each accorded one chapter. As Glissant works to rewrite those philosophemes, now well-worn with age and use, he imbues each with Caribbean-derived paradoxes, gradually developing his own approach to them over the decades. Glissant's rethinkings of totality, alterity, teleology, and philosophy form a conceptual archipelago, a cluster of interrelated, key terms that relate and relay to one another. They do so as his many, and many-voiced, narrators relate the story of his thought's unfolding.

The strategy of taking up ideas that are central to the Western intellectual tradition and reformulating them with a Caribbean inflection is, moreover, central to Glissant's long-term critique of the West. By the "West" Glissant does not mean the physical space occupied by the nation-states that have collectively come to be known by that name, but rather what those countries have done and, at times, continue to do. In his apt phrasing, "The West does not lie to the west. It's not a place, it's a project" (DA 14). That "project" has taken on a host of forms, from slavery and colonial expansion to neocolonialism and what Glissant saw as today's pernicious globalization. What is more, those military and economic moves have their reflections in the depredations of colonial and neocolonial reason in the epistemological register. A, perhaps *the*, example for Glissant of the West-as-project is the French *mission civilisatrice*, the banner under which the French colonial project unfolded. The "civilizing mission" brought about the eliding of the other's difference, via a forceful assimilation into modes of governance, education, and jurisprudence that were somehow very French but also purportedly "universal." If we are to avoid repeating and prolonging history's errors, Glissant tells us, we need to find alternatives to the West-as-project. But in order to do that, it is incumbent on us to work up a different way of imagining our world.

On the other hand, it is crucial to note that the West was not a simple and unadulterated evil for Glissant. As if in response to Audre Lorde's oft-misquoted admonition to the effect that the "master's tools will never dismantle the master's house," Glissant has taken a markedly different tack in his critique of the Western tradition. In fact, he is not concerned only or even principally with tearing down the "house" with respect to which he, and Francophone Caribbean writers more generally, occupies a position of simultaneous interiority and exteriority. Glissant's critical mission, in other words, is not mired in the stage of negation. On the contrary, it is deeply and abidingly concerned with creation, with bringing new ideas into the world, with crafting new literary genres and means of expression, and with striving to open up a space for an unabashedly utopian politics. The tools that Glissant has taken up for that task are paradox and contradiction, and he has begun his own dismantling—and rebuilding—using materials from his own particular place: the place, at once (and paradoxically) one and multiple, that is the Caribbean.

Postcolonial Paradoxes, Caribbean Contradictions

The appreciation that there is something of the paradoxical in the very fabric of Caribbean reality is made manifest in scholarly titles such as Jeannie Suk's *Postcolonial Paradoxes in French Caribbean Writing* (2001) or Natasha K. Barnes's *Cultural Conundrums: Gender, Race, Nation and the Making of Caribbean Cultural Politics* (2006), both of which foreground the idea of culture-as-dilemma. Similarly, in her essay on authorship in the Francophone Caribbean, Dominique Chancé alerts her readers early on that contradiction is germane to the Caribbean condition.

> One of the terms that will no doubt return the most often over the course of this essay is perhaps the word "contradiction." [Contradiction] is, it would seem, at the center of a universe where cultural tensions are extreme, where the shock of cultures and races, of Histories and languages, leads each person to be diglossic, or bilingual, bicephalous, at times schizophrenic, always ambiguous. The Antilles, drawn taught between France and the Caribbean, between their diverse origins and their multiple cultures, cannot but be contradictory. (*L'Auteur en souffrance* 5)

It is not difficult to comprehend why Glissant might consider his own Caribbean island to be an exemplary space of paradox and contradiction when one takes into account the politico-cultural situation of the parts of the French nation-state that lie within the Caribbean basin. Glissant's home of Martinique maintains a peculiar relationship to Europe: it is politically a part of Europe, but of course physically quite distant from Europe. Given that it shares continental France's educational and legal systems and is economically controlled by France, Martinique can of course be said to be *of* the West in various ways. But one need not look far to see all that is other-than-European in Martinique. In short, Martinique finds itself in something of a contradictory *both/and* position with regard to the

West. One might say that it is *in* but not *of* Europe, but the converse is also quite true.

Consequently, if there is to be found on this earth a fetishized space of pure and radical difference with regard to the West, we can be reasonably sure that such a space does not lie within the Francophone Caribbean. The now well-known first lines of the *Éloge de la créolité* (*In Praise of Creoleness* [1990]) point to this contradictory state of being and not-being at once, as they define their "creoleness" through negation. The *créolistes* proclaim that creoleness entails being "Neither Europeans, nor Africans, nor Asians . . ." (13). But by the same token, and given the near-ubiquitous celebration of mixing, blending, hybridity, and/or creolization among a highly visible number of Caribbean authors and their academic critics, those now well-known lines could just as well have been written otherwise, by expunging the "Neither" and substituting an "and" for each "nor." Creoleness, which Glissant finds himself at pains to distinguish from creolization (to his great chagrin, the créolistes had claimed him as their source of inspiration), would therefore constitute something radically new, but also something familiar, at one and the same time (PR 103).

If the Francophone Caribbean is to be taken as contradictory in itself, compelling arguments have been made to the effect that the lived experience of the Caribbean writer is emblematic of that "bicephalous," "schizophrenic" way of being (Chancé, *L'Auteur en souffrance* 5). The sentiment that the Caribbean writer him- or herself lives and works within a state of suspended contradiction has been shared both by critics and by some of the luminaries of Caribbean literature alike. Chancé, for example, has cast the lived experience of the Caribbean author as being *en souffrance*. *En souffrance* in a literal sense might refer to a body experiencing real, physical suffering, perhaps even mortal agony. But the phrasing is also an official formula used to describe a letter that is still in transit, not having arrived at its destination. Similarly, a debt that is *en souffrance* is an outstanding debt, and by definition one whose nonpayment presents a problem. Hence, the multiple relevance of the phrasing *en souffrance* to Chancé's fundamental sense that there is something profoundly troubled and unsettling about the state of the Caribbean writer today.

Chancé opens her *L'Auteur en souffrance*: *Essai sur la position et la représentation de l'auteur dans le roman antillais contemporain (1981–1992)* (*The Author* en Souffrance: *Essay on the Position and the Representation of the Author in the Contemporary Caribbean Novel (1981–1992)* by citing a forcefully blunt claim from the *Éloge de la créolité*'s second page: "Caribbean literature does not yet exist. We are still in a state of pre-literature . . ." (1). Glissant shared that sense of being a writer who somehow did not exist, engaged in the production of literature that was likewise nonexistent, defining himself humbly as a mere "writer of prefaces for a future literature" (Chancé, *L'Auteur en souffrance* 1). Such claims are of course themselves paradoxical. As Chancé quite rightfully points out, Caribbean authors obviously do write and see their work published; it is clear that one can with all reasonableness speak of Caribbean authors who produce Caribbean literature. But those same authors, she illustrates, tend to hold strong views on the dolorous lack of an independent Martinican nation-state and the psychological and political effects thereof, or on the tenuous and historically hierarchical opposition of written and oral language in whose shadow their work unfolds (*L'Auteur en souffrance* 2–3). For that reason, Chancé takes as her point of departure the premise that "the author of works written in the Antilles, and particularly of novels, defines him/herself in a paradoxical manner, as an inadequate, lacking figure" (*L'Auteur en souffrance* 2). There would therefore be, in other words, something always already amiss from the very moment when a Caribbean author sits down to write.

Glissant himself is no exception to this pattern of lived paradox, particularly with regard to his relationship to the "mother country" of France. Again, despite his critiques of the West-as-project throughout his career, Glissant did not, could not, and perhaps never even sought to make anything resembling a clean break with the West. As Glissant acknowledges throughout his work, his intellectual vibrancy channels energy both from his Caribbean home and from the Western intellectual tradition. What is more, some of his readers have gone so far as to imply that Glissant is himself snugly ensconced among the ranks of Western philosophers. For them, Glissant would be the most Deleuzian of Francophone writers today, or even, *pace* Glissant, more Hegelian than Hegel himself (Hallward 441–42; Leupin, "The Slave's Jouissance" 891). And Glissant of course spent the vast majority of his years in the West, publishing in a European language for a primarily European audience, and garnering the laurels offered (down?) to him by Western institutions, beginning with a set of prestigious literary prizes: the Renaudot in 1958 for *La Lézarde*, then the *prix Charles Veillon* for *Le quatrième siècle* in 1964 (Dash, *Glissant* 54).

Symptomatic of that state of ambivalence with regard to the Western tradition is one of the more innovative facets of Glissant's overall project: its conjoining of arguably non-Western, Caribbean elements with genres and ideas familiar to his Western readership. Perhaps the most visible instance of that juxtaposition is the fact that the crescendo in his self-representation as a philosopher went hand-in-hand with his persistent development of key terms that were immanent to the Caribbean: *creolization*, *archipelagic thought*, or the *Tout-monde*, to take but a few of the most salient examples. As a result, the idea that Glissant's work generated and wielded conceptual tools that he took to be intrinsic to the Caribbean in order to explore alternatives to the Western literary and philosophical traditions underlies the entirety of the present study. And yet, on the other hand, we must be careful to avoid fetishizing "radical difference" (whatever that might mean) as we engage with Glissant. Briefly put, any reader who might open a Glissantian text with an ear straining to perceive a hitherto silenced, subaltern voice, or with a palate yearning to savor a distillation of unadulterated Caribbean authenticity, is bound to be frustrated.

Indeed, one of Glissant's more striking contributions is his emphasis on understanding difference *in* and *as* relation. Rather than holding the Caribbean to be a rarefied space of radical difference, Glissant portrays the Caribbean cultural zone as profoundly and indelibly *in relation* to the West, and also to the rest of the world. Yet further, he inverts traditional hierarchies as he grants the Caribbean a status of primacy within that relationship. Like Glissant, the critic Mary Gallagher accords a position of centrality to the Caribbean in any cogent conceptualization of modernity today. Both she and Glissant posit what might be called a Caribbean ethical imperative. In other words, for Gallagher as for Glissant, the Caribbean is a sort of exemplar for what the world as a whole is becoming, but it is more importantly a model for what the world *ought to be* becoming. Her argumentation is elegant, and merits citing at length.

> The contemporary episteme connects in a special way with Caribbean writing, and this congruence explains the privileged place held by francophone Caribbean literature at the turn of the millennium. For this body of writing does not simply illuminate a particular (post)colonial relationship to place, but seems rather to constitute one of the foremost paradigms of diaspora and globalization in the (post)modern world . . . Indeed, writing from this "Other America" is perceived and often, indeed, explicitly represents itself as revealing—prophetically and axiomatically—how humanity inhabits the world today, how we all relate or how we shall shortly relate to space and time, to language and to writing. Moreover, French Caribbean writing,

driven as it is by a hypertrophied theoretical tropism, explicitly claims prophetic status and universal validity, as though the Caribbean were the laboratory of a universal future, in a world compressed by an ever-accelerating approximation of places and cultures. (*Ici-là* xvi–xvii)

The Caribbean is, here, not only exemplary of the *true* nature of the world in modernity; it is also at the vanguard of the world's becoming. Notably, Gallagher shares Glissant's sense that the Caribbean is, as she puts it, the "laboratory of a universal future." That is no small point: simply put, for Gallagher as for Glissant, the Caribbean has served as a proving ground for modernity, and now the entire world is duly coming to resemble the Caribbean in its turn.

They are not alone in holding those beliefs. In Enrico Mario Santí's talk titled "El paradigma, o paradoja, del Caribe" ("The Paradigm, or Paradox of the Caribbean"), given in memory of another Caribbean theorist and reader of Deleuze and Guattari, Antonio Benítez-Rojo, Santí seeks to justify his preconceived point of departure, inspired by Benítez-Rojo's work: that the Caribbean serves as a paradigm for the rest of the world, and for a host of reasons. Santí explains that referring to the Caribbean as a paradigm implies four different things. It means, in Santí's words,

1. that the zone and culture of the Caribbean puts on display, in effect, a paradigm from which we can understand not only these [Caribbean] realities but also other contemporaneous realities, but outside of this zone. Hence [it also means], then,

2. that the existence, the attractiveness and perhaps the predominance of the Caribbean-as-paradigm dictates that, in effect, the entire world is becoming Caribbean. The idea may appear harebrained to us. But let's think, however, about some facts that tend to confirm it. One is, as we know, global warming. Another, more serious and important, is the [migration of] the Caribbean diaspora towards other developed zones of the globe, principally of the north. That displacement . . . has had the effect of transporting, with the people, their way of being, their vision of the world, and their culture . . . For that reason the relational paradigm of the Caribbean that Édouard Glissant has outlined . . . consists in a foundational encounter—violent, total, traumatic—that today

cannot be avoided. It was not in vain that Benítez-Rojo said, in his essential *The Repeating Island*[,] that the Caribbean, in its lack of a stable cultural origin, contains the seeds of a "postmodern perspective." . . .

3. Another example that suggests that the world is becoming Caribbean would be this epiphenomenon of postcolonialism and globalization that we once called hybridity [*mestizaje*] and that today, with greater precision, we refer to as creolization. . . .

4. that the Caribbean as paradigm supposes that the world *should become* like the Caribbean; which is to say, the world should take on its paradigm. Because if the Caribbean has managed to survive 500 years of violence and historical and ecological depredation (recall the all-too-recent Haitian earthquake), and has survived thanks to the assimilative mechanisms of creolization, then the rest of the world . . . should learn from it and take on or adopt its paradigm. (58–60)

Creolization has allowed the Caribbean to survive, and it could take on a similarly salubrious role for the rest of the world. Whether we are to agree with Gallagher and Santí or not, the exuberance driving their argumentation is palpable. But if a notable group of Caribbean writers and their academic critics have also, as we have seen, framed Caribbean cultural output as itself paradoxical, a difficulty ensues. How, we are led to ask, might the Caribbean be paradigmatic *and* paradoxical, at one and the same time? After all, Santí additionally points out that a sea separates those two words, given their fundamental semantic contradistinction. As he argues, "*paradigm* signifies pattern, outline, example; *paradox* means 'contrary to opinion or expectation,' which is to say, contrary to the pattern, outline or example. Therefore, they are opposed words, and opposed concepts" (58). The kinship suggested by their shared prefix *para* is belied, then, by the fact that the two words have opposite meanings. And a conflicted representation of the Caribbean, as both troublingly paradoxical and exhilaratingly paradigmatic, emerges out of Santí's conceptual pairing. For Glissant, however, that contradiction proves not to be an obstacle at all; indeed, he seems to draw inspiration from it.

Each of the following four chapters analyzes Glissant's twofold emphasis on the Caribbean as both paradigm and paradox. Chapter one scrutinizes one of Glissant's more striking postulates: his idea that the Caribbean can impart to us new ways of thinking the idea of totality, both in an abstract sense and in its concrete reality in our interconnected world today. That Glissantian hypothesis is, moreover, quite anomalous in the contemporary intellectual climate favoring fragmentation and multiplicity over wholeness or oneness. Drawing inspiration from the creole expression *toutt moun*, meaning "everyone," Glissant's idea of the *Tout-monde*, or Whole-world, is all the more relevant when read in the context of the discordant chorus of voices critiquing "globalization" in its various avatars today. Yet more pointedly, Glissant casts his understanding of the contemporary world as *the* example of what a different, post-Hegelian vision of totality might look like. His staunch insistence on a fundamental unity characterizing all existence is all the more noteworthy given that he voices it within the divided house that also shelters the fraught, malleable discourses of World Literature, *Francophonie*, *littérature-monde en français*, or Francophone Postcolonial Studies.

In this as in other things, the Caribbean serves as an archetype for Glissant: as he has repeated for decades, "the entire world is becoming an archipelago and creolizing" (TTM 193–94). That stark assertion is at the center of Glissant's meditations on the relationship of particular places to the totality, and in particular on the role of writing within that place-totality relationship. As we track the unfolding of Glissant's idea of the *Tout-monde* over time, we can see that he contradicts himself as he weaves paradox into that all-encompassing idea. Glissant holds that the *Tout-monde* is our contemporary world at times, and maintains that it is decidedly not that world at others. Elsewhere, he posits that the *Tout-monde* is at once a part of the world and the whole of the world. And the *Tout-monde* may, in the final analysis—if one can properly speak of finality in Glissant's thought—prove to be a *new region of the world*, a world of which one could be forgiven for thinking that there is no corner left unexplored. Glissant's decades-long tinkering with the idea of the *Tout-monde* provides the setting for chapter 1's rereading of Glissantian keywords, such as *Relation, creolization*, and *Place*, through the lens of their relationship to paradox.

For Glissant, the globalized state of modernity has brought about, and in fact demands, what he calls a "new category of literature." That new literature yields the backdrop for Glissant's elaboration of his written ethics of alterity. Chapter 2 analyzes Glissant's reading of Faulkner, where Glissant reads the author of the South against the accumulated weight of criticism over the years. That critical tradition has, to Glissant's mind, become stymied by its focus on Faulkner's racism. Reversing that critical current, Glissant's asseveration is that Faulkner's is in reality a sort of antiracist. As Faulkner's novels fail to develop and breathe life into their black characters, they in fact constitute a testament to a real sincerity on the Southern author's part: painfully aware that the people of African descent who surrounded him would remain forever opaque to him, Faulkner knew them as profoundly unknowable, and so he eschewed representing them. Cognizant that slavery and the plantation system had continued their rot even after their downfall, inexorably poisoning the present, Glissant's Faulkner spoke that unspeakable truth to his white readership. In both of those ways, as Glissant put it, Faulkner "said without saying, saying all the while" (PhR 156).

Whereas Faulkner sought to know the unknowable *as* unknowable (or, better, to un-know the seemingly knowable), and to say the unsayable, Glissant makes visible the invisible in his novel *Sartorius*. *Sartorius*—whose title conspicuously recalls that of Faulkner's novel *Sartoris*—is dedicated to Félix Guattari, and is a visible flirtation with the Deleuzo-Guattarian idea of a minor literature's bringing into being a people who is missing. *Sartorius* also foregrounds a provocative play on the idea of influence, both literary and philosophical: were Faulkner and Deleuze Glissant's intellectual forbears, or was the converse (anachronistically) true? Glissant's literary criticism, when read alongside his own literature, shows us his refiguration of the philosopheme of alterity. In his criticism as in his literature, Glissant highlights the influence of opacity, underscoring in parallel the opacity of influence. Living with(in) the opacity of the other, writing in the shadow of literary and philosophical forefathers (who can at times play the role of antagonists), reaching out to a people that both exists and does not exist: all of these paradoxical yet necessary actions represent Glissant's efforts to set forth an ethics of alterity.

That ethics, both derived from literature and put into practice there, "demand[s] for everyone the right to opacity" (cf. PR 209, et passim). In line with Glissant's overall optimism, his ethics of alterity promises more harmonious ways of being in the world. Glissant is correspondingly Panglossian in his stalwart belief that understanding and living what he calls worldwide *Relation* is as necessary as it is inevitable. Truly embracing what he terms the *imaginary* of Relation is a sine qua non not only of the poetics of Relation but also for a future *politics* of Relation. In the worldwide *polis* that has embraced the imaginary of Relation, there would no longer be even the possibility of repeating the historical aberrations of the twentieth century, from Stalinism to Sarajevo or the Rwandan genocide (IPD 90–91). This plainly teleological schema of progression toward a positive transformation begs the question of attainment. Otherwise put, how, concretely, might we go about reaching such a clearly desirable state of being?

The goal of chapter 3 is to demonstrate that Glissant has already offered one possible answer to that question, through the peregrinations of his Martinican protagonist Mathieu, in two novels written decades apart: *Le quatrième siècle* (1964) and *Tout-monde* (1995). In the first novel, the young Mathieu seeks to come to terms with the concrete and final truth of his ancestors, those who lived in Africa and those who were brought from there by force across the ocean to Martinique. Mathieu consults Papa Longoué, a *quimboiseur*, or practitioner of a syncretic, Caribbean magico-religious tradition, at the beginning of his quest. What Mathieu learns is that he gains more as he searches than he ever could through obtaining the object of his desire. The novel *Tout-monde*, published a full thirty years later, stages a similar quest narrative as the same Longoué sends Mathieu off into the *Tout-monde* in search of *something*, the nature of which he finally discovers—or not. Insofar as both quest narratives frame attainment as nonattainment, they constitute a rethinking of teleology. Mathieu will never truly and finally arrive at an understanding of a past that is at once lost and lingering on, but his search is valuable in itself. I go on to argue that Glissant's rewriting of the idea of teleology provides a model for our interpretive engagement with his texts as puzzled readers. Like Mathieu, in other words, we readers of Glissant might do well to focus not on the *products* of our engagement with his texts, that is, on what we might grasp in them or get out of them, but rather on the *process* of reading them, of experiencing them and experimenting with them.

Glissant's last book-length essay prolongs that experimentation with the purpose of the interpretive act, and provides the central object of analysis for chapter 4. The very title of *Philosophie de la Relation* (2009) (hereafter *Philosophie*) functions as a performative speech act, affirming its author as a philosopher and his written products as belonging to the philosophical genre. Yet *Philosophie* undermines those moves just as swiftly as it makes them. What would at first glance appear to be a traditional philosophical treatise proves to be a fragmentary text, intermingling definitions of various Glissantian ideas with autobiographical snippets and musings on Martinican landscapes, and ending unpredictably with a paean to William Faulkner. *Philosophie*, I go on to illustrate, amounts to a paradoxical representation of its author's own authority. In *Philosophie* as elsewhere, Glissant establishes himself as what Foucault called a "universal intellectual," authorizing himself to pronounce on topics ranging from physics to cosmology, by way of visual art and world history. But *Philosophie* also underscores the book's authored-ness, illustrating that its arguments emanate from an embodied, fallible individual, as it pauses intermittently to reflect on Glissant's mother and childhood. In light of *Philosophie*'s recurrent moments of speaking against itself, I ask what we as readers ought to *do* with this excess of quite literal contra-diction in Glissant's thought. Taking a clue from the confluence of Glissant's thought with that of Deleuze and Guattari, I propose a new translation of their injunction that is commonly rendered as "Experiment, never interpret" (cf. Deleuze & Parnet 60). The French *expérimenter* means "experiment" but also "experience," and I argue that the *Philosophie* calls not only for experimenting with the text but also for a particular kind of interpretive experience. The text's closure, I show, is in the last analysis an opening—and for that reason there can be no last analysis. "[T]he imaginary of the world," *Philosophie* explains to its readers, refuses to deal in possession or even in knowing. "It concludes nothing. It supposes in an archipelago" (PhR 109).

In conclusion, I return to Glissant's notion of "archipelagic thinking," using it as a lens through which to reread the play of paradox and contradiction, both willed and unwilled, in Glissant's oeuvre. The term *play* is appropriate, as this study's closing suggests that Glissant consistently embraced the ludic dimension, encouraging and at times even provoking his readers to toy with and use his conceptual tools in order to create ideas and artistic products of their own.

One Man Was Islands

Glissant, but *which* Glissant? It can be argued without exaggeration that the name *Glissant* points to many authors just as much as it does to one. Glissant wore many hats as a writer, producing poems, novels, essays, pamphlets, anthologies, and theater, in addition to myriad interviews, many of which were later republished as essays. He welcomed playing the role of the engaged, public intellectual in a host of speeches, academic gatherings and interviews, and maintained a pronounced web presence via the websites *edouardglissant.fr* and *tout-monde.com*. Additionally, throughout his nearly sixty years of writing, Glissant metamorphosed recurrently: there was the reflective young student of philosophy and later ethnography, not incidentally a published poet, from the 1950s on, and later the encyclopedic commentator on virtually all aspects of Caribbean life in the mammoth, 503-page *Le discours antillais* (1981). After *Poétique de la Relation* (*Poetics of Relation*; 1990) Glissant came to write more and more as a theoretician. In 2006 he launched the Institut du Tout-Monde, a center for arts and culture in Paris named for his rethinking of the idea of totality. The Institut would become an institution in itself as it began to grant its own literary prize, the Prix Carbet de la Caraïbe et du Tout-monde.

Glissant's self-positioning with regard to the government and academia also shifted multiply over time. He was at times visibly close to the French government, most notably at the moment of his appointment in 2006 by French President Jacques Chirac to begin work toward the creation of a national center devoted to the memory of slavery and abolition. That project would later mutate into a short book, *Mémoires des esclavages: La fondation d'un centre national pour la mémoire des esclavages et de leurs abolitions* (*Memories of Slaveries: The Foundation of a National Center for the Memory of Slaveries and their Abolitions* [2007]), and subsequently into a website, lesmemoiresdesesclavages.com. Dominique de Villepin, then the French Prime Minister and a multifaceted author in his own right, would write the foreword for that text. Previously, Villepin had made approbatory references to Glissant's ideas of Relation and creolization in his 2004 collection of poetry *Le Requin et la mouette* (cf. Bongie, *Friends and Enemies* 56).

At yet other times, however, Glissant played the gadfly. *Quand les murs tombent: l'identité nationale hors-la-loi?* (*When the Walls Fall Down: National Identity Gone Outlaw?* [2007]), a pamphlet that Glissant produced with Patrick Chamoiseau, amounted to a blistering attack on then-President Nicolas Sarkozy. Or rather, it was an assault on Sarkozy's decision to begin his mandate with the creation of a controversial "Ministry of Immigration, Integration, National Identity, and Co-Development." Chamoiseau and Glissant lamented that the very idea of establishing a "Ministry of Identity" betrayed a misunderstanding of what identity meant. Their underlying implication was that Sarkozy and his cohorts had been led astray by the siren song of an all-too-facile ideological (read: right-wing nationalist) inflexibility as they sought to nail down the meaning of French national identity: "One could not know how to establish a ministry of identity. Otherwise the life of the collective would become mechanical, its future sterilized, made infertile . . ." (1). Decades earlier, Glissant had of course also become implicated in the push for Martinican independence well before he was even of voting age. It is just as difficult to assign a stable meaning to his relationship to the French political establishment as it is to align Glissant with a single genre.

That elusiveness has its auspicious echoes in the author's own surname, which means "sliding" or "slippery" in French. The name *Glissant* was not at first his own, however. Born in 1928 in the commune of Sainte-Marie in Martinique, Glissant shared his mother's legal surname of Godard for the first eight years of his life (Loichot, *Orphan Narratives* 72; cf. TTM 78). Glissant's father would recognize him and pass his surname down to his son after the latter obtained his Certificat d'études. Tracing his genealogy back yet further, Glissant has claimed that his father's surname was in fact a phonetic inversion of a slave master's name, "Senglis," one that would have been transferred to one of Glissant's paternal ancestors generations earlier (Loichot, *Orphan Narratives* 73). In light of that once-absent, perhaps forever-deferred *nom du père*, the author's recurring returns to the abstract themes of filiation and obscured origins in both his fiction and his essays prove to be quite personal as well.

Alongside Frantz Fanon, with whom he would later become fast friends in Paris, Glissant went on to study at Martinique's Lycée Schoelcher for the duration of World War II. Although he was enrolled at the same time that Aimé Césaire was teaching there, Glissant would later insist that he never studied directly under the great poet and statesman (Britton, "Souvenirs des années 40" 100). That said, he and the other students inevitably lived in Césaire's ever-expanding shadow, and Glissant pitched in for Césaire's election campaign in 1945 (Britton, "Souvenirs des années 40" 101). Glissant moved to Paris for his studies in 1946, the same year in which Martinique became an overseas French Department. *Soleil de la conscience* (*Sunlight of Consciousness* [1956]), the first of many essays that Glissant would go on to publish, chronicled his experience as a young, Caribbean student in Paris. It testified to Glissant's ambivalent relationship to continental France, where he felt himself to be at once at home and an immigrant.

Glissant worked toward his undergraduate *licence* degree in philosophy at the Sorbonne from 1946 on (Dash, *Glissant* xi). Among his friends at the time were Gilles Deleuze and Félix Guattari, and Glissant studied there under Jean Wahl, the great French interpreter of Hegel. In 1958 Glissant would publish *La Lézarde*, the novel that made his literary name when it won the prestigious Prix Renaudot. And by 1961, at the age of thirty-three, Glissant had added theater to his output in the poetic and the essay genres.

From 1959 to 1960 Glissant found himself in the odd predicament of being forced into exile in what was supposedly his own country. Due to his outspoken political commitment to Martinican independence, his right to return to Martinique was taken from him and he was ordered to remain within continental France. Finally, and shortly after receiving the Prix Charles Veillon for his novel *Le quatrième siècle* in 1964, Glissant was allowed to return to Martinique, where he took up a position as a professor of philosophy at the Lycée de Jeunes Filles in Fort-de-France in 1965 (Dash, *Glissant* xii). In addition to his no doubt considerably time-consuming work as a teacher, Glissant channeled his abundant energy in other directions. He went on to found the Martinican Studies Institute (Institut Martiniquais d'Etudes) and the literary journal *Acoma*, writing profusely all the while. At roughly the same time he continued to compose poetry, in addition to publishing the dense and markedly theoretical essay *L'intention poétique* (1969) (*The Poetic Intention*), and the novel *Malemort* (1975). His worldwide peregrinations, primarily within the triangulation of France, the United States, and Martinique, began in earnest in 1980 as Glissant left Martinique for Paris to become editor of the *UNESCO Courier* (Dash, Glissant xii). His novelistic and poetic output remained strong during his years in Paris, and followed hot on the heels of the publication of the most-cited of Glissantian essays, *Le discours antillais*, shortly after his arrival there. Named Distinguished Professor at Louisiana State University in 1988, Baton Rouge became his base as he put together the essay *Poétique de la Relation* (1990). His time there as well as his travels in the Gulf South region would later inspire his reading of Faulkner in *Faulkner, Mississippi* (1996). Glissant's entrenchment in the Anglo-American academy only intensified with his appointment as Distinguished Professor of French at the City University of New York in 1995. The rest of his productive life would be spent principally between CUNY and Paris. There, he founded an institution of his own, the Institut du Tout-monde (Tout-monde Institute), with the support of the French governmental subdivisions of the Ile-de-France Region and the Overseas Ministry (Ministère de l'Outre-mer) ("edouardglissant.fr/rayonnement"). In April 2010, at the Institut du Tout-monde, Glissant recited there what he described as the "Great poem" that he had long labored over, titled "*Rien n'est Vrai, tout est vivant*" ("Nothing Is True, All Is Living"). It was to be his last public talk at the Institut before his passing in 2011.[3]

Glissant is multiple in yet another sense. Faced with the panoply of genres in which Glissant worked as well as the sheer duration of his productive life, critics have diverged around the periodization of his vast oeuvre. That is, they have disagreed on whether it is appropriate to speak of Glissant as one author with a consistent set of concerns, or rather as an author who took a "turn" late in life, becoming cleaved into two, an "early" and a "late" Glissant. That division, between those who stress the overall consistency in the long arc of Glissant's production and those who insist on a scission between the early and the late Glissant, is perhaps the most significant source of debate among Glissant's readers today. (Celia Britton and Michael Dash are at the center of the former camp, whereas critics such as Chris Bongie and Peter Hallward have staked out their place in the latter.) J. Michael Dash, the first translator of Glissant's work into English and the author of the first academic monograph on him in English, has maintained that "Since Glissant's oeuvre does not evolve in the normal sense—in terms of either theme or genre—his major preoccupations are apparent from his earliest writing and return obsessively throughout the various phases of his work" (*Édouard Glissant* 27). Glissant himself corroborates that position, playfully asserting in 1997 that he sees the same "momentum" ("*balan*") in his work from 1956 on (TTM 20). The analyses in the pages that follow share that conception of Glissant as an author of both multiplicity and repetition, one whose thought was in flux just as much as it manifested consistence in its returns to a cluster of key ideas. There was one Glissant in other words, one who, as Celia Britton phrased it in her tribute to him, was paradoxically "Always Changing, While Still Remaining."

Others among Glissant's critics, however, would disagree strongly. Again, Chris Bongie has cited a growing critical consensus that would perceive a worryingly sharp curve in Glissant's intellectual trajectory in the wake of his *Poétique de la Relation* (1990). For Bongie, such critics approvingly read the work of the early Glissant as being characterized by "partisan position-takings" and "principled politics" (*Friends and Enemies* 339). They see the late Glissant, however, as opting instead (read: disappointingly) for what Bongie calls "utopian poetics," and his critics have accordingly come to feel an "unease" in light of his post-1990 reorientation (*Friends and Enemies* 338, 339). Bongie goes on to hold that Glissant's critics have, as their malaise took root, tended to "downplay or ignore the later work" (Bongie, *Friends and Enemies* 338, 339). It is not too much to say that what is evidently a critical aporia with regard to the work of the "late" Glissant has at times teetered on the brink of becoming a critical impasse. Since the pioneering monographs on Glissant by Dash (1995) and Britton (1999), no book-length study in English has been devoted exclusively to Glissant's writing—a marked contrast with the proliferation of works on Glissant in French during the same period.[4] Bongie is correct, then, in pointing out that in the Anglo-American academy the "late" Glissant's work has largely been denied critical attention, at least in the form of the traditional academic monograph. That fact is all the more surprising given that those years were an extraordinarily prolific period for Glissant, one in which he published seven book-length collections of essays and interviews, six shorter essays, and two novels, in parallel to his numerous speeches, presentations, and interviews.

Implicit in the case for a Glissantian "turn" is the sentiment that after 1990 Glissant became less—or less satisfyingly (to his critics)—political. Alongside Britton and Dash, however, the present study argues that Glissant's work did maintain its politics as well as its principles, albeit through shifting them onto a different plane. In her 2009 article "Globalization and Political Action in the Work of Édouard Glissant," Britton convincingly argues that while the "late" Glissant *has* changed his approach to the political, he is far from *a*political. After 1981, Britton holds, "Glissant's work undergoes a marked change: of focus, of mood, and of political position" (1). "The pessimism of *Discours* is replaced by exhilaration," she continues, and Glissant progressively focuses on "a view of the world—influenced by chaos theory and the 'nomadology' of Deleuze and Guattari—as a dynamic totality of interacting communities, all aware of each other and constantly changing" (1). In *Poétique de la Relation* and thereafter, Britton holds, Glissant "invent[s] a variety of more or less synonymous names for this phenomenon: *creolization, chaos-monde, Tout-monde*. Another name for it is *Relation* . . ." (1). To put it all too simply, since 1981's *Le discours antillais*, Glissant has retained his political concerns and ambitions, but has enlarged their emphasis and scope, from the local (Martinique) to the global.

Crucially, Britton draws attention to another pivot in Glissant's political work: that is, his growing conviction that change in thought must precede change in life, and that it falls to the artist (and hence to Glissant himself) to bring about the first of those two metamorphoses. In Britton's words, "All these later texts reiterate his belief that all political progress depends, beyond intervention in local situations, on the long-term development of this transformative consciousness of totality—depends, in other words, on 'changing mentalities'" ("Globalization" 10). Britton adeptly cites the "late" Glissant at a moment when the centrality of "'changing mentalities'" has become an article of faith in his thought. As the Glissant of the *Treatise on the Tout-monde* puts it, "Our actions in the world are cursed with sterility if we do not change, as much as we can, the imagination of the humanities that we constitute" (TTM, 29–30; ctd. in Britton, "Globalization" 10; Britton's translation).

Rather than shrugging off his lifelong political concerns in the 1990s and thereafter, Glissant increasingly (although far from exclusively) wrote from a perspective grounded in a strong belief that his most effective political work could be done in the realm of what he calls the "*imaginaire*." In the preceding citation, Britton has used the English word *imagination* to translate *imaginaire*, perhaps due to the fact that French term *imaginaire* has no direct equivalent in English. The French language allows for a contrast between the nouns *imaginaire* and *imagination*, whereas the latter cognate operates alone in the English lexicon. Given the semantic contrast between the two, and particularly in light of Glissant's persistence in claiming that they are in his thought quite distinct from one another, the pages that follow will translate each occurrence of *imaginaire* in Glissant with the English neologism "the imaginary," in order to maintain the grammatically nominal quality of the French original (cf. PhR 109–10, 148–49, et passim).

The dictionary *Le Grand Robert de la langue française* defines the noun *imaginaire* as "the set of products, [or] domain of the imagination," whereas the *Petit Larousse* glosses it yet more simply as the "domain of the imagination." For Glissant, however, the word takes on a new life. (First, however, if we are to understand what Glissant means with his use of *imaginaire*, it must be emphasized that he did not have in mind the imaginary register of Lacanian psychoanalysis, or Luce Irigaray's subsequent appropriation and reformulation thereof; his use of the term is altogether different.) John E. Drabinski has adroitly translated the meaning of "imaginary" in Glissant's thought as "that precarious aesthetic sphere of knowing and being that structures a relation to the world" ("What Is Trauma to the Future?" 304). The imaginary would be, in Drabinski's reading, the site where knowing and being come together, within the context of aesthetic production. As is already apparent in Drabinski's exegesis of the term, the sheer vastness of the category "imaginary" speaks to just how useful it can be to Glissant. What is more, the imaginary for Glissant also entails the potential to *change* the self's relationship to her or his world. For that reason, Drabinski has elsewhere parsed the imaginary as a human faculty, and one with considerable transformative potential: the imaginary would thus also be "the *ability* to imagine, conceive and know the world otherwise" (*Levinas* 152; emphasis added). For Glissant, it is the imaginary, and not the imagination, that has the capability to know the world more wholly and accurately. In his words, "The world as representation is given in the imagination, but insofar as it is also the Tout-monde, which is to say a non-totalitarian totality, whose details and multiplicity are not lost, it opens itself up to the imaginary" (PhR 112).

It was this expanded sense of the imaginary, a cozy union of thought and being emphasizing potential and possibility, that would lead Glissant, and later Chamoiseau, to employ the compelling formulation "insurrection of the imaginary" (CL 25). Indeed, in his later years, Glissant would write as if political change in the world could *only* be effected if it was preceded by that insurrection of the imaginary. In consequence, Glissant, a rare optimist among postcolonial thinkers, is adamant in holding that there *will* someday be a new imaginary, available to everyone everywhere, and that the entirety of the world will one day exchange in the same languages (*langages*), ones that will surpass the contemporary multiplicity of languages (*langues*), thus allowing for a harmonious communion in the *Tout-monde* (IPD 127). It is on account of the importance of language to Glissant's thought that art, and literature in particular, plays such a key role in shaping and transforming the human imaginary. The central, even causal role that Glissant accords to aesthetics in changing our imaginaries and consequently bringing about political change is what leads Britton to explain pithily that for Glissant, "poetics is the politics of the future" (Britton, "Always Changing" 111).

While the imaginary did come to take on an ever-more politicized role as Glissant's thinking progressed, it is not the case that his work toward change in the imaginary became his sole avenue of political expression and engagement. Throughout his life, Glissant remained visibly engaged in the political sphere. Beginning in 2007, Glissant published, often in collaboration, a set of highly polemical pamphlets, a demonstration of his profound belief that his abstract concepts such as Relation or creolization had real relevance on the contemporary political scene.[5] As he wrote with one foot suspended in the ether of abstraction and the other firmly planted on the terrain of the activist pamphleteer, Glissant's political thought oscillated smoothly between the theoretical and the concrete. In another, yet more striking example of that oscillation, Glissant believed even some of his more utopian longings to be within the realm of political possibility of his day, pushing for what he rather audaciously called a "realizable utopia," by which he had in mind the establishment of Martinique as a zone of exclusively organic and non-GMO agriculture (TTM 226–29). While that project would later be abandoned, it demonstrates amply that anyone who might find the political to be evacuated from Glissant's last two decades of writing need not look far in order to locate counter examples. For that reason, I will strive to reconcile the two camps of Glissant's critics, reading the shift in his thinking within the context of a greater continuity. There is, in other words, not a schism in the Glissantian corpus but rather an amplification post-1990 of tendencies and concerns that were to varying degrees latent in his earlier work. A paradox that Glissant has repeatedly sighted in the Caribbean archipelago is pertinent to our reception of the author himself: he is consistent and unified, but also multiple, shifting, at one and the same time.

On Scope and Methodology

The genres in which Glissant has produced reflect that melding of unity and diversity, in content as in form. The essay form is the principal though not the only focus of this study, given that it is most often in his essays that Glissant launches and develops the keywords for which he has increasingly become known. While Britton recalls in her posthumous tribute to Glissant that "it is his novels that for me represent his greatest achievement," she accords that for better or for worse, by the end of his life Glissant "became more famous as an essayist" ("Always Changing" 108). That bias in reception reflects the fact that while he transposed them into various genres, the conceptual tools that Glissant's critics found most useful, whether for appropriation or for objection—for example, Relation, creolization, archipelagic thinking, counterpoetics, or rhizome-identity, to name only a few—have their home in his essays. What is more, although it has received relatively little critical attention, the essay form is far from a tangential offshoot Glissant's vast oeuvre. Even though he began as a published poet, Glissant's first prose text was an essay, as was his last. Indeed, from 1958 to 2009, Glissant published twenty essays, of which fourteen are now packaged as full-length books and the rest are in shorter form. In contrast, he published eight novels during roughly the same period. Obviously, the sheer quantity of his essays is no reason to accord them a place of preeminence within his production. Their abundance does, however, suggest that they merit attention, at the very least in momentary isolation, as a body of work unto itself within the greater Glissantian corpus.

The outwardly simple act of isolating one genre among the many in which Glissant has worked is a problematic one, however. Throughout his oeuvre Glissant has taken delight in genre bending: fiction does the work of philosophy, purportedly philosophical treatises incorporate characters from Glissant's fictional universe, and his philosophical essays regularly take highly narrative, even whimsical detours. Testing, challenging, undoing and redoing generic boundaries were all abiding concerns of Glissant's. As a result, one would be hard pressed to draw an impenetrable, hygienic line of difference demarcating the various genres in which Glissant has produced. Glissant's lionization of the figure of the poet, for example, does not amount to a declamation of that writer's ascendancy over, say, philosophers, or novelists, or storytellers. In parallel, Glissant has held that he sees certain manifestations of the essay form (namely his own, for example his *La cohée du Lamentin*) as being in all actuality a style of poetry (IL 74). Elsewhere, as if to hammer the point home, Glissant has crisply spelled out that "As far as method is concerned, I do not separate theoretical thinking from novelistic or artistic creation" ("L'Europe et les Antilles"). Glissant's observations on his own methodology imply that he could do the work he sets out to do in virtually any genre. The Glissantian corpus, taken as a whole, functions as a great coming-together of genres, which overlap at times and diverge at others. In testament to Glissant's long-term insouciance with regard to the platonic distinction of philosophy and poetry, critics have combined philosophy and poetics in their interpretations of his work. For instance, Jacques Coursil refers to Glissant's "Philosophy of a Poetics" (though Coursil could have justifiably inverted his word order, that is, as "Poetics of a Philosophy"). Similarly, the subtitle of Manuel Norvat's scholarly monograph on Glissant titled *Le Chant du divers* (*The Song of the Diverse*) coins a new word to accommodate Glissant's undertakings: "*Introduction to Édouard Glissant's philosopoetics.*"

Like the selection of Glissant's essays as a primary object of analysis, the choice to read Glissant as a philosopher, or at the very least as a multifaceted author deeply engaged with the philosophical genre, also bears some explanation. Would such a move not constitute the imposition of the Western category of "philosophy" on the "O/other," which is to say, on a thinker who generates ideas marked by radical difference, one who is himself a veritable incarnation of said radical difference? Marcien Towa has asked, "But where are the [Aimé] Césaires and the Chinua Achebes of philosophy?" (5). Towa first posed his question in 1971, and responses to it now abound. Glissant notably offers himself as one. He has, after all, clearly earned the institutional legitimacy that is a sufficient if not a necessary criterion for doing so: a university student and later a teacher of philosophy, his early years in academia revolved around the formal study of philosophy. Moreover, his engagement with the names, terms and genres associated with the discipline of philosophy saw a crescendo throughout his productive life. As early as the 1950s, for example, Glissant had declared his admiration for Hegel (SC 21). That early affinity would take on a more critical tone as Glissant grew older, positioning himself as a critic of Hegelian philosophy with his unmitigated rejections of the very idea of universals or systematic thought, as well as with his repeated insistence that "Hegel can be wrong" (cf. NR 152, et passim). Moreover, Glissant's appropriation of Deleuzian and Deleuzo-Guattarian themes such as the rhizome, or the role of minor literature in creating a people that is missing, has led other academic philosophers to situate his work firmly in the philosophical register. Rosi Braidotti has labeled Glissant a "Deleuzian philosopher" (84), and Peter Hallward has hailed him to be "the most thoroughly Deleuzian writer in the Francophone world" (441–42).

Yet further, Glissant has candidly and self-consciously represented himself as a participant, albeit a quite singular one, in the philosophical enterprise. By way of a justification of his dabbling in chaos theory, for example, Glissant proclaimed that "I feel myself to be entirely authorized . . . to paraphilosophize around the science of chaos" (IPD 82). His decision to "paraphilosophize" rather than "philosophize" is true to the form of Glissant's methodology, as it paints Glissant's methods and ambitions as being simultaneously philosophical and not-philosophical, or perhaps as something other-than-philosophical, at one and the same time (the subject of chapter 4). And yet, whereas Glissant uses the term *paraphilosophy* to grant himself creative license in his philosophical work, Georges Desportes found Glissant's self-positioning on the territory of philosophy to be so misplaced that he took the word *paraphilosophy* to be pejorative in his scathing *La Paraphilosophie d'Édouard Glissant* (2008). There, Desportes impugned Glissant for the latter's flouting of what Desportes saw as the strictures of clarity and rigor that are proper to the discipline of philosophy. Desportes trumpets that "we will not allow ourselves to be seduced by Glissant's literary—and paraphilosophical—graces" (62). In his polemic, Desportes often refuses to heed even most basic constraints of academic decorum. Oddly enough, however, his critiques read at times like backhanded compliments, and one wonders whether Glissant would not have been flattered by the accusation that his thought, as Desportes puts it, "in all respects, is sinuous, wily, active, fertile and passionate on demand, even raging through intimate conviction, just as slippery as his name, sly and clever" (62).

Desportes's attacks notwithstanding, Glissant's meditations on, say, the difference between Being and beings, or his allusions to figures from the philosophical pantheon (Hegel, Heidegger, Plato), be they tacit or explicit, demonstrate that he is both sincere and self-aware in his choice of genre (cf. PhR 61, 70, et passim). The very title of his last work, once more, inducts its author into the ranks of the philosophers. After all, what nonphilosopher would dare pen a treatise titled *Philosophy of Relation*? And it is, moreover, no coincidence that the title *Poétique de la Relation* of 1990 was spun, nearly twenty years later, into *Philosophie de la Relation* (2009). From poetics, then, to philosophy: Glissant has overtly sought to condition his scholarly reception, to repackage and authorize himself as a producer of philosophy—and more importantly, as an innovative and revolutionary one, one who cannot but (re)affirm the Caribbean origins and ends of his thought. It is incumbent on us as readers of Glissant to take those moves into consideration.

It cannot be stressed enough, however, that the present analysis in no way seeks to frame Glissant as simply a postcolonial purveyor of "high" philosophy or theory. While Glissant may be a "Deleuzian" or a "Hegelian," he is not always or only so. Undeniably, the question of intellectual influence, one of the subjects of chapter 2, is a thorny one in Glissant's work. While there are indeed instances of direct and avowed intellectual appropriation in Glissant's thought, he is not above repudiating the Western tradition on one page while embracing it on another.[6] His relationship to Deleuze and Guattari is, true to type, an opaque one. Glissant did base his concept of "rhizome-identity" on what he called an "image" drawn from the work of Deleuze and Guattari ("L'Europe et les Antilles"). But early in his career, Glissant would set in motion ideas remarkably similar to those are now customarily associated with Deleuze (and lather with the Deleuze-Guattari dyad), although well before the Parisian philosopher would see his own in print. Glissant's figure of Relation, for example, which appeared in a nascent form in the 1950s, appears to anticipate Deleuzian relationality (cf. SC 13–14). Similarly, Glissant's vitalism, or his sense that all reality, and aesthetic production in particular, is properly understood in terms of interconnection and flows of force, was unmistakable well before Deleuze and Guattari would publish in a similar vein (PR 173). In short, if we are to reduce Glissant to a Deleuzian, then we must be prepared to grant that he may very well have been one before Deleuze himself.

One wonders, however, to what extent Glissant's ideas may have been formed in his conversations with Deleuze—and the same can be asked of Deleuze with regard to Glissant. Glissant, Deleuze, and Guattari did of course know and exchange with each other from their university days on, and there was no doubt a triangulated flow of ideas among them that took shape within a greater intellectual milieu. As a result, this book will frame the relationship between Glissant and others writing in the philosophical genre as one of *confluence* rather than *influence*. That is, Glissant's relationship to Deleuze and Guattari, and to the Western philosophical tradition taken more broadly, is best understood as one of exchange, of points of contact and confluence—and also, lest we forget, of moments of divergence and resistance.

In the opening pages of her *Postcolonial Paradoxes in French Caribbean Writing* (2001), Jeannie Suk alludes to the all-too familiar, hierarchized framework wherein "Theory" takes precedence over literature, and does so yet more conspicuously when the former emanates from the West and the latter is a product of the postcolonial world. On account of its unstable correlation to the discourses of "French theory," the postcolonial is haunted by paradox, in Suk's view. And the Francophone Caribbean is paradigmatic in that regard.

> [T]he postcolonial has come to "represent" the idea of the margin made familiar by post-structuralism. How is this a paradox? That the abstract signs of theory could find grounding referents in the plight and people of the postcolonial world seems at once a somewhat anti-climactic relief and a disappointment. The "dangerous supplementarity" of the in-between doesn't seem so dangerous when revealed to have been an allegory of a concrete situation. (2)

Might the lived reality of Caribbean subjects really be a reservoir of concrete referents that lend meaning to the "abstract signs of theory," and could poststructuralism be an "allegory" of a postcolonial reality? The idea is an intriguing one. And there was, for Glissant, a harmonious correlation between (what he believed to be) the lived experience of Caribbean subjects and much of the theoretico-philosophical work of Deleuze and Guattari. His use of their figure of the rhizome to explain Caribbean subjects' experience of their identity is but one example. But a cohabitation of ideas for Glissant was just that: in other words, it was an amiable (perhaps even an amorous) living-together of (at least) two currents of thought, and one that need not be reduced to hierarchical structures. In that framework, the lofty abstract and the lowly concrete might suddenly find themselves *in Relation* (as Glissant would put it) and on the same level. There, the teeming repository of unrefined referents that Suk sees some theorists taking the postcolonial world to be could undertake its own work of abstraction, creating different ways of doing philosophy, or forging wholly new literary genres. Glissant himself, after all, created his own, Caribbean-derived abstract signs, and went on to locate their referents far afield, at times on a worldwide scale. His idea of creolization, or his repeated insistence that in modernity "the entire world is creolizing," constitutes but one example (cf. TTM 194).

But Glissant is not, he maintains, interested in merely flipping the hierarchy, or in ceding to the Caribbean the authority that the West formerly held. (Although the implications of his adherence to the idea of what Santí so gingerly calls "*perhaps* the predominance of the Caribbean as paradigm" remain a matter for discussion [58; emphasis added].) Glissant insists that not opposition but rather *a*pposition is his preferred interpretive framework, calling for us to relativize our many different ways of knowing the world. In his words: "Plato's city is for Plato, Hegel's vision for Hegel, the griot's city for the griot. It is not forbidden to see them in confluence, without confusing them in a jumble or reducing them to one another . . ." (PR 208). The realities of the "postcolonial world" and of "high theory" might converge at some points, but they diverge at others, in Glissant's thought as elsewhere. Glissant was influenced by the Western world in which he principally lived and worked, and by the tradition in which he was educated—it could not be otherwise. But as we will see, what is most interesting about Glissant is his long-term effort to create an alternative to the tradition that he knew so well: that is, his endeavors to use paradoxical ideas drawn from the natural and cultural realities of the Caribbean in order to make thought do something altogether unexpected.

ONE

A Wholly New Totality

Glissant's *Tout-monde*

How might one take up the task of speaking about absolutely everything, all at once? That ambition lies at the heart of Édouard Glissant's idea of the *Tout-monde*, or *world-as-Whole*. In one of his many elaborations of the term, Glissant defined the *Tout-monde* as "the realized totality of the known and unknown elements of our universes"—in other words, quite simply everything that is, the Whole in its most fundamental sense (CL 87). Fittingly, the content of that Glissantian category is vast, and the *Tout-monde* takes on a panoply of forms in Glissant's thought. It is first and foremost Glissant's pronouncement on the present state of the world in its entirety, but it also represents Glissant's sense of the future of the world, or where it is going. The *Tout-monde* is thus a way of speaking about all of our lived human reality, both present and to come. On the one hand, the *Tout-monde* can be seen to constitute Glissant's intervention in debates falling under the rubric of the term *globalization*. On the other hand, the word *Tout-monde* means much more, as it is additionally the name Glissant gives to an abstract, theoretical model, his effort to rethink the philosopheme of totality in a post-Hegelian context. Yet more concretely, the term *Tout-monde* is also the title of a lengthy, fragmentary novel (*Tout-monde* [1993]) and the subject of a subsequent treatise, *Traité du Tout-monde* (1997) (*Treatise on the Tout-monde*), in addition to furnishing the impetus for an essay supplementing both of those texts, *Une nouvelle région du monde* (2006) (*A New Region of the World*). The *Tout-monde* has inspired a brick-and-mortar institution, the Institut du Tout-monde in Paris, as well as the literary honor it grants, the Prix Carbet de la Caraïbe et du Tout-monde. And the *Tout-monde* has proven highly inspirational, even seductive, to readers of Glissant ranging from Patrick Chamoiseau to a host of academic critics, as well as the forty-four authors who signed the "Pour une littérature-monde en français" ("For a Literature-World in French") manifesto, which appeared the French newspaper *Le Monde*'s literary supplement *Le Monde des livres* in March 2007.

The phrasing *Tout-monde* stands out in its singular resistance to translation. Bearing a felicitous resemblance to the Creole expression *toutt moun*, or "everyone," the French *Tout-monde* represents a pairing of two sets of ideas, both of which invite myriad interpretations and translations. *Tout* can be rendered in English as "all," "whole," "everything," or in the adverbial senses as "wholly" or "altogether," whereas the *-monde* postposition is even more rich with meaning. Appending *-monde* to the abstract *Tout* could be read as indicating the materiality of an otherwise abstract vision of totality: the abstract Whole is *this* world, our world. Or, the *-monde* could serve as an intensifier, emphasizing the truly worldwide breadth of the term *Tout*'s referent. A nonexhaustive list of translations of *Tout-monde* might therefore include "World-whole" or "Whole-world," or "Everything-world," or "All-world," to take only a few examples. The hyphen between the two words multiplies yet further the possible meanings of this core idea in Glissant's thought. On the one hand, it connects *Tout* and *monde*, melding them into one discrete idea. On the other, it could be seen as serving a distancing function, illustrating that the two ideas do not mean the same thing, do not point to coextensive spaces or categories. In that interpretation, *Tout-monde* is not one but rather two different words, which are paradoxically combined and kept apart with one and the same hyphen. For all of these reasons the term *Tout-monde* is one that ought to be cited rather than translated, in order to preserve its semantic richness.

Making sense of this term requires a plunge into the multiplex universe of Glissant's thought. For as Glissant takes up what Frantz Fanon called the "colossal task" of working up an "inventory of the real" in his approach to the question of totality, he is led to coin other terms: *mondialité* (*globality*), *totalité-monde* (*totality-world*), *chaos-monde* (*chaos-world*), *Relation* (*Relation*), and so on (Fanon 173). A closer look at any of those keywords will demonstrate that each draws its meaning from the others, making the definition of any particular term impossible without reference to other terms. That process of relaying creates a hermeneutic network that Glissant would call a rhizome, another core idea in his theoretical work. The idea that stable meanings might be pinned down and isolated is a problematic one for Glissant, and one that his work will consistently undermine. The very term *Relation*, for example, to which Glissant devoted a work of poetics

(*Poétique de la Relation* [1990]) and a philosophical treatise (*Philosophie de la Relation* [2009]), is declared to be indefinable in the latter text, despite its prominence throughout the essays written after 1990 (PhR 97). The fact that the enterprise of definition proves to be just as impossible as it is unavoidable is only one example of the paradoxical groundings of much of Glissant's thought, and in that regard the *Tout-monde* is exemplary.

For Glissant, understanding the global, the totality or the *Tout*, implies attention to the local (or Place, in Glissantian rhetoric), which in turn is meaningless without robust theoretical consideration of the totality. In that feedback loop or schema of circularity we can locate Glissant's translation of the Hegelian universal-particular relationship (more on this subject below). That rewritten universal-particular relationship (or *relation*) is fundamental to the other, often paradoxical attributes of the global reality that is the *Tout-monde*. Glissant refers, for example, to the *Tout-monde* as an "order-disorder," and an "immobile movement" (CL 23; TTM 12). He repeats his aphorism that the world is "creolizing," before going on to explain his sense of creolization as being synonymous with unpredictability—all of which is of course tantamount to predicting that the world will become ever more unpredictable. Even more deeply imbricated into the notion of the *Tout-monde* are a cluster of other contradictions that become apparent over the decades of Glissant's repeated returns to the *Tout-monde*. At times he asserts that the *Tout-monde* is the world, in its entirety, whereas at others he adds that it is rather a smaller part of a greater whole that we know as the world. Similarly, Glissant often holds that the *Tout-monde* is a, if not *the* defining feature of our present reality, but he elsewhere frames it as a utopian future that is yet to come. The *Tout-monde* would thus at once be whole and part, at once one thing (the whole world) and not that thing, at once present and future. These paradoxical truths are accessible only through a very particular sort of imaginary (*imaginaire*), one that Glissant's essays both make manifest for his readers and encourage them to partake in, in their own way and in their own place.

Given the difficulties inherent in thinking, or rather *rethinking*, in the way that Glissant invites us to do, the following pages will address these Glissantian key words through a strategy that is immanent to his own methodology. That is, they will ask not what the *Tout-monde is* but rather what it *does*, privileging phenomenology over ontology. As a result, our first task will be to look into what Glissant means with his oft-repeated aphorism on what the world taken in its entirety is doing: *le monde entier s'archipélise et se créolise*. That is, the entire world is archipelagoizing and creolizing. One could be forgiven for understanding that what Glissant means by that assertion is that the whole world is increasingly coming to resemble the Caribbean. Indeed, central to that schema of resemblance is Glissant's consistent emphasis on what he calls Relation, a notion that he frames as being a direct derivation from the lived reality of Caribbean subjects. Accordingly, Relation will be the second focus of this analysis. Next, we will look to the sporadic definitions that Glissant has offered for his term *Tout-monde*, with a view toward sketching out its foundational features. Key to that endeavor is a gloss of the central role that aesthetics, and literary production in particular, play in Glissant's development of the *Tout-monde*. The subsequent section is devoted to a critique of the *littérature-monde* movement, of which Glissant was a member and for which he provided inspiration, with a focus on the troubling contradictions at the heart of that supposedly new and exhilarating mode of literary production.

The first of the novel *Tout-monde*'s long suite of narrators proudly proclaims that "[o]ur science is detour and coming-and-going" (TM 18), and in the spirit of that whimsical science we will return in conclusion to the contradictions that make up the very fabric of Glissant's model of the *Tout-monde*. Far from constituting weaknesses or oversights, these literal contra-dictions, where the author speaks against himself, prove to be fundamental to his overall (which is to say, global) project. Literature, and more specifically the literature of the Caribbean and of the postplantation zones of the Americas is, as it happens, the proper home of this contradictory mode of thought for Glissant. And literature can, he suggests, point us to a new or different imaginary, a new way in which the imaginary might function. What is more, the new category of literature that Glissant both calls for and puts into practice is both—and paradoxically—the cause and the effect of that new imaginary.

Le Monde Entier S'archipélise et Se Créolise

"The entire world is archipelagoizing and creolizing" or, alternatively, "the entire world is making itself into an archipelago/becoming an archipelago and making itself creole/becoming creole": this dictum constitutes a sweeping claim with regard to the ensemble of the world's cultures, alongside a prediction as to what they will all one day become. It is also one of Glissant's many articulations of his idea of totality. The natural and cultural qualities of the Caribbean would, in this formula, epitomize the nature of the entirety of the world, and serve as a sort of archetype that would indicate, if not finally predict, its future. The term *creolization* has come to be increasingly associated with Glissant; indeed, he goes so far as to claim that he invented it in its multifarious, pliable modern form (cf. PhR 64). For those reasons, Glissant's arguments regarding creolization produce a fruitful point of entry into the evolution of the *Tout-monde* in his work.

When Glissant uses the term *créolisation*, he is of course referring to specific spatiotemporal contexts: that is, to the plantation and postplantation societies of the Americas and to a lesser degree of the Indian Ocean, where European cultures and languages collided and melded with those already present in the region as well as others from Africa and Asia. What came into being there were new lived experiences, new forms of identity, and new languages (or dialects, depending on one's politics). Creolization in Glissant's writing is a way of describing all of those phenomena, but it is also much more. That it should be necessary to point out that Glissant's sense of creolization is at least to some degree a reference to those concrete historical contexts may at first glance appear odd. Ultimately, after all, the term clearly points toward its root, the creole, in French as in English. Surprisingly, however, Glissant insists that the formula *le monde se créolise* is not tantamount to saying that the world is becoming creole. That rather puzzling claim shows to what extent his sense of the creole has made a definitive departure from the word's cultural and historical connotations. Shrugging off the constraints of grammar, Glissant assigns a wholly different meaning to the expression *"se créoliser"*: "The world is creolizing, it is not becoming creole, it is becoming this inextricable and unpredictable (*imprédictible*) that each process of creolization carries within itself and that neither supports nor authorizes any model" (CL 229). Making reference to the creolization of the world would, then, both mean *and not mean* that the world is coming to resemble the Caribbean. If we are to take Glissant at his word, then the creolization of the world would thus refer not to an increasing similarity to creole cultures and languages per se, but rather to the ever-increasing prevalence of certain characteristics that those cultures share and exemplify.

In another instance of something approaching a definition of his keyword *creolization*, the Glissant of *Traité du Tout-monde* declares "I present to you as an offering this word creolization, in order to signify this unforeseeable (*imprévisible*) of unheard-of results, which keeps us from being persuaded of an essence or from being locked into exclusions (*raidi dans des exclusives*) (TTM 26). Creolization, here, has left creole cultures far behind, and is portrayed in purely abstract terms: the unpredictable, the antiessential, and so on. Creolization, of course, implies mixing or hybridity (*métissage*) to some degree, but what distinguishes Glissant's term from the intermingling for which the cultures of the Caribbean remain, for him, an archetype, is an added value to creolization: that of unforeseeability (*imprévisibilité*) (IPD 19).

Glissant often found himself called on to flesh out exactly what he meant by this increasingly overdetermined term. In one of his many responses, he affirmed that "I call creolization the meeting, the interference, the shock, the harmonies and disharmonies between [*sic*] cultures, in the realized totality of the world-earth [*monde-terre*]," going on to list four characteristics that define creolization for him (TTM 194). First among them is the "striking speed," in other words, because with new technologies of communication and transportation, people in previously isolated places have come to find themselves in an ever-increasing communion with others, in interactions that would have been unthinkable, or at the very least unthinkably slow, mere decades earlier. Second, there is the "consciousness of consciousness" that we have of that speed and those interactions. In other words, there is now the fact that human subjects know that we are implicated in those phenomena, in addition to knowing that we have this awareness of being caught up in them: we are conscious of our consciousness of creolization. (If this formulation looks very much like the Hegelian schema of absolute knowing coming to consciousness of itself in history, that is no coincidence—more on this below.) Third, creolization is characterized by the "intervalorization" that is a result of the first two characteristics, which requires that we all reevaluate the "components that are put into contact": through his use of the term *creolization* Glissant is enjoining us to undertake the Nietzschean project of a revaluation of all values, of a rethinking of all of our value judgments. That task is made possible due to the *Relation* of all values, which is to say, a utopian and relativistic framework where no culture's or individual's values are superior to any others. In creolization, simply put, there would thus be no "hierarchy of values" (TTM 194). Fourth, once again, Glissant hammers home his emphasis on the "unpredictability of the results" of creolization (TTM 194). Glissant opposes his notion of creolization to the "hybridity" (*métissage*) cherished by postcolonial criticism, arguing that hybridity is the product of two purportedly pure and knowable origins, and that its outcomes can be easily foreseen. In Glissant's vision of a creolizing world, the products of creolization have multiple and often obscured origins. And, finally, Glissant takes the notion of unpredictability to its utmost lengths, so much so that he holds quite simply that "Creolization is the unpredictable," that the word itself is synonymous with the unpredictable (IPD 89).

The second part of Glissant's claim as to what the world is becoming is rooted in the geographical model of the archipelago. *Le monde entier . . . s'archipélise*, of course, does not mean that the world is becoming a cluster of islands in a sea. Rather, Glissant's point is that the there is something about that geographical formation that is allied with particular ways of thinking and being in the world, and that those ways are becoming increasingly widespread. In the Lesser Antilles, of which Martinique forms a part, the links between geography and culture are abundantly visible. Primarily a volcanic island chain, these small islands have remarkably fertile soil thanks to the accumulation of centuries of volcanic ash. That feature, in addition to seasons of high and consistent rainfall coupled with bountiful solar energy, meant that the islands were exceedingly propitious to agriculture—a characteristic that was an unfortunate sine qua non for the slavery-based plantation system and the cultures it would influence. Nonetheless, the creolization that was born of that system would in turn lend an archetypal status to the Caribbean archipelago for Glissant. Creolization and archipelagoes go hand in hand. As Glissant puts it succinctly: "The most human, the densest and most intense form of metamorphosis is creolization. Its privileged environment [*entour*] is the Archipelago" (CL 74).

Glissant's recurring meditations on archipelagoes reflect the central importance of landscape to his thought. For Glissant, archipelagoes by definition are a group of islands with no center, with each island related to, relaying to, each other island. The very idea of an archipelago is, in a sense, itself somewhat paradoxical, in that it uses one word to describe a multiplicity. In other words, in the archipelago form a group of disparate and diverse islands exhibits sufficient interconnection and coherence such that a singular descriptor can be used to describe their multiplicity. In that sense, the archipelago is exemplary of the notion of unity within diversity.

That archipelagic structure is mirrored in the novel *Tout-monde*. Made up of a series of vignettes that are at times intertwined, and at others an apparent succession of non sequiturs, and with no shortage of red herrings, there is nevertheless one narrative arc that lends coherence to the whole: that is, the character Mathieu's quest for something, the nature of which is entirely unclear (the subject of this book's third chapter). The interwoven stories contained between the two covers of *Tout-monde* are numerous just as much as they are one, insofar as they are contained in *one* novel, by *one* author, with *one* principal, reappearing protagonist. This fragmentary narrative, which Glissant has called an "exploded novel," is in that way a literary archipelago as well (IPD 129).

The narrative structure of the work of fiction titled *Tout-monde* reflects the *Tout-monde* in that it is a unity that relays to a diversity, which in turn relays to a unity, ad infinitum. Glissant sees this phenomenon of unity-diversity as peculiar to the countries of the Caribbean but also as a common feature of the literatures of the Americas as a whole (IPD 12). And moreover, the methodological strategy of foregrounding unity-diversity is, as Lydie Moudileno has pointed out, a defining characteristic of Franco-Caribbean literature in general (*L'écrivain antillais* 113). That is no doubt why Glissant holds archipelagoes to be "good vantage points," where "if, standing up, each person on one of these islands, each person in her country, we look to the horizon, we see not just another country but the entire Caribbean, which changes our gaze and teaches it not to underestimate anything in this world, not even the smallest pieces of land . . ." (CL 85–86). And if the whole world *s'archipélise*, if it is becoming an archipelago, the lesson that archipelagoes teach us would hold for the entirety of the world as well. Archipelagoes would therefore teach us that "even the most miniscule of components" of the *Tout-monde* is "irreplaceable," that there is no whole without each and every part (CL 87).

The whole world then, like the Caribbean, increasingly exhibits fragmentation *and* interconnected multiplicity. But there is more to archipelagic thought than that: for Glissant, it implies a rejection of systematic thinking and an ancillary embrace of ambiguity. The problem with system-thinking, for Glissant, lies in what he perceives to be the exclusiveness and predictability implied by systems. System-thinking is a mode of thought proper to continents, and is for Glissant irrevocably connected to European colonial efforts, and equally to contemporary US hegemony, both of which would impose particular ideas and ways of thinking on the O/other. Such ways of thinking are "no longer adequate," whereas "archipelagic thought fits the speed of our worlds" today (TTM 31). Archipelagic thought is not only more open and more timely, it also constitutes a challenge to one of the foundational characteristics of Western reason: the fetishization of clarity. "We can sum up," Glissant explains, "by positing the opposition between an archipelagic thinking and a continental thinking, with continental thinking being a system-thinking and archipelagic thinking being the thinking of the ambiguous" (IPD 89). If the world is becoming archipelagic and if the way of thinking proper to archipelagoes is ambiguous, then it follows that ambiguity will increasingly be the case, and on a worldwide scale. Therein lies a key point for readers of Glissant: ambiguity in thought and exposition, rather than constituting a defect, is a reflection of the nature of the world. With that argument, Glissant has built a self-defense mechanism into his nonsystem of thought, in that to accuse it of being unclear is to acknowledge it as a faithful representation of the world.

All Is Relation

The state of interconnectedness within diversity that is epitomized by the archipelago form is what Glissant calls *Relation*, an idea whose importance to Glissant's thought cannot be overstated. In her groundbreaking 1999 monograph on Glissant, Celia Britton noted that his theory of *Relation* underlies all of his theoretical work (*Édouard Glissant and Postcolonial Theory* 11). Glissant has indeed found the meaning of Relation to be exceptionally pliable, alluding to an "aesthetics of Relation" (IPD 81), a salubrious and very modern form of identity he calls "Relation-identity" (PR 157–58), to a "thought" or a "thinking of Relation" (PhR 72), to a "politics of Relation" (NR 85), and most visibly to a "poetics of Relation" and a "philosophy of Relation," formulations that provided the titles of two book-length essays (1990 and 2009 respectively). That semantic polyvalence is carried over into English translations of Glissant's work. Indeed, as Britton points out, *Caribbean Discourse: Selected essays* (1989), J. Michael Dash's landmark translation of Glissant's *Le discours antillais* (1981) dealt with the broad concept of Relation by rendering the term three different ways in English: as "creolization," as "cultural contact," or as "cross-cultural relationships" (Britton, "A Note on Translation," *Édouard Glissant*).

In an etymology that Glissant is wont to repeat, he affirms that Relation "relie, relaie, relate" (PR 183–77). Relation, in other words, links and connects (*relie*) as it relays (*relaie*) from one term to another. It relates (*relate*), both in the sense of activating and maintaining relationships among terms and, crucially for Glissant's insistence on the centrality of aesthetics in the *Tout-monde*, it also relates in the sense that it narrativizes, telling stories in both oral and written forms. Relation is all-encompassing, touching on everything and everyone: indeed, for Glissant, "there are no limits to Relation" (PhR 45–46). Characteristically, Glissant casts Relation in a verbal rather than a nominal form, telling readers what it does rather than what it is. Thus, fifteen years after the publication of the *Poetics of Relation*, Glissant would include in his essay *La cohée du Lamentin* (2005) a phenomenology of Relation. Due to its use of capitalization, that particular approach to Relation was evocative of a divine proclamation from on high, engraved in stone—and marked by an appropriately mystical tone: "RELATION CONNECTS, RELAYS, RELATES. IT DOES NOT RELATE ONE THING TO ANOTHER, BUT RATHER THE WHOLE TO THE WHOLE. THE POETICS OF RELATION THUS ACCOMPLISHES THE DIVERSE" (CL 37).

A fledgling form of Relation can be discerned even in Glissant's first essay, *Soleil de la conscience* (1956), where he alluded to a moment of epiphany, his moment of realization that no culture exists in isolation, that the particularity of each culture could not exist without attention to that culture's relation to the totality of the world's cultures: "there will be no culture without all cultures" (SC 13–14). That early intimation of diversity and multiplicity within a totalizing, unifying framework hinted that Relation would become the engine and defining trait of what Glissant would later call the *Tout-monde*. What is more, his affirmation of radical interdependence not only in theoretical terms but also on the scale of real, human cultures is typical of the effortless oscillation between philosophical abstraction and attention to cultural particularity that characterizes much of Glissant's theoretical work.

That merging of the abstract and the concrete is also detectable in Glissant's recurrent meditations on the figure of the rhizome, which he acknowledges having borrowed from the work of Deleuze and Guattari, and which undergirds his thinking of Relation and of the *Tout-monde* (IPD 132). The rhizome is, moreover, the foundation for his approach to that proverbial bee that has never quite departed from Postcolonial Studies' collective bonnet: that is, the question of identity. Whereas Deleuze and Guattari contrast the rhizome with another figure borrowed from the world of botany, the root and tree system, Glissant shifts his emphasis almost entirely to the root, which he reads as a metonymic term for the tree. Setting up a distinction between two sorts of identity, Glissant pits the rhizome against the root. When taken metaphorically, the root has proved, he argues, unvaryingly harmful for figurations of identity throughout human history. "Root-identity" appeals first and foremost to the past, to a certain territory that an individual or a supposedly homogeneous group would make exclusive claims on, and as a result it constitutes a territorialism (PR157–58). In addition, it is important to recall that Glissant's critique of the idea of root-identity is an indictment of any political discourse that would sanctify the figure of roots, from Nazism to Negritude.

In contrast to that deleterious form of identity, what Glissant calls Relation-identity would forego the (futile) quest for an authenticity enshrined in the depths of the past or in territorialism.[1] Relation-identity is, rather, an ever-expanding embrace of the contemporary reality of cultural interconnection and exchange (PR 157–58). In other words, rather than plunging vertically along a temporal axis into the past, it would reach out horizontally on a spatial axis to other, contemporary cultures in the present. These opposing ways of thinking and living identity have their counterparts in two forms of culture, the composite cultures of locales such as the Caribbean archipelago or northern Brazil and what Glissant calls atavistic cultures, which are for him typified by those of the West. (Curiously, given the lingering legacy of slavery in the United States, Glissant excludes the cultures of the United States from the ranks of composite societies, calling US society a "multiethnic" one, albeit one where "the interchange among ethnicities . . . more or less does not take place" [TTM 39]).

What makes some cultures atavistic, he writes, is the fact that they "draw their authority from a Genesis, from a Creation of the world, from which they had taken inspiration and from which they had learned how to make a Myth, the home for their collective existence" (TTM 35). Glissant's overall critique of the fetishization of origins lies behind such thumbnail histories, particularly with regard to Western, colonizing nation-states: "Filiation and legitimacy are the two teats at which this sort of divine Right of property sucks, at any rate as far as European cultures are concerned" (TTM 35). In contrast, the impact of slavery on those whose ancestors suffered through it changes their relationship to the past, to their past. Theirs, that *other* relationship to origins, has brought into being an entirely different set of cultures: "The Genesis of the creole societies of the Americas melts into another obscurity, that of the slave ship's belly. That is what I call a digenesis (*digenèse*)" (TTM 36).

The pasts that shape such composite cultures thus usher them into an embrace of Relation. Trauma has begotten a gift of sorts. Those who live within such cultures cannot do otherwise than to live Relation; indeed, their experience of it is the most intense one available to anyone. It is their tripartite experience of what Glissant calls the *chasm* (*gouffre*) that makes their experience of Relation unique: they are faced with the chasm of the slave ship's hold, with the chasm of the Atlantic into which enchained Africans were cast, and with the epistemological chasm that is their nonknowledge of the past (PR 17–21). "The peoples who have frequented the chasm don't boast that they are chosen. They don't believe that they have given birth to the power of modernities. They live Relation ... as the forgetting of the chasm comes to them and also as their memory becomes stronger" (PR 20). Forgetting and memory, seemingly contradictory actions, go hand in hand for these peoples. This portrayal of the absence of knowledge shows that *not* knowing can paradoxically be fecund, generative of more ethical ways of being and knowing in the world—an argument that will prove central to Glissant's ethical reasoning in *Faulkner, Mississippi*.

Relation thus envelops apparent opposites: forgetting and memory, the emptiness of the chasm as well as the plenitude of the *Tout-monde*. Relationality is, furthermore, an abstract, philosophical perspective on totality where the truth of a term, whether that term be a person, place, thing or idea, lies not in it but in the relations connecting it to other terms. Relation is all of that, just as much as it is a lens through which to view concrete, lived, human existence. Fundamentally, Relation for Glissant *is the case*; it is perhaps the one term that explains all reality for him. It is the truth being, and by extension of human being. He asserts tersely that: "And yet Relation is there, it *is*. Whether I want it or not, whether I accept it or not—and there are people who accept it and people who don't—, I am determined by a certain number of relations in the world" (IPD 48).

The refusal to accept Relation, for Glissant, is at the root of many if not all of the world's evils. Those who reject Relation are the same ones who have labored at the slaughter bench of history. Conversely, an embrace of the imaginary of Relation is a precondition for change in the world. Glissant warns us that "No global operation of politics, economics or military intervention is capable of even beginning to glimpse the tiniest solution" to the world's problems, "if the imaginary of Relation does not resound in the mentalities and sensibilities of today's humanities to push them to overthrow the poetic vapor, that is, to conceive of themselves, humanities, and not Humanity, in another way: as a rhizome and not as a unique root" (IPD 90). Without that shift in our thinking, "no intervention in Burundi, in Rwanda, nor in Yugoslavia" could "'resolve' situations" that bring about suffering in the world (IPD 90). We ignore Relation at our own risk.

Nothing Less than Everything: Taking the Measure of Glissant's Measure of the World

Glissant could not have put it more plainly: "What makes the Tout-monde is the poetics itself of this Relation" (IPD 88–89). And the meanings of each word, *Relation* and *Tout-monde*, are so fundamentally imbricated into one other that they act at times as near-synonyms, relaying signification back and forth to one another in an infinite dialogue—or what Glissant would call a relating. Relation is what makes the *Tout-monde* possible, and the *Tout-monde* is the foremost instance of concrete Relation in the world, of Relation *as* the world. Just as the *Tout-monde* is the utmost totality, Relation reflects in turn Glissant's abiding insistence that his idea of totality is one in which the whole has no meaning without each and every one of its component parts.

Nearly fifty years after his initial reflection in *Soleil de la conscience* that no culture could exist without the totality of all other cultures (SC 13–14), Glissant repeats the same argument in his *Introduction à une poétique du Divers* ("Introduction to a Poetics of the Diverse"), but only after giving that argument a name: "Because just as one cannot save one language while letting the others perish, one cannot save a nation or an ethnicity while letting the others perish. And that's what I call Relation" (IPD 99). Radical inclusion then, with a keen emphasis on particularity: that is what Glissant frequently refers to as "the inextricable" in his elaboration of the *Tout-monde* (cf. CL 15, et passim).

With few exceptions, concise definitions are rare in Glissant's essays, for reasons that are germane to his overall rejection of systematic thought in favor of a cluster of ideas that remain active, malleable, constantly changing, and difficult to pin down. In the case of the formulation "*Tout-monde*," however, Glissant has suggested what he intends his curious word-pairing to point to: "Tout-monde: the realized totality of the known and unknown elements of our universes, the feeling that they matter to us infinitely . . . the certitude as well that the most infinitesimal of these components is irreplaceable to us" (CL 87). That rare instance of definition shows that the *Tout-monde* denotes a totality that is quite simply not to be outdone. This Glissantian theory of everything encompasses "known *and* unknown elements," not only the universe but "universe*s*," and the import of these elements and universes to us humans is no less than infinite. In his reference to the "known and unknown elements of our universes" Glissant has in mind a host of things: for example, particular cultures, languages, countries, and landscapes would constitute the beginning of a nonexhaustive list. In the *Tout-monde*, then, all is related and all is one. The *Tout-monde* is, in the most basic sense, *everything*, and as such it allies both the abstract and the concrete, both thought and life. The material earth (*monde*) is an abstract whole (*tout*), and conversely the abstract idea of totality is actualized in the reality of modernity.

Crucial to Glissant's understanding of the *Tout-monde* is what he describes as its novelty. His idea of the *Tout-monde* is also a gesture of periodization, and Glissant maintains that this phenomenon of "world Relation," or Relation on a global scale, is unprecedented in history. "Only today," he insists in 1996, can we both witness and partake in these phenomena (IPD 34). In this epochal shift, "For the first time, human cultures in their semitotality are entirely and simultaneously put into contact and into ebullient reactions with one another . . . For the first time, peoples have consciousness completely of the exchange" (TTM 23). Where there was once separation, now there are interconnection, contact, and mutual influence. This multifaceted *rapprochement* is also reflected, Glissant tells us, in the shrinking of time. Quick to point out that he is not speaking of the founding myth of the "melting pot" in the United States, Glissant goes on to explain that the "novelty" of our time lies in the transition from immense to immediate temporal fields (*plages*): "influences" and "repercussions" (he does not specify of what sort) are today felt immediately, without the delays that were, in the past, imposed by distance (IPD 82–83). The world's peoples are thus increasingly drawn into the schema of Relation.

One could be forgiven for hearing in such celebrations of connection, speed, and a shrinking world the echoes of another, now-familiar word. It will be clear by now that Glissant's *Tout-monde* sounds very much like what in other circles would be called "globalization." Perhaps in anticipation of the knee-jerk reaction such an association would no doubt elicit in his readers on the French intellectual left, Glissant circumnavigates potential criticisms by coining a new term to describe this new state of the world. The object of his praise, he insists, is not globalization but rather "globality" (in French, not *mondialisation* but rather *mondialité*). Globality and globalization exist, he clarifies, in a relationship of stark, binary opposition. As he weighs in on the ongoing debates surrounding globalization, he allows that globalization is now inarguably ubiquitous, but argues that it is at bottom a profoundly negative feature of the modern condition. Globalization constitutes "low-quality standardization, the reign of multinational corporations, savage ultraliberalism on world markets (a company advantageously moves its factories to a faraway country, a sick person does not have the right to buy his or her medications at a favorable price in a neighboring country) and so on . . ." (CL 15). So as to avoid any confusion of his *Tout-monde* with that other, "low-quality" and "savage" global phenomenon, Glissant clarifies that globalization is quite simply the "negative flip-side" of the "prodigious reality" that is globality (CL 15). *Globality* "projects itself . . . into an adventure without precedent that has been given to all of us today to live, and in a world that for the first time, and so truly and in such an immediate way, striking, conceives itself as multiple and one, inextricable" (CL 15).

Glissant's purportedly "new" vision of totality, where the abstract concept would overlap more or less perfectly with the concrete reality of his time (globality, again, and most emphatically *not* globalization), cannot help but recall the work of another thinker of totality and world history: Hegel. That is no coincidence, as Glissant has made clear his long-term and at times ambivalent position with regard to Hegel's work. On the one hand, Glissant has voiced his affinities with Hegel on various occasions throughout his career. On the other hand, his points of departure from Hegel are remarkable, and he has also rejected Hegel with a candor that is commensurate to his enthusiasm for the German thinker elsewhere. As recently as 1997 Glissant suggested that his life's ambition was to be a Hegelian. And in his youth as a poet he and many of his cohort had insisted that they shared that desire (TTM 142). Glissant saw in Hegel's work a "promise even of life," which Hegel set into "high logic"—just as much, Glissant adds in something of a non sequitur, as Valéry (TTM 147). Inklings of his admiration for Hegel had also surfaced nearly a half century earlier in Glissant's oeuvre, when he had confidently proclaimed that "it is known that all truth is dialectical consummation" (SC 21).[3]

In another example of his Hegelian affinities, it is impossible to overlook his recurrent use, in many of his arguments regarding the *Tout-monde*'s role in history, of the French term *"dépassement." Dépassement* represents one of the various ways the Hegelian idea of *Aufhebung* has been explained (if not translated) in French. Signifying "surpassing" or "overtaking," it points to the very engine of the teleological process described in Hegel's *Phenomenology of Spirit*, whereby human reason progresses toward Absolute Knowing.

Dépassement takes on a similarly central role in Glissant's exposition of the *Tout-monde*. For example, Glissant explains that the chaotic and unpredictable nature, the "upheavals" of the *Tout-monde*, "do not cause us to lose our way." On the contrary, they are "the very matter of our mutual *dépassements*" (CL 17, emphasis added). Glissant has indicated elsewhere that the world's progression toward the *Tout-monde* can be best understood in terms of *dépassement*. He employs the term, for example, to demonstrate that the entirety of his work has long been marked by a deep concern for the advent of the *Tout-monde*, framing the latter in Hegelian language: "I have always been concerned," he tells an interviewer, "with the *dépassement* towards the 'Tout-monde'" (IPD 141).

Indeed, and despite Glissant's recurring attacks on the very ideas of systems of thought or the category of the universal, critics have gone so far as to argue that Glissant may be a truer Hegelian than Hegel himself. For Alexandre Leupin, Glissant's peculiar variety of post-Hegelianism can explained by the fact that, despite Glissant's rejection of systems and systematic thinking, "Paradoxically, Glissant criticizes Hegel for not being universal and systematic *enough*" ("The Slave's Jouissance" 891). That is because a Glissantian totality would, in Leupin's reading, be yet more total than the Hegelian version. Leupin goes on to suggest in no uncertain terms that "One can even posit that [Glissant's] entire thought is a response to Hegel that forcefully tries to go beyond all the important Hegelian themes" (ibid.). What is more, Leupin muses in conclusion, "Maybe, also, the *Tout-monde* and the Relation poetics will be a manner of *completing* Hegel" (ibid.). For Leupin, then, Glissant's rebellion against Hegel is in the final analysis a wholehearted acceptance. What makes Glissant a truer thinker of totality in such readings is his insistence that nothing should be excluded from the *Tout-monde*, neither Africa (*à la* Hegel) nor the small countries of the Caribbean and elsewhere.

Peter Hallward's interpretation of the Hegelian currents in Glissant's thought largely dovetails with Leupin's. For Hallward too, Glissant's periodic attacks on Hegel in reality constitute a sort of implicit endorsement. For Hallward, "Glissant is hostile to Hegel's '"totalizing Reason"' (IP 7) only to the degree that it is not totalizing enough. . . . Glissant writes an eminently Hegelian critique of Hegel, Hegel negated and surpassed by a dialectic which includes him" ("Édouard Glissant between the Singular and the Specific 445). When the Hegelian vision of world history neglects Africa, setting it outside of the progress of history, it sets limits for itself, leaving its totality narrower than Glissant's (ibid.). The same is true as Hegel consigns the Americas to the far-off future of world history. Glissant's *Tout-monde*, in contrast, sweeps up each and every particular place. And Glissant would consequently be, if we are to follow Leupin's and Hallward's analyses, a Hegelian despite himself.

Glissant's supposed ultra-Hegelianism notwithstanding, there are marked points of departure separating his thought from Hegel's. It was later in his productive life that Glissant would make outspoken attempts to distance himself from Hegel. In *Une nouvelle région du monde*, for example, Glissant would insist in no uncertain terms that Hegel is far from infallible.

Hegel can be mistaken . . . : there is a novel in there somewhere, and there has been one for more than two centuries now, if we set the lucid and meticulous complexity of Hegel's system in apposition with his blindness when he applies it to the totality world.[4] He elevated beauty, but it was without vision and without Relation. He knew history, he recognized it, but it remained sick, without the memory of any far-off place that would also be near. (NR 152; emphasis and ellipses in original)

Earlier, in *Poétique de la Relation*, Glissant would also cut Hegel down to size as he relativized him through his remark to the effect that, again, "Plato's city is for Plato, Hegel's vision for Hegel, the griot's city for the griot. It is not forbidden to see them in confluence, without confusing them in a jumble or reducing them to one another . . ." (PR 208).

It is, however, in his approach to the relationship of the universal and particular that Glissant breaks most radically with Hegel. Where Hegel's progression toward Absolute Knowing unfolds within a relationship of particulars to a universal, Glissant grounds his idea of the *Tout-monde* in a pairing of place and totality. The dialectical relationship that structures Glissant's conception of the *Tout-monde*, in other words, is that of the whole and its constituent parts, of the *Tout-monde* (the totality) and particular places (or cultures, languages, etc.). That alteration, of the particular-universal binary opposition into a relationship of place and totality, allows Glissant to frame his idea of the worldwide progression toward the *Tout-monde* in markedly different terms, translating the Hegelian particular-universal dyad into what he believes to be a more properly modern formulation.

"The true relation," Glissant maintains, "is not of the particular to the universal, but rather of Place to the totality-world, which is not the totalitarian but rather its contrary in diversity" (IPD 105). Before looking more closely at Glissant's place-totality relationship, his aversion to the very idea of universality calls for explanation. That eschewal is best understood in the context of his cautious handling of the concept of totality. For Glissant, the abstract notions of both the universal and totality have clear and proven potential to bring about dangerous political realities. Through his invocation of "the totalitarian" in opposition to the totality-world, Glissant establishes a causal relationship between the abstract thinking of totality and totalitarian political regimes.

Such a connection is, in its turn, far from obvious, and it merits contextualization within the overall political orientation of Glissant's thought. Glissant feels that previous forms of totalizing thought have allowed the flourishing of totalitarian politics and, yet further, that thinking in terms of universals has immense and proven potential to lead to political and ethical disasters. When

Glissant refers, to take one example, to "the generalizing universal, which is always ethnocentric and absolute," he has in mind Stalinism's murderous tenure on the Eurasian landmass, but also the French "Civilizing Mission" and the suffering it inflicted on France's colonies (PR 235).

The dangers of one particular group declaring its values to be universal and then imposing them on others extend even to the very role of systematicity in thought for Glissant. And in his many critiques of systematicity and system-thinking lies another of his critiques of Hegel. For Glissant, neither "systems of thought" nor "thoughts of systems" have any meaningful purchase on the real; they can offer "neither the comprehension nor the measure" of what happens in historical conflicts and contacts (IPD 87). Systems of thought are closed; they seek to formulate a reality that would be wholly subject to reason, predictable, and therefore fundamentally unreal. Faced with the specters of humankind's violent past that were indelibly linked to systematic thinking (again, Stalinism, or Western colonial and neocolonial projection), Glissant substitutes what he calls the "erratic" dimension. In French as in English, the word's roots connote mobility and wandering. That "erratic dimension," which Glissant frames in scientific language as "the dimension of deterministic systems with multiple variables," is all the more important in that it has become "the dimension of the Tout-monde" (IPD 87). Possessing nothing of the fixity of a closed system, the erratic dimension of the Tout-monde strays from the path of reason. It allows the *Tout-monde* to be present all over the world just as a colonial power might, but without the goal of domination.

Long before his outright rejection of universals Glissant had articulated a sense of the universal-particular relationship that shared much with Hegel's. In lieu of Hegel's emphasis on a universal that would subsume particulars as it unfolds, Glissant emphasized the lingering presence of the particular within the universal, essentially foregrounding the particular and according to it an importance equivalent to that of the universal. That move is of course not entirely without justification in Hegel's thought: at bottom, the Hegelian universal does not simply do away with the particular; rather, it subsumes and elevates the particular into it. That fact was not lost on the young Aimé Césaire, and Glissant's reading of Hegel may very well be an echo of Césaire's. Recalling the euphoric early days of Negritude in Paris, the author of the *Cahier d'un retours au pays natal* explained to Jacqueline Leiner in a 1975 interview that

> I have always been dominated by this Hegelian idea, that Senghor and I used to emphasize at the time, and I recall our joy when

we found this sentence of Hegel's: "It is via the particular that there is access to the Universal." We discussed the Universal, we tried to see how one can get to the Universal and we used to say, no no, it's Hegel who said it, that the Universal is not the negation of the particular, rather it's via the particular that there is access to the Universal, that the Universal is a deepening [*approfondissement*] of the particular. (qtd. in Leiner 139–40)

For the young Glissant as well, that robust emphasis on particularity would transform itself into an inevitable copresence of the universal and particular, an idea that would lay the groundwork for his later sense of the place-totality relationship. Glissant saw the universal and particular relationship not as one of a binary opposition to be resolved, but rather as an *a*pposition, a placing of two terms side by side without hierarchy or synthesis. Already displaying a marked discomfort with the very term *universal*, but sensing it to be necessary nonetheless, in *Soleil de la conscience* Glissant affirmed that "[E]ach being comes to the consciousness of the world through his/her world first; just as universal (to use grand terms) as it is particular" (SC 23–24).

What is true for every being is all the more so for the writer—and indeed, that particular being's lived experience of artistic production is key to Glissant's understanding of the place-totality relationship. Once again, the place-totality pairing is a key feature of the modern condition that Glissant has branded "globality." And writers, Glissant insists, have much to teach us about what it might mean to live and produce in the modern world. Place and poetics are indissociable for Glissant, and it is on account of that deep connection that the writer is no less than the modern condition incarnate for him: "Every poetics *of our times* signals its landscape (*paysage*). Every poet, his country (*pays*): the modality of his participation" (IP 73; emphasis in original). The particular form that all writing inevitably takes always departs from, just as much as it is irrevocably tied to, a particular place (IPD 133). Therein lies the meaning of Glissant's oft-repeated aphorism "*Le Lieu est incontournable*" ("Place is unavoidable/impossible to circumvent"): all writing, all expression, issues from a place. That is, the fact of all writing's grounding in, and continued relationship to, *a* place cannot be gotten around. There is consequently no writing of no-place, and by extension no universal knowledge hygienically separated from the physical and cultural context in which it was created. (Readers of Glissant will doubtless recognize therein the persistent attention to context shared by the French readers of Nietzsche known to English speakers as the poststructuralists, an emphasis that would subsequently become central to the work of Spivak, Bhabha, and Said, the early triumvirate of postcolonial criticism.)

There is no writing that could escape its situated specificity and moreover, for Glissant, no writing ought to make such an attempt: their situatedness is to be embraced. Poets, who live in and work from a particular place, cannot do otherwise but to speak the "rooted necessity of relation to the world" (IP 72). Coupling writing with place is not tantamount to limiting meaning through a sort of semantic provincialism, or to holding that writing can *only* speak a particular place, however. On the contrary, such rootedness in place is something to be celebrated, as it can become an opening onto greater creative possibilities. Rethinking the relationship of writing to place can make everything that is old new again, and can bring novelty into the world as more and more places are brought into relation with each other within the totality that is the *Tout-monde*. In characteristically sanguine language, Glissant contends that this way of framing the relationship of place to totality has transformative potential: "The passion and the poetics of the totality-world can indicate the new relationship to Place and drive out, change, old reflexes" (IPD 101). As writers turn inward to their own place they are always already turning outward; both occur simultaneously, and each directionality relays back to the other. That directionality is a paradox. And understanding and producing art within that paradoxical directionality, that "new relationship to place," is a way—indeed, it would seem to be *the* way for Glissant—of bringing change and novelty into the world.

This recursive pattern, where turning inward means turning outward, which in its turn implies turning inward, ad infinitum, is visible in Glissant's intellectual returns to his own place, the island of Martinique within the Caribbean archipelago. The archipelago form is, we must recall, fundamental both to Caribbean landscapes and increasingly to the world as a whole. In the landscapes that archipelagoes give birth to, human subjects sense at one and the same time a profound sense of belonging to a particular place and its culture, alongside an awareness that their island (read: their place) is but one among many other islands, all of which have vast, continental powers as their neighbors (CL 85–86). That paradoxical belonging, at once here and there, at once rooted and in relation, gives life to a particular sort of imaginary: "The imaginary of my place is linked to the imaginable reality of places in the world, and the inverse is also quite true. The archipelago is this source-reality, non-unique, whence these imaginaries are secreted: the schema of belonging and relation, at one and the same time" (PhR 47). The imaginary of the Caribbean subject is thus as much singular as it is dual, here and there at the same time, *ici-là*.

Glissant's emphasis on this "archipelagic thought" is emblematic of what J. Michael Dash has identified as a "major and complex issue in Caribbean writing—the temptation of cultural difference and intellectual containment on one hand and the impulse towards relativity and interdependence" (*Glissant* 23). The peculiar situation of the Caribbean writer is an archetype of the place-totality relationship that, for Glissant, characterizes all writing, as well as all human being, today.

Crucially, Glissant has described this now-archetypal relationship as having a circular structure in the context of a discussion of his novel *Tout-monde*. When posed, in the context of an interview, the deceptively simple question as to "who is speaking?" in that ludic, postmodern narrative, Glissant counters that it is impossible to know exactly who the narrator of *Tout-monde* might be. He shifts the focus of the conversation to the question of place, preferring to explain that, despite the novel's multiple, globe-trotting settings, "The paradox is that all of this departs from a place and returns to that place, in circularity" (IPD 131). The novel *Tout-monde* is in this way representative of the imaginary of the *Tout-monde*, a way of thinking that Glissant rephrases in simpler terms as "the fact that I can live in my place while being in relation with the totality-world" (IPD 91). That way of thinking also represents a way of *re*thinking Hegelian dialectics, at the very least in terms of their emphasis on teleological progress. Instead of a departure from a place that subsumes that place's particularity (though retaining it in some form per the Hegelian model), Glissant's schema is structured by eternal returns to place. In short, there is no departure without return. And conversely there is no rootedness without relation. Paradoxically, to say one term is to say its other.

Although the young Glissant had maintained that reality was fundamentally dialectal, the question arises as to whether Glissant's recursive circularity can properly be called a dialectics at all, or whether it moves toward the utmost truth of "dialectical consummation" that Glissant envisaged in *Soleil de la conscience*. Otherwise put, how might this infinite loop of returns and relations go anywhere, and where might it be going? The response, for Glissant, lies in the radical potentiality of literary production. It is literature, Glissant maintains, that both brings about and signifies to us the reality that is the *Tout-monde*.

The Book of the World: The *Tout-monde* and Aesthetics

It is no coincidence that Glissant often refers not to Relation *tout court* but rather to the *poetics* of Relation, to the *aesthetics* or to the *philosophy* of Relation. And it is, once again, not Relation but rather the *poetics* of Relation that produces, that makes up the very stuff of the *Tout-monde* (IPD 88–89). Such formulations attest to the fact that for Glissant there is something about how Relation works in the *Tout-monde* that connects it intimately to language: no Relation without its poetics, or its articulation in philosophy. Yet more pointedly, Relation and the *Tout-monde* that it creates go hand in hand with literary production. All literature takes as its object the *Tout-monde*, and it falls to us to discern that fact. The *Tout-monde* is, Glissant affirms succinctly, "THE HIGHEST OBJECT OF POETRY" (CL 37). Poetry, at its best (its "highest"), would thus take the *Tout-monde* as its object, would speak the *Tout-monde*. While that intimate link between literature and the *Tout-monde* is an effect of the modern condition, it has also been to some degree latent in poetic production throughout history, since the *Tout-monde* is something that "Poets throughout the ages have sensed" (TTM 176). Poetry, and literature more broadly, have always pointed toward the greater totality that is the totality-world, and the only difference today is that they do so yet more intensely. "The poem," therefore, "forms the framework between the density of place and the multiplicity of the diverse, between what is said here and what is heard over there" (TTM 182). Put otherwise, it is literature that bridges the gap between particular places and the totality, and it is the writer who, through language, articulates the *Tout-monde*, bringing readers closer to it.

> Writing today is not only telling stories to have fun or to bring forth stirrings of emotion, or to amaze; to write is perhaps first and foremost to seek out the trustworthy link between the mad diversity of the world and what we desire, within ourselves, in terms of balance and knowledge. This world is there in our consciousnesses or our unconsciousnesses, a Tout-monde, and although we may have said it time and again, it calls out to us more each day and we must try to experience our own scope within it. *The writer and the artist have summoned us to it. Their work is marked by that vocation.* (TTM 173; emphasis added)

The connection between language and the fiber of the physical world runs deep for Glissant, and resonates with the Judeo-Christian tradition as well as with Heidegger's sense of the relationship of poetics to Being. Hence the subtitle of *Philosophie de la Relation*, "poetry in extension." The opening pages of that text go yet further, depicting poetry in a geophysical sense, as a force that was present at the planet's creation, bringing it into being. Poetry would thus be coextensive with the very matter of the earth, and what poetry produces, as Glissant wrote twenty years earlier in the *Poétique de la Relation*, is an "expression" of the "becoming of the planet Earth" (PR 44). In this quasi-mystical framework poetry would therefore lie at the origins of the world just as much as it points its readers (back) to the world-as-totality, in a circle. In this neo-Romantic conception of the poet, it is thus the creator of art, and of written texts in particular, who is granted the greatest proximity to the world, who enjoys a privileged access to the truth of the physical landscapes that surround him or her, and to reality in the plainest sense.

While in Glissant's thought poetry has always enjoyed this profound connection with the very fiber of reality, its historical role has shifted, or rather become amplified, with the advent of the *Tout-monde*. Glissant does not give a precise date for the onset of the *Tout-monde*, although he does suggest that the Atlantic slave trade and its aftermath were key in bringing it, along with the creolization and Relation that animate it, into existence. But another marker for the dawn of the *Tout-monde* is a corresponding revolution in the poet's role with regard to his or her community. Before the *Tout-monde* came to be, the poet's function in society was one of affirming and thus reinforcing the coherence of his or her community. That enterprise was predicated on the exclusion of other communities and the languages they spoke. In the past, serving as the bard of one community was, then, a way of deprecating other communities, of staking out a distance from them. Likewise, literary production served the purpose of establishing one community's dialect as a sort of chosen language, with the added implication that other languages were minor, or even barbarous (IPD 47).

The *new* literature of the *Tout-monde*, however, does something entirely different: it "will establish relation and not exclusion" (IPD 68). Rather than founding the nation-state, rather than delineating the boundaries of a community and reinforcing them, this new literature is an opening, an invitation to commune with others. Individual, discrete communities do of course continue to exist in the *Tout-monde*. But the latter is characterized by a new form of collective, and one that proves to be imperiled today: a collective that Glissant names, in another use of what will by now have become a familiar affix, the "community-world" (*communauté-monde*) (IPD 79). That community, which is both one and many, is what today's writers are called to defend. And with this new community-world comes a wholly new literary genre (the subject of the next chapter).

Glissant's sense of a larger, interconnected literary community that would somehow be more in touch with the reality of today's world has proved appealing to many of his readers. Most visibly, one group of writers who are associated with the far-flung and contested lands of "Francophonie" have taken up Glissant's torch, seeking to name and thereby activate a purportedly "new" mode of literary production. What they call a "literature-world in French" (*littérature-monde en français*) would constitute a new way of writing and understanding texts, one characterized by a more profound, a truer connection to the world itself. That ambition is as compelling as it is problematic, and it tests the limits of Glissant's vision of globality.

A Visit to Malarkeyland? The *Littérature-monde* Movement

For the forty-four signatories to the "For a literature-world in French" manifesto, the time had come to "find anew the ways of the world" ("PLM" 5). In order to understand how it is that the ways of the world might have gotten lost in the first place, it is beneficial to look more closely at the text's Glissantian imprimatur. The manifesto was published in *Le Monde des livres*, the weekly supplement to the French newspaper *Le Monde*, in 2007. Critics have noted that the formulation *littérature-monde* looks very much like a Glissantian turn of phrase (Porra 34), so much so that some have gone so far as to assume that he in fact coined it (Hocine and Marin 23). (On the other hand, the term's origins are further obscured by the fact that one of the movement's leaders, Michel Le Bris, has suggested that he was the first to use the word, in 1992 [24]). Not surprisingly, much in the manifesto dovetails with some of the more basic, the most optimistic, and even the most utopian aspects of Glissant's *Tout-monde*.

The manifesto can be summarized in broad strokes as a dual gesture: it first is a sort of performative speech act, whereby the very fact of proclaiming the demise of *la Francophonie* is tantamount to killing it off. That move of negation is followed by the positing of a new genre or regrouping of literary works along linguistic and geographical lines, the eponymous "littérature-monde en français" or "literature-world in French." The manifesto seems to take a cue from the Judeo-Christian tradition, where creation of a new (literary) world follows a two-step process: (1) name a new world and by virtue of doing so breathe life into it, and (2) rest, and allow it to flourish. (The signatories are presumably busy with this second step now.) The impetus for their dissolution of the francophone world lies, they clarify, in their realization that French-language literature is produced in a multipolar world and on multiple continents. The manifesto's authors explain that they were inspired to join together by what their first lines hold to be an unprecedented "historical moment": in that year, the Goncourt, the Renaudot and a handful of other French literary prizes were all won by French-speaking writers from "beyond-France" ("*outre-France*"). "The center, the fall prizes tell us, is everywhere from now on, at the four corners of the earth." Whereas Glissant heralds the dawning of the *Tout-monde*, of the "time-world" (*temps-monde*; cf. IPD 132), they (and he along with them) announce "The end of Francophonie. And the birth of a literature-world in French."

That doing away with Francophonie should be such an urgent matter stems from the fact that, for the signatories, so-called francophone literary production has always placed metropolitan France at the center of the francophone world. That tendency was visible even in the supposedly open-minded literary milieu, which possessed a "vision of a Francophonie in which a France as mother of the arts, as mother of arms and of law would continue to dispense her enlightenment, as a universal benefactor, one concerned with bringing civilization to the peoples living in darkness." That lingering, neocolonial bias, they suggest, led to a degeneration into formalism, the navel-gazing in which the contemporary French novel has been caught wallowing: "Instead of rubbing up against the world in order to capture its breath, its vital energies, the novel, in short, only had to watch itself being written." Such contemporary French novels from continental France, ignorant of the world, "from then on only point to other texts, in an endless play of combinations." They name and shame this putatively postmodern, excessive French textualism in order to proclaim that "The world is coming back. And that is the best of news. Won't it have long been conspicuously absent (*le grand absent*) from French literature?"

The hyperbole evident in these dreams of a new "Copernican revolution" also shines through in the signatories' rather startling usage of the language of astrophysics: *Francophonie* is a "dead star," and as we witness the birth of a literature-world we are in effect gazing on the "formation of a constellation." The aspirations of Glissant's own essay in the *Pour une littérature-monde* book, which nearly thirty authors under the direction of Le Bris and Rouaud published in the wake of the excitement generated by the manifesto, seem humble in comparison. They do, however, reflect Glissant's critiques of Francophonie and World Literature (cf. TTM 120). Christopher Miller explains that in Glissant's "more philosophical critique" of Francophonie, the Martinican renunciant of Francophonie demonstrates that Francophonie, which would seek to pass for a champion of diversity, is in actuality a forceful assimilation of former colonies and their writers to France and its variety of the French language (*Theories of Africans* 197). "The value of Glissant's contribution," Miller writes, "lies in his unveiling of the monolithic substructure of an ideology that claims to be pluralistic" (ibid. 198). *That* Francophonie would thus be "an ideological wolf in sheep's clothing, inviting dialectical exchange but subtly domesticating and assimilating to an unchanging standard" (ibid.).

Camille de Toledo's is perhaps the most eloquent and insightful of the now-plentiful reactions to, and rebuttals of, the *Pour une littérature-monde* manifesto and the ardor it generated. The very title of his *Visiter le Flurkistan ou les illusions de la littérature-monde* (2008) (*Visiting Malarkeyland, or the Illusions of Littérature-Monde*) makes plain that his response will not be kind. Toledo's riposte points to the central problem of the manifesto: what is cast as a gesture of global inclusion (via, in an echo of Glissantian rhetoric, the *-monde* affix) proves to do exactly the opposite. And the *littérature-monde* that Le Bris et al. herald as something altogether novel displays, as Toledo illustrates, a troubling continuity with the past.

Toledo shows that the manifesto sets up a new politics of exclusion that continues in the path of the old one. First and foremost, the world-loving forty-four signatories are in effect drawing and defending boundaries, excluding from their *monde* anyone who would foolhardily continue to bear the banner of Francophonie aloft. What is more, the manifesto separates *its* authors from much of the rest of the literary world: that is, from writers not working in French (read: those who work in the language of perfidious Albion in particular), but also certain currents within "French" literature itself. What is more, the manifesto fetishizes a particular *sort* of "Francophone" writer. As Eric Prieto has rather cuttingly put it, "Michel Le Bris (the primary author of the manifesto) seems also to be looking for a way to co-opt some of the minoritarian mojo that has made postcolonial literature such a hot commodity in the United States and Britain" ("Édouard Glissant, *Littérature-monde*, and *Tout-monde*" 111). Prieto's argument is validated by the conspicuous invocations of ethnicity and color in the essay "Pour une littérature-monde en français" written by Michel Le Bris in the collection of the same name. To take only one example, Le Bris vaunts the restorative powers of a literature-world that would be "multiple, diverse, colored" (41).

Elsewhere, Toledo casts doubt on the ability of French (which French?) to be a true world language, skeptical that the French language could ever acquire the same global footprint that English has. Because they meet French speakers at academic gatherings all over the world, Toledo explains, the purveyors of *littérature-monde* "take what is no longer any more than a secondary language for a language-world" (*"langue-monde"*) (70). Besides, the proponents of *littérature-monde* ignore one of the more important material constraints on the globality of world literature in French, one that keeps it enduringly attached to the French capital, despite the forty-four's claims to the contrary. As Toledo emphasizes, even in the twenty-first century the most prominent "editorial structures" for literature written in French remain located not just in metropolitan France, but almost exclusively in the city of Paris (68). Whereas few today would perceive English-language literature to be eternally attached to London, French-language literature, it seems, cannot shake off its Parisian yoke. Alas, while Paris may be an increasingly cosmopolitan city, it clearly is not a world.

Toledo points out a yet more striking gesture of exclusion couched in the heralding of a *littérature-monde*: while the manifesto would appear to be an open-armed embrace on a world scale, it is also haunted by a "limit, a lack of opening." That limit is exemplified by the fact that the partisans of *littérature-monde* exhibit just as much adoration for the writers whom Toledo terms "the postcolonials" as they do disdain for "the postmoderns" (69). For as Toledo insists, "we need Césaire *and* Beckett, Bouvier *and* Perec" (78). The need to read writers from former colonies *and* their metropolitan counterparts stems from the fact that "Césaire's 'vast words' are not enough to re-found, to authorize, to open and liberate the novel. They need, alongside them, 'hole-words,' 'stutter-words,' 'stupid-words'" (90). In other words, Toledo reminds us of what should go without saying: that the *monde* of *littérature-monde* should exclude no part of the world. It ought, as Glissant says of the *Tout-monde*, to be guided by Relation. Above all, as the Glissant of *Philosophie de la Relation* explains, "Relation is here understood as *the realized quantity of all of the differences of the world*, without being able to exclude a single one" (PhR 42).

Appending *-monde* to other words (*littérature-monde, Tout-monde, chaos-monde, identité-monde, communauté-monde*, and so on) is an ecstatic gesture. That is, not only is it marked by exuberance, it is also an ek-stasis, a standing outside of oneself and one's context. But as Toledo points out, as they gush over the "*frisson* of the outside" that they feel as they witness the birth of a *littérature-monde*, the prophets of *littérature-monde* forget that the world is already total, that it is already one (31). They have let slip from their recollection the fact that today, as Toledo puts it, there is no longer any outside (31). And finally, in his coup de grâce, Toledo illustrates that the forty-four's yearning to shake off the "grand ideologies" of the past does not open up for them a new world where all ideologies have been hygienically swept away. Quite to the contrary, it betrays a treacherous embrace of yet another, now-familiar ideology from the past. That way of thinking, what Toledo calls the "ideology of afterwards" (39), or the sense of epochal closing and the dawning of a new era, carries with it its own dangers and deceptions.

In Glissant's writing and in its echoes in the *littérature-monde* movement, the addition of the *-monde* suffix would seem to have a sort of enchanting effect on a word, whereby its very presence signifies a direct conduit to the reality of the world, and to the unified entirety of that world. Yet such *enthousiasme-monde* is, as Toledo and Prieto adeptly show, as problematic as it is seductive. The contradictions that are operative in its elaboration would appear to be reactionary, regressive, and incongruous with Glissant's optimism. But there are ways in which Glissant's *Tout-monde*, in whose shadow the *littérature-monde* movement unfolds, shares some of those problematic characteristics. That figure of exuberant thought carries with it its own contradictions, both avowed and unspoken.

By Way of Conclusion: Letting the *Tout-monde* Slip Our Grasp

> Our science is detour and coming-and-going.
> —Glissant, *Tout-Monde*

Glissant's *Tout-monde* is alive with paradoxes. On the one hand, some of those paradoxes are clearly integral to his development of his broad and flexible tool for thought. As we have seen, the *Tout-monde* is at once unity and multiplicity, it is produced (at least in part) by a creolization that does not mean becoming-creole, it is characterized by a local belonging that is simultaneously a global one, and it is fundamentally an "order-disorder" (CL 23). Likewise, the "globality" that describes the whole of our world today, and therefore the *Tout-monde*, is "unique and multiple" (CL 23). And Glissant also holds that what allows us to know and understand the *Tout-monde* is its "immobile movement" (TTM 120). This "fixity of the Tout-monde's movement" is what allows us to make some sense of it, to know it as something other than a ceaseless and daunting agitation, or an incomprehensible chaos (TM 145). As an unnamed narrative voice of the novel *Tout-monde* affirms, in yet another paradoxical lesson, the *Tout-monde* whirls and swirls (*tourbillonne*), but it does so in order to teach us immobility (TM 455). Self-contradictory though it may appear, the reality of modernity that Glissant calls the *Tout-monde* nonetheless does not give birth to an intellectual nihilism or an uninterrupted, chaotic upheaval. It is, Glissant tells us, as chaotic as it is grounded, a "moored whirling" (*tourbillon amarré*) (TM 179).

There are other paradoxes in the *Tout-monde*, however, that pose greater challenges to understanding. Each one of Glissant's numerous references to the *Tout-monde* begs one question that is as simplistic as it is inevitable: *is the Tout-monde the world*? Glissant's answers to that question swing wildly from the categorical to the contradictory. And in concordance with the overall tenor of his thought, they articulate a set of paradoxes that remain unresolved, deploying language and ideas that are thoroughly saturated with opacity. The seemingly simple question as to whether the *Tout-monde* can be said to exist in actuality conjures up a host of other questions, all of which can be loosely organized around the axes of space and time.

With regard to space, we might ask whether what Glissant calls the *Tout-monde* describes the totality of the world as it exists today, or whether it is a part of the world, or whether it might even be a larger whole of which our world is only a part. Confusingly, Glissant has at times made each one of those arguments. The temporality of the *Tout-monde* is similarly undecided, as Glissant at times implies that the *Tout-monde* describes the state of the world today, whereas at others he describes the *Tout-monde* as a far-off, utopian future. Yet elsewhere, he has suggested that we ought to think beyond a simple distinction between "now" and "then," insisting that there are multiple temporalities associated with the *Tout-monde*, insofar as some of us in some places are moving toward it more quickly than others (cf. TTM 23; IPD 83–84). Similarly, some individuals are more acquainted than others with the *Tout-monde* and, or rather as, a "new region of the world." In a brief aside, Glissant indicates that Rimbaud was a prime example of that latter sort of person, as is presumably Glissant himself (NR 97).

Oscillations between clarity and opacity are ubiquitous in Glissant's theoretical work, and Glissant continually introduces yet more key words or ways of framing what he has in mind when he writes, and speaks of, the *Tout-monde*. There are moments, however, when a remarkable clarity is on display as Glissant fleshes out his *Tout-monde*. For example, Glissant spells out at various times that the *Tout-monde* is at once a signifier whose referent is the entirety of the planet earth, *and* that it is the way in which human consciousness knows that space. The *Tout-monde*, in other words, would therefore at once be a thing and our knowledge of that thing. In a radio interview shortly after the publication of *Tout-monde*, Glissant was asked whether the *Tout-monde* can be described as "this desire to know, to approach the totality of the world" (IPD 130). His response was remarkable for its forceful clarity. The *Tout-monde* is, he explains, "the totality of the world as it exists in reality (*"dans son réel"*) and as it exists in our desire" (IPD 130). The entirety of the planet we humans inhabit would in consequence be the "Tout-monde," and its extension is continued even into our own psyches. *Une nouvelle région du monde* is similarly unequivocal with regard to the nature and extent of the bounds of Glissant's totality, referring to "the Tout-monde, which for us always includes the entirety of the world" (96).

Such lucidity, however, is short-lived and scarce in Glissant's theoretical work. In the *Traité du Tout-monde* (*Treatise on the Tout-monde*), whose title manifestly suggests that it will be a reasoned inquiry into that subject, Glissant chooses to describe the *Tout-monde*, once again, by invoking not what it *is* but rather what it *does*: "The Tout-monde, which is totalizing, is not (for us) total" (TTM 22). The *Tout-monde* is something that totalizes without being itself total: as if this notion were not sufficiently slippery in itself, Glissant has elsewhere declared (and repeated) that the *Tout-monde* is "the realized *totality* of the known and unknown elements of our universes" (CL 87; emphasis added). If we are to *a*ppose all of these claims, we are left with a somewhat befuddling proposition: the *Tout-monde* is a totalizing totality that is not total.

In order to dispense with the conceptual difficulties that such semantic somersaults inevitably engender, Eric Prieto reads the *Tout-monde* not as a place but rather as a way of thinking.

> [T]he *Tout-monde* is not so much a geographical concept as an epistemological concept. The *Tout-monde* is most emphatically not the world itself, in the geographical sense of the planet's spatial configuration. It implies, rather, a certain *vision of* the world in the phenomenological sense of a consciousness that is simultaneously aware of and awash in the world around it. (*Literature, Geography and the Postmodern Poetics of Place* 176)

Reading Glissant against himself, Prieto is adamant in his belief that the *Tout-monde* must not be a descriptor for a physical space. Prieto's desire for a noncontradictory Glissant leads him to that compromise, one that is far from unsubstantiated in Glissant's work. After all, Prieto cites the character Longoué from *Tout-monde*, who reiterates his insistence that "the world is not the Tout-monde . . . Because the Tout-monde is the world that you tossed around in your thoughts while it was tossing you in its swell" (TM 208; ctd. in Prieto 176). Indeed, elsewhere in that same novel, the *Tout-monde* is held to be something other than the world by a host of other narrators (cf. TM 330, 49).

Whether it is to be a place, a space, a way of thinking, an idea or playful turn of phrase, the *when* of the *Tout-monde* remains similarly unresolved. As readers of Glissant we cannot help but wonder whether the *Tout-monde* is no more than his name for the present state of affairs; let us not forget that he has sung the praises of his contemporary *temps-monde*, or *time-world* (IPD 132). Or, on the contrary, we might ask whether the *Tout-monde* is better understood as a utopian future, one not yet attained but one that will someday be attainable. The latter question is all the more pressing given the stark contrast between the happy and harmonious space that Glissant depicts as the *Tout-monde* and a contemporary reality that is, to say the least, less than utopian. Which is it to be?

As Celia Britton noted as early as 1995, years before Glissant's preoccupation with the *Tout-monde* would reach its zenith, Glissant "increasingly writes as though the values of relation, chaos and diversity have already prevailed" (*Édouard Glissant* 9). And Britton's sense of Glissant's optimism with regard to the present is indeed increasingly corroborated by his late work. Yet in 2006, Glissant's *Une nouvelle région du monde* ("A New Region of the World") would weave even more complexity into the question of the *Tout-monde*'s temporality by drawing a third term into the fray: the eponymous "new region of the world." In that text, Glissant would assert that "it is the case that this Tout-monde is also in our times *another region of the world*" (NR 96; emphasis in original). Taking that assertion into account, it becomes evident that in Glissant's thought the *Tout-monde* is one thing (that is, the whole of the world, excluding nothing) and it is not that thing (not the whole of the world, but rather a part of it). And it is also, and paradoxically, both of those things simultaneously.

The difficulties involved in thinking through exactly what Glissant might mean by "Tout-monde" are neatly reflected in a set of remarks Glissant made during an interview with Lise Gauvin. There, his language contorts visibly as it struggles to come to terms with the play of clarity and ambiguity that are the very fabric of his idea of the *Tout-monde*. Returning to his then-new idea of a "new region of the world," Glissant explains his shifting and multiple understandings of what exactly the words *region* and *world* mean.

> The region is new because it's a region that some of us have already entered into, Rimbaud and many other individuals, but it's a region that we are all led to enter into together. That's why it is new. It's a new region of the world because we live in the world, the world is in front of us, in us or beside us, but we have not yet conceived that there is a part of the world that we see or that we do not see and into which we must all enter together, that is to say in which we must relate our differences without these differences causing catastrophes. These differences in us and for us signal the beauty of the world. That's why there is a Tout-monde, a new region of the world, next to the world itself, in the world itself, beyond the world itself, within the world itself, and confused with the world itself. (IL 89–90)

"Confused with the world itself": the term *confused* is fitting, as such excursions into linguistic opacity leave the reader at pains to obtain any final understanding as to whether, or where, or when, the *Tout-monde* exists.

For Glissant, that is precisely the point. Glissant foregrounds paradox in his ludic manipulation of the world/*Tout-monde* relationship, taking pleasure in asserting the truth of a contradiction.

> So then, the world is of course known, and the Tout-monde includes the world totally, however and for us the Tout-monde remains to be discovered and known. It's a part of the world, one that here-there (*ici-là*) surpasses (*dépasse*) the world and points to it. The world is the known and the Tout-monde is the unknown, but the contrary is just as true, and what is more, the world is the whole and the Tout-monde is the part, but the opposite makes just as much sense to us (*nous parle autant*). (NR 97)

Glissant's language in such passages invites readers to rethink some of the basic foundations of Western reason: whether something is or is not, the relationship of the part to the whole, or the relationship of the present to the future. The *Tout-monde*, Glissant insists, both is and is not the world. It is of the present, but it is also still to come. And it is at once part of the world and the entirety of the world. If his totality is to be more total than Hegel's, as Hallward and Leupin have argued, it is nonetheless evident that there is nothing of Hegelian systematicity here, neither in Glissant's language nor in his conceptual maneuverings.

The key both to understanding the *Tout-monde* (whatever that might mean) and to partaking in it proves, for Glissant, to be bound up in literary creation. Hence the gloss Glissant gave of his suite of plays entitled *Le monde incréé* (*The Uncreated World* [2000]). When asked in the context of an interview to shed light on the question of whether the "uncreated world" of the title was also a world that was "to be created," Glissant responded with a contradiction accompanied by a return to the *chose littéraire*. The "uncreated world," he argued, is "a world remaining to be created but which is already there, and one of which we don't have, let's say, an obvious awareness. Consequently, it's a world that one can only reach with the powers of the imaginary and the poetic intention" (IL 63). *Le monde incréé* writes into being a world that is at once uncreated and already quite extant. But Glissant's invocation of that "uncreated" world points to a key characteristic of the *Tout-monde*: the crucial role of the imaginary and what Glissant calls the poetic intention in any understanding of it. Indeed, they are the *only* means of reaching this uncreated creation. The novelty of the *Tout-monde*, the novelty that *is* the *Tout-monde*, thus goes hand in hand with novelty in the realm of literary creation.

Literature is the site where the elaboration of Glissant's contrast of the totality and particular places takes place. Their relationship is what Jean-Louis Joubert rightfully recognizes as a contradiction in Glissant's thinking of totality: the fact that the Caribbean subject's strong sense of belonging to a very particular place makes sense *only* in the context of that place's belonging to the greater whole, and vice versa (Joubert 318). As Glissant has repeatedly argued, the Caribbean is the privileged locus of that contradictory imaginary. Its geography is reflected in Glissant's idea of totality, as Glissant shows that landscape is thus productive of particular modes of thought.

The very fact of thinking through what Glissant means by "*Tout-monde*" places considerable demands on some of our most basic ways of knowing. Glissant describes his own literature as part of the effort to "reach" the *Tout-monde*, as he writes that

> [W]e are entering into the Tout-monde, which always for us covers the totality of the world, but now it is the case that this Tout-monde is also in our times *another region of the world*, a wholly new region, and the world is there, it is here-there (*ici-là*), it is before us, we who say it without saying it, saying it all the while, *undertaking a new category of literature*. (NR 96; emphasis added)

In this "new category of literature" that Glissant (and presumably others) are in the process of forging, then, a world can be both "remaining to be created" and "already there." And a writer may write in relation to a world that is at one and the same time the entirety of the planet and a smaller part of it (IL 63).

In such passages, Glissant seems not to have made up his mind. But therein lies what he would have us take to be his ultimate authority: for if Glissant seems undecided with regard to the nature of the world, it is because the world too is undecided. Indeed, in Glissant's words, the "thinking of ambiguity reigns from now on over the imaginary of the chaos-world and the imaginary of Relation" (IPD 89). The ultimate truth of the world, Glissant tells us, is that the world, like our understanding of it, is fundamentally unclear. Glissant concludes his explanation of the world by holding it to be finally and fundamentally unexplainable. With such enigmatic proclamations, Glissant toys with our understandings of his texts, prodding us to think differently. His message, as he does so, is a vitalist one. Vitalist, in that subjecting the *Tout-monde* to the machinations of reason, reducing it to a stable and graspable truth, would mean putting an end to its living and flourishing.

Like the world itself, the self's other is most accurately known as unknowable, and preserving the unknown means protecting the life of the other. The next chapter will examine more closely what Glissant has in mind with the *Tout-monde*'s "new category of literature," paying particular attention to how that new literature might point us toward new ethical modes of being toward the other—in other words, to ways of being that would seamlessly prolong the harmony, the nonhierarchical interrelation, and the interconnectivity that characterize the *Tout-monde*.

Chapter 2 will approach that experimental Glissantian literature from two angles: first, by examining Glissant's reading of Faulkner, whose work he considers to be a remarkable precedent for this new literature that would speak the *Tout-monde*; and next, by turning to Glissant's own literary production, via a Glissantian novel that shares much with (what Glissant portrays as) Faulkner's approach to alterity. Glissant's Faulkner is deeply engaged with saying what is unsayable, with saying what cannot be said in his time and place. And Glissant's novel *Sartorius: le roman des Batoutos* (1999), whose title is a riff on one of Faulkner's titles, will in response go about visualizing the invisible. Paradox and contradiction, in both cases, set a new way of knowing the other and the world in motion; paradox, in both, provides an aesthetic gateway to the *Tout-monde*.

Two

Writing a Caribbean Ethics of Alterity

FAULKNER, MISSISSIPPI, AND SARTORIUS:
LE ROMAN DES BATOUTOS

Édouard Glissant's demand that all be granted "the right to opacity" resonates throughout his work. For Glissant, one way that literature can deploy opacity is to engage in a set of paired, paradoxical operations. It can say the unsayable, or make the invisible visible—or, more accurately put, present the absent. With his literary-critical text *Faulkner, Mississippi* (1996), Glissant sees both of these operations at work in the novels of an author whom he has hailed as the greatest of the twentieth century (FM 54). This poetics of paradox is born of what Glissant sees as the shared cultural zone made up of the Caribbean and the US Gulf South region (cf. FM 134, et passim). It is a poetics proper to that space; indeed, for Glissant, a literary method characterized by paradox and contradiction is necessitated by the particularity of that place or group of places.

In this chapter, I would like to propose an analysis of two texts that constitute theoretical meditations on, and experiments with, the figure of opacity: *Faulkner, Mississippi* (1996) and *Sartorius: le roman des Batoutos* (1999). For Glissant, Faulkner's novels say the unsayable, whereas Glissant's own novel *Sartorius* undertakes to make present a people that is absent (or, in the Deleuzian language that Glissant echoes, missing). *Sartorius* and *Faulkner, Mississippi* are linked in more ways than one. Through their repeated engagements with Deleuze, they conjure up a triangle of three authors, and three corresponding vectors of thought. *Faulkner, Mississippi*, for example, is a reading of the quasi-totality of Faulkner's work. And in it, Glissant's preferred Deleuzian theme, the rhizome, plays a customarily crucial role. "Faulkner writes in rhizomes," Glissant holds (FM 244), in a formulation recalling the first line of Deleuze and Guattari's *Kafka: pour une littérature mineure* (1975) (*Kafka: Toward a Minor Literature*):

"How to enter into Kafka's oeuvre? It's a rhizome, a burrow" (7). The title *Sartorius*, moreover, alludes to Faulkner's novel of almost the same name, *Sartoris* (1929), and is prefaced with a quotation from Deleuze, one that would seem to spell out precisely what the novel will undertake: that is, the invention of a people that is missing. That apparent clarification of the novel's aims is one that, as we will see, Glissant quickly puts under erasure. This seemingly clean-cut triangulation of the authors Deleuze-Guattari/Glissant/Faulkner belies, however, the complexity of the relationship that Glissant institutes among them. For if this constellation of authors is a triangle, it is an open one, opening up onto other relationships of influences, other voices, other stories. Paradoxically, as Glissant might say, it is at once a triangle and a rhizome. Reading *Faulkner, Mississippi* alongside *Sartorius* shows that it is the possibility of paradoxes that makes Glissant's thought rich, in this pairing of texts that always proves to be more than two.

The opacity that Glissant demands serves as a sort of protective mechanism insulating the radical difference of the other from the self's at times depredatory search for knowledge (TTM 29). Opacity dictates that in the other, an unknowable remainder will always persist. Glissant's figure of opacity, as I will show, also comes to work on his own ideas—including the idea of opacity itself. Glissant uses opacity and the set of paradoxes that accompany it as part of a larger enterprise of creation. That is, not only the engendering of an ethical mode of being between self and other, but also the impetus for the creation of new literary forms. Through accommodating contradiction and allowing paradox to perdure, opacity points us toward possibilities for new forms of literary creation. The importance of such literary innovation to Glissant cannot be emphasized enough. For in his thought the causal link between new forms of writing and new forms of ethical life is spelled out quite explicitly. The formula for launching this sequence of causally linked creations, however, is somewhat less clear.

In a rather contentious literary-historical formulation positing Faulkner as the genitor of a multilingual, pan-Caribbean poetics, Glissant holds that Caribbean writers ranging from Wilson Harris to Alejo Carpentier to Glissant himself have borrowed the *langage* (language) of Faulkner's literary practice ("La 'créolisation' culturelle du monde").[1] While this literary practice is peculiar to the US Gulf South––Caribbean region, this shared, paradoxical poetics has the potential to extend outward into other spaces and places. Glissant thus implies that literary and philosophical lessons drawn from the Caribbean, and by extension the shared US Gulf South–Caribbean cultural zone, can indicate an ethics of alterity, pointing the way toward new and more desirable forms of thought and, subsequently, life.

Paradoxes of Locution:
Saying the Unsayable in the Faulknerian Corpus

Composed during his stint at Louisiana State University in Baton Rouge, Glissant's *Faulwkner, Mississippi* undertakes a survey of the entirety of Faulkner's oeuvre. It distills a reading that, as can be seen in Glissant's literary-critical work on other authors, brings Faulkner's thought into line with Glissant's own (cf., in particular, IP 96). Glissant's efforts in that regard run counter to Faulkner's views on race, or what many take to be his views (cf. Weinstein 117–18). For in his chronicle of a journey through the past and present of the American deep South, which he situates in a history of profound and continuing race-based antagonism, Glissant reads Faulkner's work as laying, perhaps despite itself, the groundwork for an ethics of alterity.[2]

The term *opacity* has appeared throughout Glissant's oeuvre, and most notably in his *Le discours antillais*, which includes the now well-known discussion of counterpoetics, as well as "forced" and "natural" poetics (DA 399–418). Celia Britton's landmark study *Édouard Glissant and Postcolonial Theory* (1999) focuses on these issues, and more broadly on the role of language in Glissant's work. It concentrates particularly on the way in which the literary language of his earlier, fictional texts helps to further a political project of resistance and self-affirmation. The title of Marie-José N'Zengou-Tayo's review of Britton's text, "Can Language Free Us from Subordination?," poses the question that drives Britton's analysis, a question that Glissant attempts to answer concretely in his appropriation of Faulkner's work. As Patrick Crowley points out, Glissant's demand for the right to opacity for all has gone beyond its earlier form in *Le discours antillais*. The right, or claim, to opacity has, almost ten years on in *Poétique de la Relation*, left the colonizer-colonized opposition behind, extending the right of opacity not only to the oppressed but to *everyone* (Crowley 107). For Crowley, this shift proves that, *pace* Britton, Glissant's main concern is less "postcolonial resistance" than "the capacity of poetic language to unsettle categorical systems of thought that are allied to power" (Crowley 110). In *Faulkner, Mississippi*, I submit, Glissant shows the potential of (his sense of) opacity to do both. In other words, Glissant uses opacity in *Faulkner, Mississippi* with both epistemological and political goals. Indeed, his use of the term epitomizes the extent to which the political and epistemological dimensions are intertwined in his thought. And therein lies the entry point into Glissant's rehabilitation of Faulkner as an antiracist, white Southern novelist: in Glissant's reading, it is in Faulkner's epistemological opacity (his refusal or reluctance to make black subjects finally readable to his white characters and readers) that his political leanings (that is, his fundamentally antiracist poetics, his critical stance toward much of what his novels identify as Southern culture) can be discerned.

Transparency is, for Glissant, characteristic of the way in which what he calls "Western humanism" saw the world. By that Glissant is referring to a conquering knowledge that would take possession of the world with each act of understanding (PR 206), functioning alongside the advance of warlike civilizations that assume nothing can escape the ever-augmenting triumph of reason: Glissant's arguments resonate with the founding moves of the genre of Enlightenment critique. Yet further, Glissant holds that rather than seeing the truth of the world, Western humanism was in fact gazing on itself. This argument is strikingly similar to Luce Irigaray's in *Ethique de la différence sexuelle* (1984), if we substitute "the Western" for "the masculine." For Irigaray, masculinity has heretofore merely pretended to make contact with the feminine other, trapped in a reflexive loop of self-love that excludes woman-as-other in favor of woman-as-self, woman subjugated to and refashioned in the image of man. By the same token, the transparency of the other thus amounts to a transparency of the self to the self—one which is, moreover, a false transparency.

In Glissant's thumbnail sketch of epistemological shifts throughout world history, he emphasizes the stage at which the non-Western other has begun an irruption into the West. Not only has this other refused to be a product of Western fashioning and thus proved opaque, thereby demonstrating the falsity of the transparency that preceded this obscurity, he or she has also disrupted Western humanism's vision of itself.

> Transparency no longer appears to be the depths of the mirror where Western humanism reflected the world in its image; in the depths of the mirror, now there is opacity, a whole slime left by the people who have come up from the hidden face of the earth, fertile slime but, to tell the truth, also uncertain, most often denied or dominated. ("Au fond du miroir")

For Glissant, Western humanism's efforts to project itself into the world and know itself as it comes to know the world—and it is clearly Hegel's "consciousness of consciousness" that he evokes—are in modernity irrevocably blocked. And the domination implicated in this project has been replaced with a "slime" ("*limon*"), a very material, fluid substance (again, Glissant's confluence with Irigaray here is uncanny) that will, once acknowledged and engaged with, allow the totality of the world's peoples to accede to states of greater health. This slime is fertile, in that it generates possibilities for the birth of life forms. It is uncertain (*incertain*), in line with Glissant's veneration of the unpredictable. In Faulkner's novels of the American South, African-American characters, one of the peoples whom this category of otherness represents, can be seen to be both denied/negated and dominated, just as Glissant's fluid figure is. And it is in this very same corpus that we can perceive an opacity that can undermine, or as Deleuze would have it, that can "spring leaks in," this system of domination (*Dialogues* 47).

In work as in life, Glissant tells us, Faulkner was not interested in undertaking psychological studies (FM 138). Glissant holds that Faulkner's concern, at least in his work, lay with what Glissant calls "the abyss" (ibid.). Or rather, abyss*es*, the abysses of nonknowledge and desperation that are brought about by "the refusal of creolization" and the refusal of the "Other," cardinal sins in the Glissantian worldview (FM 138). Faulkner and his people (that is, Southern whites) struggle against the current that is the creolization of the world; they are "offended" by "mixing, hybridity, and then the unpredictability of what results from it" (FM 117). As Glissant makes this point, he maintains the semantic slippage in his sense of the word *creolization*. The term denotes for him at once the creolization that Faulkner and his contemporaries would have considered to be "racial mixing" as well as the more abstract and metaphysical creolization that would signify ever-increasing interconnection, combination, and unpredictability (cf. FM 117).

As is his wont in other treatments of literary figures whom he admires, Glissant bends Faulkner's thought to meet with his own philosophy and poetics. Glissant's use of *créolisation* (creolization) as well as the *imprévu* (the unpredicted) shifts the scene of conflict in Faulkner's work from the ethnic to the epistemological realms. The "refusal of creolization" of course refers to the rejection, on the part of Faulkner's whites, who believe themselves to be of a "pure" race, of other races and of races that contain others within them (read: races that are perceived to be "mixed"). But this same refusal also refers to the rejection of a set of epistemological categories. While he is of course describing a refusal on the part of Faulkner of a certain race or of the mixing of what he perceives to be races, Glissant is also indicating that the "*sudistes*" (that is, the French term for sympathizers of the Confederates in the US Civil War) are refusing a certain way of knowing the world, one that would be grounded in Glissant's idea of creolization.

For Glissant, Faulkner both is and is not a member of that group. Glissant perceives an ambivalence in Faulkner's literary texts, where "The way Blacks are posed . . . appears to be phenomenological, which is to say that it doesn't seek any profundity, since that would have been fraud" (FM 97). It is this methodological choice of phenomenology over ontology that allows Glissant to recuperate Faulkner as a thinker of the ethics of opacity. In Glissant's reading, Faulkner is concerned not with the truth of African-American subjects' being, but rather with how these subjects appear, or more properly how they do not appear, as objects of knowledge.

In a curious foregrounding of his own subjectivity, Glissant suggests that his reading is a matter of choice, or preference, explaining that "*I prefer* to think that in this methodological choice there are the lucidity and the honesty (in sum, the generosity, both natural and systematic, which is to say aesthetic) of he who knows, who in effect admits that he will never understand neither Blacks nor Indians" (FM 97; emphasis added). Glissant intensifies his speculation into Faulkner's psychology as he insists that Faulkner also knew that it would be, as Glissant puts it, "Odious (and, in his eyes, ridiculous) to posit an all-powerful narrator and to try to penetrate these consciousnesses which would have been for him impenetrable" (FM 97).

It is through this clarity of mind (*lucidité*) (lucidity)—a curious way to praise Faulkner's understanding of the incomprehensible, the "impenetrable," which is for Glissant the opaque—and in order to avoid the "odious," that Faulkner has recourse to a language of his own invention (FM 97). Citing a critic who invokes Faulkner's "language of the obscure," Glissant holds that Faulkner "Goes back to the most obscure, the most essential, there where no one goes. He doesn't describe, he doesn't do genre painting" (FM 216). It is thus in eschewing the search for the other's essence that Faulkner's literature sets in motion the essence of the encounter with the other. This apparent contradiction in terms—abandoning an essentialist framework in order to attain to "the essential"—is made possible, once again, by Faulkner's use of language.

Noting that Faulkner's writing (in French translation) is fond of the phrasing "*en même temps*" ("at the same time"), Glissant formulates a theory of a Faulknerian methodology echoing Glissant's own, one of the paradoxical coexistence of opposites in Faulkner's work. The language that makes Faulkner's writing possible does three things at once: it (1) describes; and in that process of description it (2,) undertakes a paradoxical operation of saying the unsayable ("It seeks to say that which is unsayable in description and yet that which would fully signify (which would found in unveiled reason) that which is described" (FM 190)). Third, and *at the same time*, it leads readers to understand that the underlying reason in the text can be unveiled but never attained ("Ceaselessly lets it be understood that this unveilable reason is also quite unattainable" [FM 190]).

These three actions can be otherwise understood in terms of three figures that Glissant sees at play in Faulkner's work. The first is the "hidden truth," the shame or trauma that is the key to Faulkner's novels (FM 190). This hidden truth generally takes the form of the impossibility of establishing a series of traceable lineages. Glissant connects that latter term to root-identity, system thinking, and the cruelty of Western empires (PR 23–31, et passim). Second is the description of his project, which in Faulkner's work is necessarily "visionary," in that "It is thus decided by intuition, the premonition of primordial truth" (FM 190). Third, and finally, there is the unstable reassurance offered by the text that this secret of a lacking origin will never be revealed (FM 190).

For Glissant, slavery becomes the unsayable, the unspeakable, in Faulkner's novels: "Everything happens as if for him the defect that was slavery was a moral suffering, one of Being, an indelible decline (the absence to History), one much more maddening to carry than the physical suffering of oppression and misery" (FM 99). The lingering stain of slavery on the conscience of Faulkner's whites would thus influence Faulkner's text so profoundly that, as Glissant puts it, it is *as if* that mark were harder to bear than the more concrete pains of oppression and poverty.

That is no small point. Faulkner's emphasis on the suffering of whites, while it may seem provocative or even taboo, is connected to another unspeakable, which Glissant presents as the cipher of Faulkner's depiction of race relations: that is, the lack of transparency, epistemological failure, and the (white) subject's inability to know finally and thoroughly the other. Just as Faulkner cannot describe outright the shame, the stain that marks the consciousness of Southern whites, he cannot speak the being of Southern blacks. Two "primordial truths," thus, are and are not spoken in Faulkner's work. And the latter truth, Faulkner's inability to fully or finally know the being of Southern blacks, serves as the point of departure for Glissant's development of his ethics of opacity.

Richard Watts and Celia Britton both translate the "right to opacity" as simply the "right not to be understood" (Watts, "The 'Wounds of Locality,'" 119; Britton, *Glissant* 19). Glissant maintains that through the figure of opacity, Faulkner seeks one thing: "only and by any means to found the obscurity of the relation between blacks and whites in a metaphysics" (FM 99). As Britton points out, whereas for Spivak the opaque is a source of disempowerment, it is a figure of resistance for Glissant (*Glissant* 20). The opaque, Glissant explains, "is not the obscure, but it can be, and it can be accepted as such. It is the non-reducible, which is the most vivacious of guarantees of participation and confluence" (PR 205–6). This elevation of the obscure to the state of a metaphysical proposition figures into Glissant's larger theoretical concern with protecting the Diverse from the conquering machinations of the Same. Thus, "We therefore call opacity that which protects the Diverse" (PR 75). J. Michael Dash, using medical and biological metaphors, holds that in Glissant's work, "*Opacité/alterité (opacity/alterity)* become the diastole and systole of human relationships, the give and take of self-denial, self-affirmation and recognition of the other" (180). Opacity, when faced with the otherness of the other (alterity), thus, becomes a guarantor of continued human life. Opacity is in that sense a key vitalist instrument in Glissant's conceptual toolkit.

It is thus in literature that Glissant locates the possibility for a viable ethics. This ethics does not remain abstract, however, as Glissant links it to real, lived social interactions. The opacity that Glissant finds in Faulkner's novels is precisely what allows for the knowledge of, and participation in, the whole that is represented by the all-important Glissantian figure of the Tout-monde. Opacity makes possible the concept and lived experience of a community, while protecting the singularity of the individuals that make up said community: "It is also this very same opacity that animates every community: that which forever brings us together, while singularizing us forever. The general consent to particular opacities is the simplest equivalent of non-barbarism" (PR 209). In other words, acknowledging, and living in the (clear) awareness of, the opacity of the other is the most basic way of conceiving of a society that would stand in opposition to the barbarism of the past.

Therein lies one of the fundamental links between Glissant's abstract conception of the "poetics of Relation" and the effects of that idea on political actuality. The other resists the self's effort to know him or her in two ways: in terms of density and in terms of change. The other is thus never ultimately knowable because the entirety of his or her being never becomes apparent or readable to the self. Moreover, even if it were to become thus, its nature of constant flux would preclude any knowledge of the other that could boast mastery. As Glissant puts it, "For the poetics of relation postulates that the density (the opacity) of the other is offered to each of us. The more the other resists in his/her thickness or fluidity (without being limited to either), the more his/her reality becomes expressive, and the more the relation becomes fecund" (IP 23).

Otherwise put, for Glissant as for Faulkner, a poetics of Relation is the site where a certain, seemingly paradoxical phenomenon of perception occurs. This phenomenon is the coincidence of opposites, in this case in the form of a revelation of nonrevelation: that is, the final revelation of the other as concealed and finally unknowable. This paradox is, in Glissant's reading, decisive in the context of the elaboration of Faulkner's literary project. The *différance* of Faulkner's writing, for Glissant, lies in the fact that it stages difference in a continued pattern of deferral. For example, Glissant illustrates that the *différé* (differed/deferred) of Faulkner's writing goes back, without ever finally arriving, to a presupposition: that of "The impossible establishment, the denied legitimacy of the South" (FM 191). Given this impulse in Faulkner's work, it becomes clear that, as Glissant puts it, "The task of the writer is to reveal this presupposition, all the while exposing its painful equivalences in the present, all the while signifying that this revelation is forever deferred" (FM191).

For Glissant, then, Faulkner would realize the impossible in literature. In his novels the (black) other is made visible in his or her final invisibility to the (white) self; the other's final absence to the self is unveiled in its presence. By the same token, the impossible knowledge that haunts the South is said without being said, articulated without being spoken. And, yet more importantly, Glissant reads Faulkner as seeking political change though a literary language that undertakes the impossible. This newly invented form of writing may lead, Glissant suggests, to new political inventions. The Southern writer seeks to "Say the impossible of the South without ever having to say it, to set forth a writing of it that would go back to all that is unexpressed in this impossible, and perhaps to change something by the very force of this adventure" (FM 207–8). In his lifetime, Glissant adds, Faulkner did all but the last.

Paradoxes of Vision: Learning (Not) to See a People that Is (Not) Missing

> Literature as health, as writing, consists in inventing a people that is missing. It falls to the storytelling function to invent a people. One doesn't write with one's memories, unless one is making them the collective origin or destination of a people to come, one that is still buried under its betrayals and renunciations.
> —Deleuze, *Critique et clinique*

Anjali Prabhu has noted Glissant's "call upon the ethical subjectivity to bring together the theoretical and the social through his notion of opacity" ("Interrogating Hybridity" 82). Inherent in this call is an impulse to create new forms of social life via artistic creation, and Glissant's 1999 novel *Sartorius: le roman des Batoutos* accordingly links literary creation and a more ethical form of being-in-the-world. Glissant has given his own gloss of his text, deeming it a "modern fable of non-domination" ("La 'créolisation' culturelle du monde). *Sartorius* is a myth, he continues, "that the world needs," insofar as "the Batoutos incarnate a people who does not have the pretention of elevating itself to the status of a model, [they are] one that goes into the world not to possess it but rather to live together with others" ("La 'créolisation' culturelle du monde"). The Batoutos do not seek to conquer, nor are they "imperialist." Their invisibility (which is of course made visible as Glissant's text portrays them) makes them a people who would "protect us." Glissant's "us" is intended here to refer to the set of all "humanities" who would be prevented, thanks to the Batoutos, from returning to less ethical modes of being and knowing founded on the idea of transparency: in other words, from "the temptation of making us too visible by imposing our values, our ways of being on other peoples" ("La 'créolisation' culturelle du monde"). The invisibility of the Batoutos is thus a mechanism whose intended effect is to combat the projection of transparency (read: vulnerability to perfect knowledge) and visibility (what Glissant has elsewhere referred to as "making particular values universal" [IPD 136]).

Sartorius's depiction of the Batoutos' peripatetic existence over the centuries foregrounds the ways in which this people, at once missing and present, bears no fixed essence, and founds no discernible lineage. The space-time of the Batoutos' origin, too, is at once definite and unclear, definite enough to be known and recorded, but on closer examination, entirely bereft of scientific exactitude. As a result, the *roman des Batoutos* begins its narration with "In the year five hundred, or more or less, before this era in which we live," which was the moment of the Batoutos' apparition, in "a region of Africa central enough to be indeterminate" (15). More significantly, their origin, rather than being a specific point in time or space, is immediately a departure: Oko, one of their number, decides to "go out into the world, not to possess there," but with the noble goal of "enduring" (the term echoes Faulkner's depiction of African-Americans in the South[3]), which he will do "with everyone" (*Sartorius* 15). With Oko's migration, their genesis is an origin set in motion, and the Batoutos prove to be a people in motion, coherent as *a* people only insofar as they do not cohere, that is, insofar as they are scattered, divided, elsewhere.

Glissant describes his novel as a tool of argumentation and a spur for political change even more forcefully in a 1999 interview with Héric Libong and Boniface Mongo-Mboussa titled "Un peuple invisible pour sauver le monde réel" ("An Invisible People to Save the Real World"). When asked to explain the text's title, Glissant invokes its strange pairing of a seemingly Faulknerian allusion (*Sartorius*/*Sartoris*), followed by a subtitle that summarizes the text—for the "*Roman des Batoutos*" would appear to make the text's main focus and reason for being deceptively clear. For the text, as Glissant would have it, is intended to take on a concrete role in bringing about social change: "The whole book," he explains, "is a way of fighting against the essentialist positions that I have always rejected" ("Un peuple invisible"). Calling the book "The Batoutos" or "Batoutos" would have constituted, Glissant continues, "an extreme platitude, a redundancy, a repetition of the content in the title" ("Un peuple invisible").

Behind those justifications, however, lies a strategic argument, one that is derived from Glissant's overall politics of Relation: while the Batouto people may be necessary, he maintains, they are not an "ideological people" ("Un peuple invisible"). As such, they are marked by what Glissant has characterized as one of the more salient facets of modernity: our increasing inability to impose ideological schemas on the world (IPD 132). As for the title's first word, *Sartorius*, it is, according to Glissant (or rather, to this particular self-representation on the part of Glissant) nothing more than the name of a good friend (more on this claim and its implications shortly). In an oft-employed rhetorical strategy, that remark presents Glissant as an author who mingles the gravely serious and the whimsical with ease.

For Françoise Lionnet, Glissant's rejection of essentialism and pure origins must be placed within its historical context. The privileging of creolization/hybridity that can be seen in thinkers such as Glissant is a reaction to the earlier, contrary valuation placed un them: "It is in large part because of the scientific racism of the nineteenth century that hybridization became coded as a negative category," she explains (*Autobiographical Voices* 9). In this mode of thought, "'Pure race'" plays a role in what Lionnet calls "the West's monotheistic obsession with the "One" and the "Same" (*Autobiographical Voices* 9). If the novel *Sartorius* itself is a form of struggle against essentialism, it is in good company, joining the current of what Chris Bongie has called

> [T]he anti-essentialist, hybridizing arguments that have gained such prominence of late in postcolonial theory. Glissant's vision, elaborated over the course of the last forty years, resonates in the many recent critiques of what Trinh T. Minh-ha has termed "the identity enclosure," and it has been explicitly championed by an

increasing number of postcolonial theorists for whom it serves, in the words of Françoise Lionnet, to "demystif(y) all essentialist glorifications of unitary origins, be they racial, sexual, geographic, or cultural." Glissant's valorization of métissage holds forth for a critic like Lionnet the promise of a radical transformation of society . . . (*Islands and Exiles* 63)

In keeping with that enterprise of demystification, and with an immediacy equal to that of the Batoutos' antiessentialist appearance/disappearance, the narrative voice of *Sartorius* shrugs off its authority in its recounting of the tale of the Batoutos. This "nation, invisible as a nation" is difficult to perceive, and the narrator's preface concludes by suggesting that even the text to follow offers something less than a complete knowledge: "Thus we dream them, rather than knowing them" (*Sartorius* 15). The first Batouto to be known by readers is Oko, who will be followed in the seventeenth century by Odono Odono,[4] a name that will be familiar to readers of Glissant's other novels, and *La case du commandeur*, in particular. Through the aftermath of the slave trade, the Batoutos have been spread out throughout time and space and have become (almost) lost in the human race, appearing exclusively to those who know how to recognize them. *Sartorius*'s narrative voice—are we to assume that it is Glissant's own?—recounts a discussion with the writer Abdourahman Waberi, who says that in Djibouti the "indigenous foreigners" are all called Martinicans or Senegalese. This custom, the narrator affirms, does not stem from the colonial past, but rather represents "a practice of the Batoutos, wandering as wandering" (*Sartorius* 42). The Batoutos "have joined us and they recount in our stories/histories (*histoires*) the story/history of their disappearance" (*Sartorius* 42). This people that is missing, or that *we* have been missing, narrates to us the story of how they have come to be missing—"Perhaps," the narrator adds, epitomizing Glissantian uncertainty (*Sartorius* 42).

For "we," here again, both the text's first person narrative voice and, implicitly, the entirety of the human race, have not perfected our ways of pinpointing the Batoutos. We focus on the proud and noble Batoutos, overlooking in the process the "humble" and "unseen ones" (*Sartorius* 43). We—in this case another, much more specific *we*, as *Sartorius* demonstrates in a repeated move the slippage and obscurity of this pronoun's meaning—were transported across the "immense Waters" to the plantations of the Americas, the narrator continues. It was only subsequently that the survivors of the middle passage looked back and dreamed about what the "drama and impossibility" of the "country from before" might be (*Sartorius* 61). Throughout this time the "strength of the Batoutos, which was to appear not as a strength," accompanied them. Celia Britton, in her exegesis of Glissant's concept of opacity, traces this play of visibility/readability and invisibility back to the resistance of *all* colonized people, Batoutos or not, in the Caribbean: "Opacity therefore has to be produced as an *unintelligible* presence from within the *visible* presence of the colonized" (*Édouard Glissant and Postcolonial Theory* 25).

This strength or force did not appear as such because then as now, force was something that "so many peoples yearned to exercise against one other" (*Sartorius* 61). The Batoutos' strength, on the other hand, made possible a certain kind of knowing that laid the groundwork for a more ethical kind of being, one that in turn provides the basis for Glissant's conception of the *Tout-monde* (cf. IPD 136). The strength of the Batoutos "makes it possible to concentrate in silence and in secret on the energy of the world, without prejudice and without withdrawing," allowing them and anyone else who might learn to share this force to remain open to different sorts of knowledge and multiple conceptions of the world (*Sartorius* 61). More importantly for the Batoutos, their strength allows them to navigate a passage between the Scylla and Charybdis of being destroyed by the world of slavery and oppression or withdrawing themselves from the movement of the world altogether (*Sartorius* 61).

In a return to the epistemological rupture brought about in and by the slave ship's hold, which Glissant had discussed at length in *Poétique de la Relation*, *Sartorius* indicates why it is that the Batoutos, as well as all of the other ethnic groups taken from Africa, have lost their means of access to any sort of determining origin in the past. In the slave ship, where the "sea's swells mixed vomit with the iron chains' bites, mixed famine with the panic before the unknown" (*Sartorius* 49), all of the pillars of what Glissant has called an "atavistic" society were broken down (TTM 35; FM 159–60). At that moment, "Everything got smashed together there, origin, language, gods, forms of life, all that remained was suffocation, and the notes made in the slave ship's log" (*Sartorius* 50). This multiplicity of origins has traditionally been seen as a sort of tragic flaw in Caribbean identity, to deleterious effect. In Glissant's diagnosis, "Caribbean people, for centuries, have had a bastard complex" ("Le monde entier se créolise" 212).[5]

Barely concealed in the violence of such scenes is a critique of movements such as Negritude, which Glissant deems both "noble and generous" as well as "an insult to Africa" ("Un peuple invisible"). The quest for a clear lineage, it would seem, is not hazardous only for the empowered whites of Faulkner's novels. In lieu of the return to Africa of the sort that Negritude sought, Glissant proposes a detour, one made necessary by the chasm, the abyss of the sea.

> Not long ago we used to lie to ourselves, but it was a beautiful and necessary lie, when we claimed to find with exactitude, with a supposed science of filiation . . . Believing that we recognized, in the mirror of a wounded Africa, elders, cousins . . . where there was simply a yawning, unknowable abyss, one whose bottom the Batoutos have been digging up and turning over. (*Sartorius* 61–62)

This "beautiful lie" has masked the reality of rupture with the past, and consequently it has kept hidden what Glissant sees as the privileged position that is available to those who have been subjected to that rupture. In Glissant's words,

> We were left to believe for centuries that we didn't have an identity because the earth we were on did not belong to us. It was repeated to us that we had no real density as subjects because we didn't know if we were white, black, Chinese, Arab, Indian, etc. But that's what gives us our greatness! That's what makes the greatness of the culture and civilizations of the Caribbean, we must come to consciousness of that. ("'Supposez le vol de milliers d'oiseaux sur un lac africain' . . ." 18)

At the moment of their forced departure from Africa, the narrator surmises, some Batoutos were mistaken for Ibos, a group known for committing suicide ("they would sink into the sea," among other methods) (*Sartorius* 50). But, the narrator asks, in a questioning that falls agrammatically in the middle of a longer sentence, "how can one distinguish between so many sufferings and misfortunes [?]" (*Sartorius* 50). In the mass of so many sufferings taken together, the differences founded in and by atavistic cultures melt away. This pain, Glissant's retelling of the middle passage suggests, made all of those affected by slavery equal. Moreover, the above question seems to imply that it would be just as difficult and perhaps just as futile to distinguish among intensities of suffering or even among differing ethnicities. What is more, yet another question ensues from that one: most crucially, how to distinguish Batoutos from the other descendants of Africans that are alive today? It is through this myth of origins, which is in effect a story of the *loss* of origins, that Glissant articulates his belief that essentialism is not only undesirable, it is untenable, even impossible.

It is arguably for this reason that the Batoutos come to behave less like a people or "nation" in the traditional sense than as one among the many forms that a life can take. Rather than existing in a fixed state of being, the Batoutos would constitute, in the manner of Deleuze and Guattari, a phase along a vector of becoming. The narrator explains, "You are born Batouto, but I become one too" (*Sartorius* 65). This sense of belonging to the Batoutos, of taking part in their lineage, does not mirror other senses of belonging that have come to be part of modern policies of immigration and national belonging: "Heritage is not grounded in the *jus soli* nor in birthright citizenship nor in any exclusivity of that sort. That's the reason why the Batoutos haunt us, invisible as they are" (*Sartorius* 65).

The Batoutos would seem to exist in innumerable forms: there are, for instance, Batoutos by lineage, as well as those who are Batouto by inspiration (*Sartorius* 65). Rather than declaring the nature of the Batoutos, a move that would imply more authority than the Glissantian narrator is willing to assume, the text instead asks questions, surmises, guesses. In one of the many subtexts of *Sartorius*, a young African is purchased in the eighteenth century as a slave by a German aristocrat, who did so with an unusual goal in mind: to educate and nurture the young man as much as possible. In those heady times, the German, a "friend of the Enlightenment," is using the young "Wilhelm" to prove a point about the equality and potential of all humanity. As a result, the child will be trained and educated in the best European tradition before going out to know the world (216). Wilhelm soon changes his name to Guillermo Amo (thus continuing the Batouto custom of ending masculine names with one *o* and feminine names with two[6]) and sets off for the Americas. In the opening of this parody of a Bildungsroman, the narrator asks, rather than declaring: "Can the Batouto character be reborn in you . . . does there exist a Batouto character that would resist removal and abandonment . . . [?]" and further, pushing this line of reasoning beyond the Batoutos, "does a common character exist for each people, any people . . . ?" (215).

Near the book's conclusion, in a stream-of-consciousness dialogue almost entirely bereft of punctuation, the Batoutos' roots in Africa are further obscured, further muddled: "Black and mulatto and Coolie Batoutos Rastafarian Batoutos white slave owners yes yes that's in the Caribbean basin truly Bob Marley truly no of course we are not ashamed" (282).

Ties to Africa are severed yet further earlier on in the same dialogue, as the description and elaboration of this people's nature takes on a more teasing tone: "I believe that there have been Chinese and Tibetan Batoutos, Tibetans especially, why especially eh?" (278). Through this "I believe," once again, the authorial voice of *Sartorius* shrugs off its authority and foregrounds uncertainty. To what end? Otherwise put, what are the effects of this narrative strategy on our "phenomenological" (to echo Glissant in his reading of Faulkner) experience of the Batoutos?

One of the markers of modernity, of "our times," is the fact that, as one of the narrators puts it, "we are beginning to guess that the Batoutos are among us" (*Sartorius* 53). Aimé Césaire, in one example cited by the narrator, expressed his presentiment of their existence in his lyrical poetry (*Sartorius* 53). This "guessing," however, may very well constitute the limits of our knowledge of the Batoutos. They prove to be simultaneously present and absent, visible and invisible. Additionally, the Batoutos share the uneasiness with the notion of a division between present and past that marks Faulkner's work. Their glory "is resplendent in us, but not nearby, neither far away nor in the beyond" (343).

Exhibiting once again his affection for Italy and things Italian, Glissant places the following "truth" in the mouth of Pietro, an Italian trader in Africa who has seen much.

> Here's my truth, it's about us and about all of these peoples who make up with us a great they, *they* need the Batoutos, no, no, if I'm understanding, no one needs them, without that fact they would not be what they are, but *they* need the idea that the Batoutos exist, they need that idea, yes . . . what am I saying when I say *they* need it, *they* are already reinventing it, *they* have sung it to you, *they* are singing it to you, there is no one among us who does not need to hear it, it's their voice, it's the voice of the Batoutos. (*Sartorius* 191–92)

This is "his," Pietro's muddled truth, and not the truth; in any case, he is not sure to have understood it. His message avoids any implications of mastery, blurs the "truth" of the Batoutos' presence, and blurs the distinctions among the Batoutos, the rest of the world's peoples, himself, and the other narrator to whom he is speaking.

Similarly, Wilhelm, who later becomes "Guillaume," exhibits a parallel cohabitation of surety and uncertainty with regard to the Batoutos. This young victim-cum-chosen-one of the Enlightenment, who has learned to recognize himself as an African, still achingly lacks knowledge about his identity. For recognizing himself as a Batouto, seeing the invisible *and* incarnating a missing people, is (perhaps) an impossibility. The narrator asks, "how could he have, which is to say, recognized a Batouto, which is to say, recognized himself?" (228). This repetition of "which is to say" shows that language is failing the narrator; the use of such an expression to express Guillaume's situation in language only betrays its obscurity. He continues: "Beneath the invisibility where you are scrutinizing, another invisibility keeps vigil, it's up to you to disentangle yourself from it" (228). Just as language cannot decipher the enigma of the Batoutos' existence (in another example, who, in this scene, is the "you?"), the invisible resists being sighted and recorded as such, dropping out of, and in on, recorded history. And herein, for Daniel Aranjo, lies the bridge between the two paradoxical strategies of these Glissantian texts, which say the unsayable and show the invisible, or in his words, "The unsayable. The invisible in terms of official history" (108). The damnation of the South, which is the unsayable in Faulkner's work, and the Batoutos, who are the invisible in History, are both brought into the clearing of opacity in and through Glissant's work.

This resistance to visibility on the part of the invisible is neither total nor final. The scene of the impressionable young Guillaume's travels in Italy demonstrates the possibility of staging these paradoxes of locution and vision. For Guillaume, who is gazing on a painting, "realizing a conception of togetherness that was altogether his own [,] The Italian painting presented itself like an ocean . . . repeating the same, always reestablished waves, different each time" (226). Here, he finds "islands," images of "Africans and Moorish kings" (226). And as a Batouto, "He truly noticed them, and no one else but him did. *The invisible chooses its seers* (voyants)" (226; emphasis added). If the Batoutos, "a people who teaches you the world" were to appear outright, "it would have been as rulers," which is precisely what this tale of nondomination seeks to avoid (19).

If the world has need of the Batoutos, it is in part on account of certain pedagogical qualities that they possess. While they may wander, and while they may often manifest themselves as invisible and absent, they nonetheless never lose sight of their paradoxical goal: they "are incubating a hidden project, that of showing the invisible, or at the very least of arranging visits with it" (243). In cultures where masking plays a pivotal role in social rites, where the people "play with a ceremonial invisibility that alternates with the visible, the Batoutos expose these works of their imagination, you meet them everywhere, that's because they have the secret surety that you don't see them, at the very moment when you are looking at them" (243). Indeed, the Batoutos flee if they are sought after: their "art of the invisible" has accompanied them everywhere they have gone, "which is why you seek them in order to point them out, most often they escape" (243).

Recognizing them, to the extent to which such a thing is possible, implies recognizing a set of truths about the Relation of all human beings in its totality. The Batoutos, who teach the world, are chiefly apostles of the *Tout-monde*. Encountering the Batoutos is commensurate to "meditating on this fray, beginning to confirm the differences, without renouncing the interlacing" (*Sartorius* 233). They teach the "Unity-Diversity of the world" (PR 94), what Glissant parses as "the extreme diversity of the unity of the world" (*Visite à Édouard Glissant* 60), in short. As they learn of this "interlacing," they also come to know the totality of the world, and know the totality of the world's unknowability. For it is in the epistemological failure that the world's totality brings about that the world's beauty consists. Similarly, the Batoutos' visible-invisibility, what amounts to their opacity, points to another lesson with regard to the possibility of knowing the other: "The all-seeing eye is a handicapped one" (*Sartorius* 243).

Rather than seeking to answer the question as to *what* the Batoutos are, I have heretofore sought to ask rather *how* they are, to look into the effects of Glissant's peculiar narrative approach to them. In order to sustain this impetus of asking *how*, I would now like to look more closely at the way in which the Batoutos become present in Glissant's text, that is, the way in which they are rendered in language. As I hope to show, a closer look at the opacity that marks Glissant's narration of the Batoutos—as well as more than a few other themes throughout his work—can offer insight into the way in which Glissant presents himself and his texts in relation to other authors (most notably, Deleuze and Faulkner) and their texts.

From the Influence of Opacity to the Opacity of Influence: Triangulating Glissant, Faulkner, and Deleuze

"We too make frequent visits to the obscure," affirms one of *Sartorius*'s narrative voices, claiming to join in the Batoutos' religious belief in non-Origins, in Creation as an undoing (*Sartorius* 95). Who is this "we" who speaks at this juncture in the text? Immediately before this affirmation, the narrator offers a terse response: "we" is nothing less than "we, they, I" (*Sartorius* 95). The brevity of this explication belies the complexity and the opacity that characterize both the subjects and the methods of Glissantian narration. Celia Britton and J. Michael Dash have treated the topic of opacity in Glissantian narration in great detail, but have focused in large part on texts preceding *Faulkner, Mississippi* (1996) and *Sartorius* (1999), given their monographs' dates of appearance (1999 and 1995, respectively; cf. Britton, *Glissant* 18–25; Dash, *Glissant* 134–57). *Sartorius*, I would like to argue, continues and amplifies the ongoing process of foregrounding opacity in Glissant's work, and exemplifies Glissant's strivings toward what Deborah Hess has called the "overthrowing" of the coherence and continuity that are the foundations of traditional narrative (*La poétique de renversement* 221).

Any literary text, Glissant argues in *Poétique de la Relation*, will be caught up in a negotiation between complexity and transparency. Writing is, he argues, "contradictorily, productive of opacity. Because the writer, entering into his/her writings stacked up together, renounces an absolute . . . writing is relative in relation to that absolute, which is to say that it in effect it opacifies that absolute, bringing it about in language. The text goes from dreamed transparency to the opacity that is produced in the words" (PR 129). The same holds in the domain of the discipline of "theory," and one could fruitfully apply Glissant's remarks on "theory" to his own theoretical work: In a section of *Poétique de la Relation* titled "THEORIES," he argues that "*Theory is absence, obscure and propitious*" (PR 143). For Glissant, in other words, a given theory, indisputably present (in the text, on the page, in the reader's mind), is nonetheless absent; it never encompasses the whole of the object that it purports to explain or illuminate, nor does it communicate the entirety of its message (if such a message ever existed, either in the author's mind or in the text, in a complete and final state). Hence, its propitiousness: it reinstates obscurity as a preserver of the Diverse, or opacity as a protector of the different. Glissant's section headings in *Poétique de la Relation* push this linguistic obscurity to its outermost limits at times, demonstrating the metamorphoses that language must undergo if it is to address topics such as Relation or Being. In doing so, they stage the resultant failures both of language (to produce meaning) and of the reader's comprehension (to grasp meaning in its transparency).

The heading "Ce que ce que," is indicative of this obscuring function of Glissant's language, as is "Ce qu'étant ce que n'est." In her English translation of that cornerstone of Glissant's theoretical production, *Poetics of Relation*, Betsy Wing renders these two section headings as "That

That" and "That Those Beings Be Not Being" (159, 185). The texts that follow these agrammatical or paradoxical formulations make no concerted effort to develop, explain, or even visibly correspond to them in any way. And that is just one of the many ways in which Glissant undermines the reader's attempt to assign a final truth to his text. Lest we forget, it must be considered that this opacifying effect may extend even to the truth that the text's meaning, or intention, is to communicate an absence of truth—the opacification of opacity itself, in other words. Glissant's thought in this regard answers to the vitalist agenda of demonstrating that when human reasoning faculties are turned on the world, on the living other, or on Being itself, those faculties fall short.

Paradoxically, in Glissant's thought, it is only through embracing the opacity of the other than we can begin to see him or her clearly. The true state of affairs between self and other is one in which the self cannot know the truth of the other and vice versa. Or, otherwise put, the truth of the other's being is the inaccessibility of this truth to the self. Similarly, the very idea that I might formulate for myself of what Glissant calls the totality-world is an impediment to my understanding the world as such. That opaque, Glissantian idea could only be rendered in opaque language: "Let's say it again, opaquely: the very idea of totality is an obstacle to totality" (PR 206).

That such an argument must be "said" in an opaque way (*said*, that is, in a written text) is crucial. Here, Glissant's language performs his point. In this way, Glissant's writing inspires the thinking of opacity, which leads away from absolute truths: "The thinking of opacity distracts me from absolute truths, of which I would believe myself to be the depositary" (PR 206). Indeed, the very idea of opacity exists in a troubled and troubling relationship to its opposite, transparency. For example, Glissant sees in Faulkner's "methodological choice" to deploy opacity a deeper "lucidity" and "honesty" (FM 97). And as Papa Longué says to Mathieu in the novel *Tout-monde*, "if you don't climb into the obscure, then you won't enter into the light of the Tout-monde" (TM 178). Glissant thus cautiously utilizes his figure of opacity as something of an undecidable, keeping it in a constant and shifting relationship with clarity. Consequently, the cloudiness that is characteristic of literature and life is not a good in itself. It is not simply a substitute for clearness, either in narrative or in his theoretical writings; instead, it remains in a troubled—which is to say, opaque—relationship to transparency.

One of the rhetorical strategies evident in Glissant's numerous interviews exemplifies this reactivation and privileging of the obscure in conjunction with a desire for clarity. Glissant tends to use interviews, which are customarily seen as the site where authors, in Lydie Moudileno's words, "give readers access to illuminating aspects of their work and personality," in order to reinscribe the opacity of his thought (Moudileno, "Positioning" 132–33). Moudileno has interpreted the role of the interview in an author's self-fashioning as a matter of "positioning." In her words,

> as a discursive, performative and highly coded exercise in self-representation, the literary interview is a space of constant reconfiguration of the writer's identity. Although it obviously cannot keep its promise to give readers access to the writer's absolute, metaphysical presence, it does however reveal the writer's ability, or disposition to engage the constitutive categories of his/her projected identity. ("Positioning" 133)

Glissant's *Introduction à une poétique du Divers* (1996), to take but one example, is in large part constituted of transcripts of interviews and question-and-answer sessions. The fact that Glissant has hand-picked these interviews for publication himself intensifies the purported truth-value of his comments. Glissant's words in this text are presented both with the (apparent) relaxed frankness of a conversation and with the author's own intention to include them along his written texts (and with the rather didactic-sounding title of *Introduction* no less).

What is most striking about this particular collection of interviews is the extent to which Glissant casts himself as elucidating his key ideas in lucid and cogent language. Beginning his sentences with phrases such as "What I want to express when I say . . ." and "I call the Chaos-world—I've said it many times . . ." serves to increase this effect (141; 82). Indeed, Glissant often uses interviews as a platform from which to repeat his aphorisms. His frequent habit, when interviewers ask for clarification of a claim, is to rehash one of the slogans that resurface throughout his written works (here, "I change in exchanging myself," for example [IPD 103]). Further, Glissant enshrines his strategy of repetition by making it into an imperative: "I've already said it elsewhere but one must repeat oneself" he tells his interlocutor; or, "One must always repeat oneself" (IPD 82, 88). Thus, the author's habit of reiterating a set of axioms would in fact constitute a direct reflection of the importance of the theme of repetition in this thought. As he explains in *Le discours antillais*, "The repeated nature of these ideas does not make speech more clear, on the contrary it opacifies speech perhaps. We need these stubborn densities . . ." (DA 17).

The willful opacity of the text thus becomes, for Glissant, a strategy of protective concealment as well as of opposition. The Glissantian text ostentatiously declares that there is not an ultimate truth to be found within it, aside from the truth of continued opacification. The same holds for its author, whose thoughts are presented repetitively and frankly through the interview form and elsewhere, demonstrating a continuity and integrity that nonetheless repeats the process of opacification. This approach to self-presentation functions as a simultaneous reinforcement and deconstruction of the image of the intellectual (the literary critic, the wise author) as a bearer of universal truths, or even of truths with regard to particular ideas.

Just as Glissant's figure of opacity informs his presentation of himself and his ideas, it also impinges on the way in which he construes his relationships to other authors: in this case, Faulkner and Deleuze. Despite his overwhelmingly positive valuation of Faulkner, Glissant does acknowledge that he is aware of sharp contrasts between his own beliefs and those of the white, Southern author. To begin, Glissant concedes that Faulkner commits what is perhaps the most disingenuous and harmful offense in the Glissantian worldview: he rejects creolization. As Glissant makes this point, he maintains, once again, the semantic slippage in the word *creolization* between what Faulkner and his contemporaries would have considered "racial mixing" and the more abstract and metaphysical sense of creolization as ever-increasing interconnection, combination, and unpredictability. If it is the case that "Creolization is that very thing that offends Faulkner," this creolization is synonymous with "Mixing, hybridity, then the unpredictability of results" (FM 117).

Moreover, if Faulkner's work depicts the US South as a bleak place, it is because "In the inextricability of the world . . . Misfortune and damnation remain the only possible results, when one has pushed away hybridity or creolization with revulsion" (FM 123). Glissant proves to be an apologist for Faulkner despite all of his faults, and at times the weight of his personal desires and affections on his reading of Faulkner becomes arrestingly clear. For example, in a justification of sorts of one of Faulkner's more incendiary declarations, that is, that he would not hesitate to go out and shoot blacks in the street should the need ever arise, Glissant suggests that Faulkner must not have been "sober" when he made such remarks (FM 144).

The problematic nature of Glissant's reading of Faulkner did not escape the students of Southern University, to whom *Faulkner, Mississippi* is dedicated. Given Faulkner's famous remarks to the effect that African Americans should "go slow now" (FM 145) rather than seek rapid and revolutionary change, and given Glissant's comment that African Americans in Faulkner's oeuvre are "depositaries of suffering, guardians of the temple of the unsayable," who are never allowed the possibility to rise up, the students of this African-American college in the deep South (Baton Rouge, Louisiana) prove loath to follow Glissant's example in reappropriating Faulkner (FM 132). Glissant allows that these students taught him that "no quality in literature is worth the even emblematic thingification of a community," but responds that readers are "free to look Faulkner in the eyes, to go with him where we want to go" (FM 146). Through this retort, what Glissant holds to be the true value of Faulkner's work becomes evident: in the Faulknerian corpus, *careful* readers can make out "a disruption of unitary conceptions of being, a putting-into-deferral/difference (*mise en différé*) of absolute identity, a vertigo of speech . . ." (FM 146–47). These latter qualities constitute, for Glissant, the "revenge" of the Faulknerian corpus against its author, the "brilliant puritan who engendered it" (FM 147).

Glissant's apology for Faulkner has recourse to a claim to know the writer, the "true" Faulkner, better than other readers have in the past. Recognizing that there is a worrisome ambivalence in Faulkner's texts but continuing to champion him all the while, Glissant suggests that his interpretation of Faulkner is validated by a direct pipeline to the author's intended meaning. In an attempt to resolve the question of whether Faulkner should, we might say, be burned, Glissant writes: "Whatever it may be, blacks. Too-conventional silhouettes, as if they were invisible as masses. Was that a respect for the opacity of the Other or the beginnings of a system of apartheid? Free density of identity or negligence or disinterest? That's up to the person who is expressed in the work" (FM 93). Glissant's reading of Faulkner thus comes into line with Glissant's own understanding of the author's identity and intentions. Curiously, the explication "That's up to the person who is expressed in the work" bears with it another implication that would seem out of place in today's literary-critical climate, marked by what Roland Barthes famously named the "Death of the Author" (Barthes, *Image-Music-Text*). In basing his advocating of Faulkner on "the person," the author, Glissant perceives an author's literary corpus as existing in direct correspondence with that author's self-expression as an individual.

The riven nature of this person whom Glissant claims to know mirrors the Caribbean critic's use of Faulkner. Seizing on a comment that Faulkner made to the effect that he and Albert Camus "shared the same anguish," Glissant holds these two writers up as *good* white writers, who issued from a culture of oppression that had sprung up on contested ground. Because of a conflicted sense of belonging, Camus and Faulkner were trapped in a predicament, that of "having to conceive of justice while having to avoid crying it out (even if that means separating it from truth) because that would be against (their) own . . ." (FM 92) This conflict in moral orders (loyalty to one's own social group as opposed to adherence to one's individual conception of justice) is, for Glissant, what spawns the Faulknerian method: Faulkner "thus suspends his judgment with regard to the South. He needs the ambiguity of unveiling as a resource for the tragedy that he develops" (FM 92).

It is worth recalling Glissant's argument that Faulkner's method has influenced not only his own work but also that of many Caribbean writers, from Alejo Carpentier to Wilson Harris. Indeed, Glissant holds not only that these writers are "influenced" by Faulkner, but that the "techniques of writing" in the common language (*langage*) of Caribbean writers, whether they produce in French, Spanish, or English, were a direct influence of Faulkner.

> An Alejo Carpentier (Cuba), who writes in Spanish, a Wilson Harris (Guyana) who, as for him, writes in English, an Aimé Césaire (Martinique) or myself, who write in French, we have a common language (*langage*) that is made up of trust in words, in the power of the word, in the writing techniques that we have essentially borrowed from Faulkner: accumulation, listing, repetition, jumbles, deferred revelation. All of that constitutes a language (*langage*), a way of appropriating the languages (*langues*) that we all have in common. That constitutes a specific literary given, an aesthetics of relation, if you like! ("La 'créolisation' culturelle du monde")[7]

Glissant would thus have his readers believe that he suffers from very little of what Harold Bloom has called the "anxiety of influence." In this instance of self-representation, Glissant's relationship to Faulkner, much like his access to Faulkner's psychology, would appear to be all too transparent.

It is in his stated relationship to Deleuze that Glissant exchanges his seeming insouciance with regard to the anxiety of influence for what we might call an *opacity of influence*. Glissant makes this correlation to the French philosopher in one of his epigraphs to *Sartorius*. As Lydie Moudileno has pointed out, an epigraph has traditionally served to designate the main idea of the text to follow ("Positioning" 138). The connection between the Deleuzian invocation of a literature that would create a people that is missing (cited at this chapter's opening), and *Sartorius: le roman des Batoutos* would, thanks to the novel's epigraph, therefore appear to be quite clear. (Glissant's dedication of his earlier novel *Tout-monde* to Félix Guattari has a similar effect of eliciting comparison with the latter's thought.)

And yet, a few pages from the text's ending, Glissant places in the mouth of *Sartorius*'s narrator a curious remark that puts the relationship of his text and its paratext in doubt. The narrator explains that the text's Deleuzian epigraph was inspired by a conversation with Christian Salmon, author of *Tombeau de la Fiction* (*The Tomb of Fiction*). Salmon thought that the epigraph might be a good fit with Glissant's text, Glissant tells us, and so he brought it to the author's attention. Interestingly, the narrator of *Sartorius* confesses that he cannot quite make out what the epigraph means.

> We would have argued endlessly about the sentence from Gilles Deleuze that is at the opening of this book . . . I can't seem to decide, I may not want to, whether the betrayals and the renunciations that are emphasized at the end of the citation would belong to he who would thus have wanted to bring about a people, perhaps much later, and at least to conceive of that people in consciousness or in dreams, or if it's the people itself that would betray itself, taking too long to rise up as a people. A delightful ambiguity from Gilles Deleuze, whose words are just as precise as they are radiant with possibilities. I'm associating the thought of Félix Guattari with this ceremonious declaration. (*Sartorius* 307)

Susan Crosta has said of *Sartorius*'s epigraphs that "The citations from Gilles Deleuze and Saint-John Perse that are found as epigraphs showcase the notions of the imaginary and the diverse, but do not illuminate the identity of the Batoutos in any way" (35). That observation with regard to the epigraphs could be extended beyond the identity of the Batoutos—which, if we are to follow the spirit of *Sartorius*, ought to remain murky at any rate—to our interpretations of the overall meaning of the text.

Writing toward a New World: From a New People to a New Literature

For Bernadette Cailler, part of the novelty of *Sartorius* lies in the fact that, as she puts it, "*Sartorius* transcends multiple traditions that oppose the world of the book to the world of life" ("*Sartorius*" 269). A look at another apparent relationship of influence, that which links William Faulkner's *Sartoris* (1929) and Glissant's *Sartorius* (1999), helps to illustrate more concretely how Glissant weaves together Cailler's "worlds." Somewhat surprisingly, the content of Faulkner's novel *Sartoris*, which is mainly concerned with the past, and more particularly with the haunting absence-presence of the character of Colonel Sartoris, has very little to do with Glissant's text. In Glissant's novel, the name "Sartorius" is only one phase in a long progression of mutations of a name, and it represents neither the origin nor the end of this genealogy, which in fact is but one of the many that his *Sartorius* undertakes. As elsewhere in Glissant's thought, the use of the name/title *Sartoris* proves to be a critique of the very idea of origins. In the novel *Sartorius*, the text's narrator interviews a certain Joachim Sartorius on the history of his family, "For reasons that are in some way Batoutian" (*Sartorius* 211). The (non)explanation of the family's genealogy that ensues traces the family line, which begins, or rather which is first invoked, with the tailor Schneider. Schneider, a denizen of Frankfurt, decides in 1518 to Latinize his name (*Sartorius* 174–75). He thus becomes Sartor, the progenitor (or rather, one of the progenitors) of the clan, and in true Faulknerian fashion, he is deeply concerned with the problem of establishing a foundation for his progeny (*Sartorius* 208). In this regard, he stands in contrast to the Batouto character Aréko, who understands time differently and who is in no way concerned with tracing lines of filiation or establishing a founding origin for future generations (*Sartorius* 208).

By 1705 another member of the Sartor line has his name changed to "Sartorius," a yet more Latinate name (210). Still later, Wilhelm Sartorius, one of his descendants, decides to immigrate to the United States. There, with a brisk "OK Bill" at the immigration desk, he becomes, in a reversion to the Faulknerian spelling, "William Sartoris" (*Sartorius* 269). Such were the tangled and opaque origins that ended with Glissant's character sharing the name of Faulkner's. "I observe, or at least I suppose," muses the narrator of *Sartoris*, "that this selfsame *u* that had been removed from his name . . . was put back by the writer into his family's patronymic roughly sixty years later, from Falkner to Faulkner. *U*'s are imposing, just as much as *o*'s" (269). (Final *o*'s in names are, of course, the mark of the scattered Batouto line.) In this quick rumination lies, we are to assume, the entirety of the relationship between Glissant's text and Faulkner's. As is the case for Glissant's following novel, *Ormerod* (2003), named for his friend and collaborator Beverly Ormerod, the author would have us believe that the origins of the *Sartorius* novel's name are laid bare, just as he has done with those of the Sartorius family. Glissant explains,

> (I)n the book's mythical narrative, I bring in people who exist in my circles, friends, people I've met and whom I frequent. And Sartorius is the Director of the Goethe Institutes and the treasurer of the International Parliament of Writers. I told him about my intention to entitle the novel *Sartorius* because I wanted to make the connection between the (hi)story of the Batoutos and that of a friend. ("Un peuple invisible")

Glissant's explanation here that *Sartorius*'s title is quite simply an homage to a friend ought to be set in brackets, for things are not as simple as the author makes them out to be. While Glissant seems to be making the origins of the title clear, a look to other comments he has made on the title of *Sartorius* will prove that his elucidation here in effect proves to be an obscuring move.

As we have seen, at the "end" of the Sartori(u)s genealogy, or rather the end of the portion of it that is isolated here, Glissant hints at a relationship to Faulkner. And given what we have seen to be the concerns of *Faulkner, Mississippi* and of *Sartorius: le roman des Batoutos*, the two texts are far from unrelated. Moreover, Glissant writes approvingly that in *Sartoris*, Faulkner "had supposed that no white (by which he no doubt meant: no white from the South) would be able to affirm that he understood blacks" (FM 126). The theme of opacity is, consequently, a crucial one in all three texts, just as it is for the constellation of influence that Glissant sketches with comments such as these. Glissant's strategy in explaining the title of *Sartorius* in the text itself, in *Faulkner, Mississippi*, and in a postpublication interview, serves to multiply and obscure the text's origins, and to suggest that if we are to believe that origins determine meaning, then both origins and meanings are multiple.

Glissant's meditation on origins and opacity is by no means a willful obscurantism: as he makes clear in his response to his interviewer, "For me, it's a *new way of understanding the novel*, mixing personal relations with mythical relations" ("Un peuple invisible"; emphasis added). A new way of understanding the novel: blending the personal and the mythical in *Sartorius* has the effect, as we have seen, of putting the knowledge of origins into doubt, and in myriad senses. The origins of a people, the origins of a text (more specifically, its origins in other texts), all become as clouded and impenetrably dense as the other whom the self cannot (perfectly, finally) understand. And it is in this sense that Glissantian opacity is not a purely negative enterprise: while it may block or obscure knowledge in one domain, it hints at new possibilities for knowledge in another.

As for whether *Sartorius* is a myth of foundations, Glissant is ambivalent. Whereas he would later claim that the Batoutos story was a myth that the world needs ("La 'créolisation' culturelle du monde"), here, in 1999, Glissant holds that "we don't need a myth, rather, what we do need is a new imaginary" ("Un peuple invisible"). *Sartorius*, rather than establishing even a false or provisional origin, would therefore constitute a project of changing the role of origins in the imaginary of its readers. And although the text's nonorigin is set in Africa, Glissant maintains that its apparent return to Africa, unlike that of Negritude or US Afrocentrism, is rather a "detour" through this "country of origin" ("Un peuple invisible"). As such, *Sartorius* presents the continent of Africa as one among many Africas, for it illustrates the existence of "another Africa, which is not only that of origins but also that of the diaspora, of the moving-on/departure (*l'en-aller*)" ("Un peuple invisible"). For Glissant, *Sartorius* would thus avoid what Doris L. Garraway has called "the Enlightenment search for origins" as well as "the modernist nostalgia for lost origins," in her article titled "Toward a Creole Myth of Origin" (152).

Yet while *Faulkner, Mississippi* maintains that there is a direct and traceable lineage connecting Faulkner to a host of Caribbean writers, Glissant also holds that the Faulknerian literary corpus marks a radical rupture with the Western literary tradition. Faulkner's writing is also, in other words, the scene of a creative destruction of foundational genres in western literature: not only the novel, but also the epic and tragedy. This death and rebirth of fundamental modes of literary expression will, in Glissant's view, contribute to bringing about a more ethical tomorrow.

Seizing on two interrelated definitions of the epic and tragic modes, Glissant argues that both come to know their decadence in Faulkner's writing. Faulkner's entire oeuvre becomes a "meditation on the impossibility of the epic, in this time and in this place. Or rather a fury raging against this impossibility, a heroic effort to bring about its birth and express it, taking as a point of departure the improbability that it postulates" (FM 169). The tragic mode, just as swiftly defined, figures prominently in the Faulknerian corpus as well, a corpus that repeatedly stages the tragic mode's downfall: "Legitimacy, the drama of its exhaustion, and the course of its restoration, constitute the first principle of traditional tragic theater. Because legitimacy, in Western cultures, runs along the thread of being, the obscure path that attaches every community to a Genesis, thus establishing it in its sovereign right" (FM 177). The "greatness" and the novelty in Faulkner, for Glissant, stem from the fact that in his work both the epic and the tragic modes of literary production see their own undoing, or as he puts it, "crash into their own impossibilities" (FM 180).

For Glissant, salvation lies in the advent of a new epic form. Faulkner's work, in Glissant's view, intimates to us the possibility of that new sort of epic, one that would dispense with any effort to make whole what is fragmented, or to seek resolution in what is dissolute. An epic form that would be, as Glissant puts it, "An opening beyond suspicion, unpredictable, one that would in no way be a system. That would be fragile, ambiguous, ephemeral, but that would shine with all the contradictory explosions (*éclats*) of the world. It must be so, for otherwise the extinction of the traditional epic will have produced a death colder and harder than death itself" (FM 139–40). Might *Sartorius* be this new epic? Further along in his interview with Libong and Mongo-Mboussa, Glissant finds himself explaining that *Sartorius* ought not to be read as a rehashing of the old epic form.[8] The interviewers ask: does *Sartorius* seek to establish a genesis for the Batoutos? Does it constitute a foundation myth? Glissant replies that his novel is the opposite, a "*digenèse*" (digenesis). For Glissant, geneses give the right to conquer (*Faulkner, Mississippi* 159–60). The Batoutos, on the other hand, shun conquest and domination.

For Glissant, Faulkner can be valued as a writer who began to measure the changes that need to be made in the world and in the imaginaries of his readership. In Glissant's words, Faulkner "measures which kind of overturnings will be necessary in our sensibilities" (FM 134). Crucially, political change is, in this view, prefaced by the work of literature: "This overturning, Faulkner's oeuvre works toward it, not through moral lessons, but rather by changing our poetics" (FM 134). In *La cohée du Lamentin*, Glissant directly allies what Deleuze has called a "people that is missing" with a utopian political practice.

> Utopia is not a dream. It is what we are lacking in the world. Here's what it is: that which we are lacking in the world. Many of us have rejoiced in the fact that the philosopher Gilles Deleuze considered that the function of literature as art is first to invent a people that is missing. Utopia is the very place of that people. We imagine, we try to imagine what would happen if we could not invent *that*, even if we didn't know what it is, except that

we know that with this people and this peopled country we would be closer to the world, and the world closer to us. (16)

How might it be that, in Glissant's thought, writing comes to serve as a conduit from individual subjects to the world-as-whole, and from the world as it is in the present to future utopias? The answer lies, for Glissant, in the decadence and rebirth of established literary forms, and in their subsequent effects on the imaginary. It is this impetus toward change in the imaginary, toward change in poetics, that allows Glissant to recuperate Faulkner as an ancestor of sorts. As Cilas Kemedjio tersely puts it, "The quest for founder-ancestors . . . is part of that canonizing tendency that torments writers and critics of Antillean literature" (229).

It would seem, then, that Glissant has found in Faulkner a "founder-ancestor" who allows him to critique the ideas of founding and of ancestry. Whether fueled by "torment" or not, Glissant's choice of Faulkner is significant in that it is not based on racial or ethnic confraternity, but rather on a shared poetics and a common spirit of critique: it is for this reason that Glissant's reading of Faulkner is relatively untroubled by the latter author's race or his overt implication in the racial politics of his time. For Glissant, the imaginary would thus transcend racial or socioeconomic belonging.[9]

For Glissant, the writer or philosopher's role in the advent of the *Tout-monde* is to model new forms of thought and to breathe life into them. As is often the case in Glissant's work, progression toward a higher, future goal (e.g., the *Tout-monde*) does not imply a unilateral and conclusive departure. Rather, a relationship of simultaneous *détour/retour* (detour/return) is instated between the particular and the universal, or rather between place and the totality: in the case of Faulkner, for example, Glissant reads the writer as attaining to the "most essential" of human interaction (FM 216) precisely through his exploration of opacity and through deepening his study of Yoknapatawpha county, a very particular, very small place. Faulkner is "the greatest writer of the 20th century" for Glissant, in that he was "He who had the most to reveal of his own incontrovertible (*incontournable*) place, at the same time as of the Relation of that place to the totality-world" (FM 54). Herein lies the conduit between the particularity of Faulkner's novels and the universality (although Glissant would spurn the term) of the methodological experimentations that guide them. Through the decadence and rebirth of established literary forms that is staged in his work, Glissant's Faulkner—like Glissant himself—becomes a revolutionary ontological thinker. Glissant professes his admiration for what he calls:

> These infinite openings of the epic and the tragic (their failure, finally, but one that renews them so completely), and this effort, the most total that, since Nietzsche, a creator has undertaken in order to "rethink" *that* (Being, and by extension in the real: identity, belonging) upon which Western ontology has rested for so many centuries and with such profundity. (FM 181–82)

It is through this project of rethinking Being, identity, and belonging that Faulkner can be seen as one of Glissant's forerunners. The terms Glissant uses to describe Faulkner's literary practice, terms such as *"repenser,"* (rethinking) (FM 181–82) *"renouvellement"* (renewal) (FM 141), *"renversement"* (overturning) (FM 134), could be fruitfully applied to the Martinican author's own literary-philosophical project. Indeed, in response to Stathis Gourgouris's 2003 inquiry into the philosophical potential of literature titled *Does Literature Think?*, one might propose a Glissantian reformulation of Gourgouris's question: Does literature *re*think? If we are to take Glissant at his word and follow him in his *re*reading of Faulkner, a corollary question arises: how can a connection be drawn between thought and life, between a Glissantian rethinking of opacity in ethical relations and concrete, political changes in actuality?

Faulkner, Mississippi is a treatise on how to read opacity, on how to read opaquely, and on how to proffer an opaque reading. Reading it alongside *Sartorius*, we gather that the other is best known as radically unknowable, that Faulkner's texts say what is unspeakable most effectively by not saying it, and that the Batoutos only become visible to us when we learn that we cannot see them. In *Faulkner, Mississippi* as in *Sartorius*, it becomes apparent that for Glissant, the only real transparence *is* opacity.

Troublingly, however, Glissant's repeated demands for the right to opacity for everyone are remarkably uncontentious. After all, who could possibly disagree with either their ethical plea (*something* of the other ought to remain unknown to the self) and their epistemological certainty of uncertainty (something of the other will always, irrevocably and inevitably, remain unknown to the self)? The demand for opacity is broad enough, it would seem, as to be altogether unquestionable.

The "right to opacity" also poses problems due to the fact that it proceeds by negation, eschewing the positive near-absolutely. Glissant's opacity dictates what the self cannot know about the other, without hinting at what he or she *can* know about the other. Critics peddling the effigy of a postpolitical, late Glissant will no doubt take comfort in that apparent quandary.

After all, how might Glissant reconcile his emphasis on radical alterity and his celebration of the unknowable with the political necessities of mutual understanding and coalition building? How, in other words, to square opacity with solidarity?

The very metaphor of opacity is of course a reference to a *lack* of transparency, to what we can*not* see. And we can read the predominantly negative nature of opacity as a reflection of Glissant's uneasiness with prescriptive claims. The latter are, for him, too susceptible to a backslide into coercion. Glissant's paradoxical approach to alterity is most concerned with clearing the path for the first steps in social and epistemological transformation—and decidedly *not* with predicting the outcome of such future revolutions. It serves a protective function, preserving the life of the other, or allowing Faulkner to speak an unspeakable truth, or unseating essentialism in order to open up the world to the *Tout-monde*. Glissant's use of the "re-" prefix in words such as "rethink" or "renew," moreover, reveals his overall preoccupation with literature as a revolutionary activity whose effects extend beyond the book. As to the question of what or who might inhabit that beyond, and as for the political potentialities of "new" literary forms, for the moment the idea of creolization dictates that there is only one prediction we can make with regard to future creation, literary or otherwise: that it will be imbued with the unpredictable.

THREE

Teleology Undone

Tout-monde and *Le quatrième siècle*

As we have seen thus far, Édouard Glissant's thought posits a set of enviable objectives, suggesting that with a shift in our imaginaries an ethical relationship with the other within the framework of his or her opacity is conceivable, or that the advent of the utopian *Tout-monde* is possible, perhaps even inevitable. It thus becomes apparent that there exists a Glissantian teleology, a set of outcomes toward which the world, and we as the subjects who inhabit it, ought to move, or are already moving. All of which begs the question as to how exactly we might go about acquiring such covetable things. Glissant's answer, as I argue in this chapter, is that the question itself ought to be rethought. In two philosophical novels, *Tout-monde* (1993) and *Le quatrième siècle* (1964), Glissant demonstrates another way of approaching teleology as he reformulates the trope of desire. Taking up the novel *Tout-monde* anew, I illustrate that this text constitutes a rewriting of the classical psychoanalytic model of desire, replacing the emphasis on the attainment of an object of desire with a recognition that the search itself is fruitful and productive. The plot of *Tout-monde*, which dialogues extensively with the essay *Traité du Tout-monde* (1997), turns around the familiar novelistic trope of a young, male character who sets out into the world on a quest. The *quimboiseur*, or traditional magic man Papa Longoué, sends Mathieu away from Martinique in search of something undefined, with the opaque explanation that "What you are going to seek everywhere, it's someone, is it a man an old man a child, who connects the country of sea to the country of land, and who is spread out and shared everywhere in the Tout-monde . . ." (207–8). Rather than ending with a scene of attainment, however, the text closes on a note of paradoxical uncertainty, where readers are left unsure as to whether Mathieu has achieved his purpose.

Although it was published nearly thirty years earlier, *Le quatrième siècle* displays remarkable parallels with *Tout-monde*. Longoué and Mathieu find themselves in dialogue there as well, as Mathieu seeks to attain an ultimate knowledge of the past, a task rendered impossible by the devastation wrought by the slave trade. Mathieu's goal is twofold: that is, he endeavors to attain the meaning of the category of the past and to illuminate its content, asking, for example, "Tell me the past, papa Longoué! What is the past?" (17). As the narrative unfolds, it becomes evident that Mathieu's quest is as impossible as it is inevitable, a condition that Glissant diagnoses in all Caribbean subjects, and perhaps by extension in all members of the African diaspora in the Americas: "And none of us knows what happened in the country over there beyond the waters, the sea has rolled over all of us, even you . . ." (68). In *Le quatrième siècle* as well, it is far from clear whether Mathieu has attained what he set out for. The objective that he desires is to become himself a channel to the past, turning back in time toward the truth of Africa, of slavery, and of his earliest ancestors on the island. As he turns backward, the narrative that Mathieu creates as he speaks with Longoué, however, pushes forward into the future, as it makes up the stuff of the text.

This paradoxical temporality, turning backward into the past as it grows forward into the future, has a spatial parallel in *Tout-monde*. In that novel, the polyphonic narration exhibits a contradictory directionality as it is at once a turning-outward and a turning-inward. In other words, in a pastiche of the traditional *Bildungsroman*, Mathieu leaves Martinique to set out into the world in search of knowledge and experience. But, as the text's polyphonic narrative voices point out, the characters come to see "Martiniques everywhere" they go (20). Far from a novel of definitive departure, there are in addition repeated narrative returns to the island throughout, all of which culminate in Mathieu's final homecoming at the narrative's close.

In *Le quatrième siècle* Mathieu seems not to have gained the knowledge he sought at all; in *Tout-monde*, he seems to find the person or thing that he seeks, but the scene of discovery is oneiric, and anticlimactic at best. Teleology, in other words, is undone in these two texts. Having rendered the question of attainment opaque, Glissant shows that in both novels Mathieu's desirous quest itself is productive: as Glissant puts it in *L'intention poétique* (1969), "One never attains truth: but all poetry comes about in that quest" (225).

Writing the Teleology of the Whirlwind: The *Tout-monde* Revisited

In the novel *Tout-monde*, Félix Guattari receives alongside Gilles Deleuze the honor not of inspiring but of *anticipating* the Glissantian Tout-monde. Glissant alludes to

> [T]he extent, the multiplication of the rhizome, that the philosophers of *A Thousand Plateaus*, Deleuze and Guattari, would establish later in the landscape of imagery, a sort of prescience of the Tout-monde, and one that would 'make contact' infinitely with each thing begun anew, in a rush and in great pleasure. (TM 63)

Glissant insinuates here that the relationship of influence between him and Deleuze and Guattari is not what his readers might have expected. The *Tout-monde*, if we are to follow Glissant, is not a mere transfer or translation of the Deleuzo-Guattarian concept of the rhizome into the contemporary world-political context, or in other words, into debates on globalization—or in Glissant's parlance, "globality" (CL 15). While, for Peter Hallward, the *Poétique de la Relation* is "*dependent* upon Deleuze's example" ("Édouard Glissant between the Singular and the Specific" 455; emphasis added), this novel, if it may be so named, is on Glissant's account the further realization of something that Deleuze and Guattari had begun to articulate in a "sort of prescience."

This comment by Glissant could be read as a way of asserting the *independence* of his thought, aligning it with the very movement of the world rather than with ideas associated with particular individuals or schools. While Deleuze and Guattari articulated ideas similar to Glissant's before Glissant himself, in other words, they did so because they were merely describing the same world that Glissant is, albeit in their own manner. The most salient characteristics of this world are also made clear in Glissant's nod to his precursors: the rhizome, which he has avowed to be the "principle" of his concept of Relation, is submitted to yet greater "extension" and "multiplication" in Glissantian Relation (PR 23). And the nature of the rhizome, insofar as it describes the *Tout-monde*, is marked by "contact," by recommencements and not ends, by a flurry of movement and, lest we forget, by what the novel *Tout-monde* calls a "great pleasure" (TM 63).

Despite what I will demonstrate to be that text's efforts to project multiplicity, as well as the fragmentation that it entails, into many domains,

I would like to distill a set of features that mark *Tout-monde*, in order to better understand the peregrinations of desire that traverse its pages. These features are movement, multiplicity, and circularity. And while they are ever-present in the text, one angle from which to approach them is through an examination of Mathieu Béluse's wanderings, by which he comes to better know the world (TM 48). In them, an impressive accumulation of narratives, histories, and chronologies is held together—if it can be said to hold together—by a plot line that it shares with *Le quatrième siècle*: the desire of, and the search it engenders in, Mathieu Béluse.

When asked by an interviewer, "Who desires in this book [*Tout-monde*]?" and "Who is speaking in this novel?," Glissant responds by invoking multiple configurations of directionality (IPD 130, 131). Whereas *Le quatrième siècle* claims to direct its narrative focus toward the past (as seen in Mathieu's repeated question, "What is the past?"), while also turning itself toward the future (in that it seeks a relationship to the past that could ground a literature and a nation), *Tout-monde* refracts the tropes of desire and directionality into increasingly diverse configurations. As he continues to respond to his interviewer, Glissant seeks to undermine the logic that shapes the interviewer's questions: the speaker of *Tout-monde*, he affirms, "is multiple" (IPD 131). There is no "someone," and there is not a "that [*ça*] in the psychoanalytic sense; the speaker's origin cannot be determined, perhaps not even by [him]self, and his speech acts cannot be controlled" (IPD 131).

It is curious that a thinker who had first demonstrated a consistent concern with connecting particular places with the rest of the world nearly forty years ago in *Soleil de la conscience* would wait until 1993 to set a novel outside of the Caribbean, with the publication of *Tout-monde*.[1] The extra-Caribbean or worldly character of *Tout-monde*, however, does not constitute a definitive rupture with Glissant's *pays natal*; as Jérôme Cornette puts it, "the 'poetics of chaos' . . . could not take flight without being rooted" (91). Quite conscious of the narrative's architecture, which takes Martinique as both point of departure and point of arrival, Glissant deems that directionality to be a paradoxical one: "The paradox is that all of that departs from a place and comes back to it . . ." (IPD 131). Despite, or perhaps thanks to, the circularity of the text, Glissant identifies *Tout-monde* as a fragmentary novel that has "exploded" (IPD 129). Inasmuch as it manifests not only this circular narrative direction but a host of others as well, Glissant finds his *Tout-monde* to be exemplary of the modern novel in that it follows a rhizomatic multidirectionality: "What is enthralling in the contemporary novel is that it can take off in all directions: it travels throughout the world" (IPD 129).

This world-traveling, "exploded" novel is not, for all that, wholly unreadable. *Tout-monde* consists largely of a sequence of quasi-traditional narratives, usually involving the characters that have inhabited the rest of the Glissantian fictional universe. After a short commentary on Martinique and on an expatriate from there, Panoplie, the novel launches into an extended, nostalgic recounting of the young Mathieu Béluse's sun-drenched Italian vacation. Next comes an anecdote regarding the two *Békés* who also appear in *Le quatrième siècle*, Senglis and Laroche. Senglis is tricked into giving money to a character of mixed African and European ancestry, a young man whom Senglis has been sidestepping. The text goes on to track that young man's journeys, as well as the various names he takes on for himself, which recall the constant renaming of the Schneider/Sartor/Sartorius clan in *Sartorius* (being the son of Laroche, he becomes "Georges de Rochebrune," "Rocamarron," etc.). Then come more voyages: that of the slave ship carrying the first Longoué to Martinique, which is a recapitulation of one of *Le quatrième siècle*'s central narratives; and that of the first passenger ship from Martinique to France at World War II's end.

War stories involving Raphaël Targin, who was introduced in *La Lézarde*, in addition to various episodes from previous novels that are explored from different perspectives, some of which are enhanced with added description while skirting over other narrative elements entirely, all follow. Prefacing this fragmented narration, and situated just after the book's dedication to Alain Baudot (a friend and bibliographer of Glissant's) and Félix Guattari, is a "Reminder of the adventures that preceded it" (TM 11). Serving to reinforce the ties linking this text to all of Glissant's previous writings, this short paratext also demonstrates that *Tout-monde* in large part encapsulates all of the other, proceeding texts: it is a book of the Glissantian world. Readers are reminded of the accursed cask that *Le quatrième siècle*'s Laroche gives to the escaped slave who will later come to be "the origin of the Longoué branch," or led to recall real historical incidents such as the plane crash that killed Albert Béville (TM 11, 12). In another "adventure," the character Marie Celat "endures," a verb that Glissant discusses at length in his reading of Faulkner (FM 87). In the margins are footnotes explaining important terms in Martinique such as "*marronner*" (to become a Maroon) and "*quimboiseur*" ("The quimboiseur was a marabout, a doctor, a sorcerer . . . he held séances for you, when nothing else had worked") (TM 11, 12). Those notes purport to make this Caribbean text more "readable" to non-Caribbean audiences. All of the above events and other assorted textual fragments were, the section concludes, "the approach to the Tout-monde" (TM 13).

The above line would have us believe that all of Glissant's work heretofore may be read teleologically, as a tending-toward the *Tout-monde* that is presumably to be revealed in the eponymous text at hand. On the other hand, if the narrative voice behind this declaration were to be Glissant's own (again, which Glissant?), it is unclear to what extent that voice can be trusted to give a valid, final reading of the author's entire oeuvre. After all, as Glissant has said, *Tout-monde* is a text where the speaker (who is already multiple) "does not guide the emission of speech" (IPD 131). Parallels between claims such as that one and the liar's paradox aside,[2] this prefacing remark raises the question of what it might mean to approach the *Tout-monde*, to participate in a teleology with the *Tout-monde* as its end.

It is Mathieu's quest that launches his voyage in the *Tout-monde*; as a theme, this quest meanders throughout the text, reaching its attainment—or not—in the novel's final pages. In its most basic form, his quest recalls many of the traditional epic tropes: an individual, male hero is made the subject of an annunciation, learning that he will travel far and wide, learning much and ameliorating himself in the process, in order to finally attain the object of his desire. But this semblance of an individual's heroic expedition cannot be carried much further. As Doris L. Garraway argues, Glissant's work "has in recent years turned away from the 'we' subject and the representational authority and collective identity that it implies, adopting in his recent novel *Tout-monde* a number of subjective first-person narrators who relate to one another in a play of difference and multiplicity" (161). Moreover, as I will illustrate, almost every stage along the traditional progression of an individual hero's quest becomes blurred, obscured, and undone in this novel. The origins of Mathieu's quests are multiple, the object of his quest is unclear, and the text leaves considerable doubt in place as to whether Mathieu has attained what he sought.

Just as *Sartorius* and *Le quatrième siècle* go about the task of revealing origins in their absence, *Tout-monde* makes unclear the origin of the pursuit that is fundamental to one of its primary narratives. One evening, as Mathieu sits ruminating on a jetty in the seaside Italian village where he is spending his vacation, he is approached by an unknown woman, Amina. She asks to read his palm, and foretells the quest he will set out on: "In order to express what you want, and for so many other things still, you will encounter great difficulties . . ." (46, ellipses in text). As if glossing the book on which her textual existence depends, she suggests that Mathieu's challenge is wrapped up in a problematics of Glissantian opacity.

> It is only much later that you will be understood . . . That is, if you want to be understood . . . That's not all . . . You have a problem of relation . . . You never explain. You think that any explanation is a waste . . . And that's not all . . . You will be wounded in a fight, I can't tell you whether it will be very serious. (TM 46, ellipses in original)

Relation "*relie, relaie, relate*" ("connects, relays, relates") (PR 183). Mathieu's problem could correspond to the third term: he has trouble making himself and his ideas clear to reasoned comprehension. But the "problem of relation" that Amina alludes to could have other meanings as well, and the ellipses in this transcription of her speech suggest, along with her repetition of "That's not all," that there is much more to be told. Mathieu himself is not satisfied, and probes Amina for more detail, which she cannot grant. "And will I meet someone is it a woman a man an old man a child?" he asks, to no response (TM 46). It is for this reason that he criticizes Amina as a soothsayer. Her vision of reality is not complete; she only sees "half of things" (TM 47).

Mathieu's second annunciation comes about in a meeting with Papa Longoué, who mysteriously assures him that "We have met for all of our lives and beyond" (TM 208). Echoing Mathieu's earlier words—for Longoué has already boasted to Mathieu that he can read the young man's thoughts—Longoué emphasizes that the object of Mathieu's desire, the goal of his quest, is far from clear.

> What you're seeking, what you are seeking everywhere, it's someone, is it a woman is it a man an old man a child, who brings together the country of the sea and the country of land, and who is shared everywhere in the Tout-monde, you try to gather together the sharing, you seek you seek . . . (TM 207–8)

The objective of Mathieu's search, in this interpretation of it, is therefore a person, one who brings geographical differences into contact with one another. The specification "who brings together the country of the sea and the country of land" recalls Glissant's frequent citations of Edward Kamau Brathwaite's line, "The unity is submarine," in order to reiterate his sense of the sea as universal connector.

The word *share* is used twice in Longoué's prediction, both as an adjective derived from a verb ("who is shared everywhere") and as a noun ("the sharing"), thus invoking both omnipresence and apportionment.

Longoué's use of this word, as well his phrasing "everywhere in the Tout-monde," intimates that Mathieu's quest will lead him to a direct engagement with the totality. "Sharing" in these two senses, i.e., as the act of sharing or exchanging and as the fact of being everywhere, also describes the role played by two other, seemingly minor characters in *Tout-monde*: Panoplie, and the *pacotilleuses* (who are roving, small-time saleswomen of the Francophone Caribbean). Each of these embodies the experiences that Mathieu will gain, as each stands as a veritable bookend with regard to the rest of the text. The initial pages of the text's first section introduce the fittingly named Panoplie, who becomes many different sorts of panoplies, and the *pacotilleuses* appear near the text's final pages, where the text's narrator finally claims to become a metaphorical kind of *pacotilleur* himself.

The text, like Mathieu himself, begins with a firm grounding in Martinique. The particularity of this place, affirms the "we" who is speaking, lies in its way of approaching the whole of the world. Addressing themselves to readers, the narrators muse that the world-traveling characters see the whole through the lens of their particular place, finding multiple Martiniques no matter where they look (TM 20). In that peculiar sort of approach to the World-whole, "You fall into the bends in the world's road," "you swing you tremble," "you make speech spin not like a thread but like a whirlwind"—if we know these experiences, it is because we have come to exist as the character "Colino" does (TM 20–21). This "Colino-philosopher," who is said to possess the cursed cask that continues to resurface in this text just as it does as in *Le quatrième siècle*, is also known as "Panoplie Derien" (in other words, "Panoply of Nothing") and "Panoplie-philosophe" (TM 23). He claims to know the great actors of world history; mad, he sees that "Everywhere it's unsettled, confused, worn out, completely crazy, but what's happening is that the whole world is talking to you through my Panoplie-voice. Wherever you turn, it's desolation. But you turn all the same" (TM 25–26). His message is one of movement, of the movement of the entirety of the world in its "whirlwind." And if this world is one of misery, it is not without consolation: motion continues, the world-as-world exists in a state of flux. It is thus in change that hope lies.

When Panoplie talks in this manner, the narrators assure us, it is not because he has brought philosophy from Europe to enlighten his desolate, Caribbean homeland. Rather, what Panoplie knows comes from an awareness of the workings of the world itself, taken as a whole: "it's not from France, go Deeper, it's the Tout-monde style. Because what he's saying to you like that, it's the world" (TM 26). The world speaks through Panoplie—whose very name implies an assortment, a complete array—and he speaks the world. He is a character whose name encapsulates the whole of the novel, and the novel-as-whole.

A *pacotilleuse*, on the other hand, personifies movement as well as agglomeration. "You don't know the *pacotilleuses*," teases a narrative voice claiming to be the novel's author, one whom the character Mathieu Béluse calls "'that novelist'" (TM 544). By way of explanation, "that novelist" enumerates the activities of the *pacotilleuses*: "They go from island to island, like the Arawaks or the Caribs of long-long ago, but obviously they're more mobile"; "they weave the Caribbean the Americas, they load up the planes with this mess of boxes . . ." (TM 544, 545). They are the Lévi-Straussian *bricoleuses* of trade, "carting around enormous heaps of merchandise that you can list: rattan chairs, cow skins, necklaces that are supposedly Indian . . ." (TM 544). While the expressions the narrator employs to describe the *pacotilleuses* emphasize disorder and chaotic multiplicity ("messing," "heaps" (TM 482, 544)), their true task is a nobler one. The keywords that Glissant uses to frame their role in the world, words that are some of the most important in his cosmology, make the importance of figures such as the *pacotilleuses* evident: "They connect life to life . . . They are Relation" (TM 545).

What the *pacotilleuse* does in the joined worlds of commerce and culture, the artist does in the world of literature. As one narrative voice of *Tout-monde* ventures: "Let's say, this will be a way for me to boast, that I'm the *pacotilleur* of all of these assembled stories" (TM 545). Insofar as "that novelist" is a *pacotilleur*, presiding over a chaotic hodgepodge of anecdotes, names, and places, he and his text demonstrate a desire to *return*—and a desire that returns. And it is in this sense that the desire for departure and travel that permeates *Tout-monde* must be understood: that is, not as a linear progression toward a faraway goal but as a *detour* (*Le discours antillais* 36, 32, 29), and more importantly as a detour that always maintains its relationship to its point of departure.

As early as *Le quatrième siècle*, Glissant's characters are subjected to "this sole and intense desire to leave, to get out, to leave behind the round earth like an overflowing gourd, to swim in the space beyond the horizon" (LQ 276). Here, place and totality are contrasted in the desire for a sensuous, total immersion in that which lies "beyond" the Caribbean island. And already in this earlier text, we can see both characters and a narrative voice who come to terms with concepts that will be crucial to the figure of the *Tout-monde*. Thus, Mathieu experiences "the deaf desire to leave, to take part . . ." (LQ 294). Conjoined within his desire are an appreciation of radical diversity and the idea that this multiplicity is the truth, perhaps the unique truth, of the world. It is in this sense that Philippe Mengue's vision of Deleuze and Guattari's framing of desire is can be smoothly transferred over to Glissant's. For Mengue, Deleuze's philosophy leads its readers toward an "ethics of desire"; Glissant's does much the same (89). Most importantly, their two visions of an ethics of desire give rise to a moment in which the conjoined positing of multiplicity and oneness occurs under the banner of the keyword *world*.

Despite the distinctly teleological overtones in these ways of framing characters' movement in the world, other moments in *Tout-monde* emphasize a circular, rather than a linear, directionality. In the scene of the two plantation owners Senglis and Laroche's soak in the hot spring, *Tout-monde* stages one of its many metatextual commentaries, addressing not only the narrative strategies used elsewhere in the text and in Glissant's texts in general but also the very commentary that the text is in the process of making. As the text resurrects these two characters from *Le quatrième siècle*, it seeks to justify its abrupt shift in plot: "And because there are people who only believe in the time that is followed along a straight line, and they protest when an episode from one hundred years ago falls into a story that will only come tomorrow, and they cry that they can't understand anything . . ." (TM 72) After alluding to such bad readers of time, the text responds to these imagined critics by not responding. Or rather, it does so by simply carrying on with the narration. The issue of causality in historical events, of events following one another in a logical sequence, and of their being *narrated* in this logical sequence (as Mathieu asked of Longoué—and how long ago he did so is neither clear nor important), is once again dismantled with a carefree, almost capricious ease.

And as Longoué has already suggested to Mathieu in *Le quatrième siècle*, time may not be what Mathieu believes it to be. In what sounds remarkably like another metatextual comment on temporality in the Glissantian text overall, Longoué asks, "What tells you that time passes? And if I cry out that time is wind-whirl/a soup-hole (*trou-bouillon*)? That it turns in a circle like a lemon? And if I say that you are going to spend your time spinning in the whirlwind of the wind over who knows how many faraway countries?" (TM 207). Longoué's vision of circularity takes on a near-mystical quality, with an epigraph to the novel claiming that all history is round like the earth, and a section beginning with the declaration that "'You have to come back to it, when you have passed through it'" (TM 485, 487). Roca (alias Rocamarron, alias Roquebrune, Rochebrune, etc.) holds that "All force is in the Circle," and the narrator, summarizing a voyage throughout the Caribbean and Central then South America, affirms "The force of the Circle" (TM 552, 553).

This circularity, this infinite oscillation between departure and return, is manifested in time and in space, the various narrative voices of *Tout-monde* tell us. In an italicized footnote—penned by we know not who—we learn that this circular directionality equally applies to written texts as well. Tracing the various avatars of an expression as it is translated into various languages, following its passage through a language "from Ivory Coast or from somewhere over there," to standard French, and to other languages in turn, a footnote revels in the similarities that surface among languages (TM 471). Locutions such as "*Tché, min bé*," it tells us, "*sound so much like the creole 'tchébé mouin,' hold me . . .*" (472). Lending the appearance of a scholarly edition to the text, the footnote restates Glissant's long-term message of unity-in-diversity: "*At a certain point, all of the world's texts come together*" (TM 472).

As Roca invokes the "great Circle," a directionality that is applicable to time, to space, and to texts, Mathieu asks for clarification, as he had done earlier with Papa Longoué in the latter's discussion of the *Tout-monde* (TM 554). Invoking a quest that sounds much like Mathieu's, Roca insists that

> In the great Circle, everything is placed within everything.
>   He who finds the strength to mix, has the strength to find.
> To find what, said Mathieu.
> The Vision, said Roca. (TM 555)

It is in moments such as this one that *Tout-monde* takes on its most markedly mystical quality. *Merriam-Webster's Online Dictionary* defines "mystical" as "1.a: having a spiritual meaning or reality that is neither apparent to the senses nor obvious to the intelligence . . . 1.b: involving or having the nature of an individual's direct subjective communion with God or ultimate reality." Here, Roca's invocation of "the Vision," like that of the footnote's author regarding a universal confluence of texts, is far beyond the reach of reason. Yet more strikingly, Roca's claim, like many of the foundational features of the *Tout-monde* (e.g., oneness, flux, etc.) implies an unmitigated access to the truth of the world, of "ultimate reality."

Whether Mathieu has attained what he set out for remains undecided; the same might be said of the Vision that Roca invokes. It is, perhaps, a vision of the opaque. One of the text's final sections, "THE DREAM ONCE

AGAIN OF THAT WHICH IS," demonstrates that one of the greatest problems plaguing Glissant's conception of the *Tout-monde* extends its grasp into the text's final pages. Full of sarcasm, the narrative voice speaks as if it were chastising itself, as well as the very book in which it appears.

> We used to chant, like Mathieu Béluse in his first wanderings: 'One is all the more universal if one recognizes oneself to be particular.' Without a single damn person guessing the very least of what that universal means. And if they mean to point out the Tout-monde with that, then they should at least try to detangle that Tout-monde, and try not to forget even one detail, not one corner of existence, not one island not one river not one way of speaking or one rock in this Tout and this Monde. (TM 512–13)

The relationship between universal and particular, between the whole and its parts, lingers on as a quandary in the thinking of the *Tout-monde*. As this narrator suggests, if we are to think the *Tout-monde*, we must maintain whole and parts in a recursive relationship, insisting, as Glissant has often done (PR 44) that particularities not be dissolved in a forever-augmenting homogeneity.

The narrator who reiterates these admonitions is quite conscious that there is an unresolved dilemma here, one that (s)he broaches with an appeal to Glissant's pronouncement on the imperative of maintaining particular places in their particularity (TTM 59).

> Place is unavoidable and impossible to circumvent (*incontournable*). We don't live in suspension in an indefinite space. That is the question: how to drink from one's spring, without leaving others thirsty for it? How to consent to the other, without adulterating the spring water that you have drunk and that you will drink?
> Not only place, but also common-place (*lieu-commun*), where anguish sways.
> Impossibility that must be undone. (TM 513–14)

The problem, then, is to remain unresolved. Another imperative, furthermore, comes in the wake of the assertion that "Place is unavoidable and impossible to circumvent": the predicament, the "impossibility" brought about by this maxim must be unraveled. The text, it would seem, leaves the discussion of this crucial element in the theorization of the *Tout-monde en souffrance*, yet to arrive, and uncomfortably so.

Mathieu Béluse's situation remains equally undecided. As for whatever it is that he is "seeking," whatever he might "find" (TM 207–8) Glissant's narrative brings this quest sprung from multiple origins to a close through (at least) two endings. Along his journey, Mathieu will explore the distinction between universal and particulars raised above; he will "take up anew the work that he had never given up: traveling the distance that Longoué had marked between the world and the Tout-monde" (TM 226). But not before making a return to the place of his origins, "not before going back up [the Martinican river, and title of Glissant's first novel] La Lézarde" (TM 226).

Mathieu meets Mycéa, alias Marie Celat, a fellow Martinican, who suddenly announces to him that he is the father of her children (TM 412). "We find each other, Mathieu Béluse . . . Did you have to travel throughout the world in order to claim that you had found me? The Tout-monde whirls, Mathieu Béluse, in the very same place where you are suffering" (TM 411). It would seem, then, that Mycéa was what Mathieu had been seeking after all. After Rocamarron's revelation to him regarding his "Vision," however, Mathieu concludes that his search may have arrived at yet another end entirely. Mathieu has yet another realization, and decides that the object of his quest was something altogether different: "ah! Now I imagine what a 'what is a woman a man an old man a child' is, and it's you Rocamarron" (TM 556). This new attainment casts doubt on the importance of Mathieu's discovery of Mycéa with regard to his quest. Origins are obscured and ends are multiplied, as the text leaves unresolved the issue of whether the object of desire that Mathieu had set out to discover has been reached at all.

The narrative voices of *Tout-monde* thus undermine certainty with regard to the fulfillment of Mathieu's quest. They acknowledge the founding structure of the *Tout-monde* concept as a "question," an "impossibility" that must be "unraveled" (TM 514). As Mathieu's journey in the *Tout-monde* began, Amina foretold that Mathieu would find it difficult to be heard or understood ("*entendu*"), explaining to him that he had a "problem of Relation" (TM 46). Has Mathieu been understood by his readers, or by his fellow characters, at the text's ending? By making this understanding the object of Mathieu's desire, as well as the object of the quest that permeates *Tout-monde* and maintains suspense throughout, Glissant reinscribes the problematics of desire into a logic of process: it is the continued, lived experience of desire that he foregrounds, not desire's ultimate satisfaction and self-annihilation.

If there is a truth to be distilled from *Tout-monde*, if there is one primary and unifying meaning to be retained, it is this performance of fragmentation, movement, and circularity that Mathieu's desire leads him into (and not *to*, for it is an activity in which he is immersed, rather than a destination). Furthermore, as for whether *Tout-monde* belongs more to the corpus of Glissant's theoretical texts than to that of his fictional ones,[3] it is a (theoretical) novel whose own theoretical bases are both enacted in literature and put into serious doubt there. Uncomfortable with attainment, possession, singular objects, sole origins, and unique, conclusive ends, as well as with atomistic individuals, Glissant's text performs and prescribes connection, wandering, and the embrace of paradox. The novel *Tout-monde* admits that it does not have and cannot offer the final word on the *Tout-monde*, or on the series of ideas that it entails (e.g., the difference between "*monde*" and "*Tout-monde*," etc.). Through Mathieu's quest, which may or may not have come to fruition, through a turning-outward (toward the world-as-whole) that is also a turning-inward (toward Martinican particularity inasmuch as it is turned-outward), *Tout-monde* uses paradox in order to demonstrate that it is a continual process of working through.

On the Simultaneous Impossibility and Inevitability of Time Travel: *Le quatrième siècle*

The very title of *Le quatrième siècle* [*The Fourth Century*] is a gesture of periodization: the narrative will play out from the vantage point of four centuries of oppression in the Caribbean, where the early institution of slavery has metamorphosed into neocolonialism and economic oppression. The text is dedicated to the memory of Glissant's friend Albert Béville, the Guadeloupian poet and partisan of the Negritude movement better known by his *nom de plume* of Paul Niger. *Le quatrième siècle* is at its core a treatise on memory, on the imperative of remembering experienced by Caribbean subjects, and on the inaccessibility of that which they seek to remember. Where *Tout-monde* exhibited a paradoxical directionality, this novel proves to be a space of paradoxical temporality. First, *Le quatrième siècle* is directed into the past: set around a dialogue between Mathieu Béluse and Papa Longoué, the text repeats the question "what is the past?," placing it in the mouths of various characters. And throughout, multiple answers to this question are set forth, setting in motion a quest whose ultimate goal is the attainment of knowledge of the past. And yet, it is not the case that *Le quatrième siècle* is purely concerned with the past. In Patrick Chamoiseau's rather polemical phrasing, "Those who take the date 1940 or 1950 or slavery in order to say, 'it's a text from the past,' are, in my opinion, people who do not understand literature. Literary modernity is founded in problematical terms" (727). *Le quatrième siècle*'s interrogation of the past, of the very notion of the past, occurs in the context of a profound concern for the relationship of this past to the lived present and to the future of the geopolitical entities of Caribbean and the groups of people that populate them.

Although it is deeply concerned with the past, *Le quatrième siècle* is also forward-looking in that it weaves the universe that Glissant's future characters will inhabit, raising many of the paraphilosophical concerns that will reverberate throughout his oeuvre. For Glissant, Béville's memory lives on in the present, and instills purpose into the quest that Glissant and his characters are undertaking today. As he puts it, Béville's "name and his example are for me inseparable from the quest that we are conducting" (LQ 9). Glissant explains neither what he means by Béville's "quest," nor what the object of that quest might be. It is clear, however, that the quest has its teleology, it is in other words guided by a purpose, and as such it is directed toward a particular end.

Béville/Niger had passed away only two years before *Le quatrième siècle* was to be published. Glissant recalls a moment of shared memory with his friend, one that was predicated on a bidirectional temporality. As the two encountered the concrete, material vestiges of painful historical memory, "*We were talking about the Slave House . . . he showed me the irons that they used to attach to their ankles*" (LQ 9). And yet, Glissant continues, "*But he also looked towards the future: and the present is now forever forbidden to him*" (LQ 9). Béville, it would seem, incarnated the contradictory directionality that *Le quatrième siècle* sets in motion.

Much like Glissant's other books, this novel melds philosophical speculation with a meditation on the landscapes and cultural singularity of Martinique. Its plot is held together by a long, ongoing conversation between Mathieu and Papa Longoué, where the young man incessantly harries the *quimboiseur* with questions both practical and theoretical. Mathieu treats Longoué as if the old man were a reservoir of historical truth. Early on, he eagerly prods Longoué with questions that are in fact commands: "Tell me the past, Papa Longoué! What is that, the past?"

(LQ 17). Much like Glissant, Longoué believes that if such questions are to be fruitfully addressed they ought to be rephrased: Mathieu might have asked, he imagines, "'What remains to us of the past,' or, 'Why do we have to return to the past?'" (LQ 18). Longoué realizes that the boy will be swept away by his quest and by his line of questioning. A line of questioning that at first seems quite simple is in fact a trick, a "detour" (LQ 18). This Glissantian teleology, Longoué implies, will not be a linear accession to a fixed objective.

Mathieu is in search of the knowledge of his island's past in its plenitude. But his quest is also very much a personal one. And the search for origins, for a clear line of filiation, is as unavoidable as it is problematic. In response to Mathieu's persistent questions about the past, Longoué launches into a listing of names that echoes the Old Testament: "And Anne begot Saint-Yves and Stéfanise, who lived with Apostrophe, the son of the brother of the man whom his father had killed. And Saint-Yves begot Zéphirin . . ." (LQ 19). Longoué is himself the last of that particular line (LQ 20). But the knowledge that Longoué offers is not what Mathieu seeks. Mathieu is in search of a transparent channel toward the unmediated truth of the past. And, as he insists, neither the speech that has become fixed in books as writing nor Longoué's ludic, oral exposition are satisfying to him. The seemingly infinite series questions that Mathieu puts to Longoué prove to cohere solely on account of the younger man's assumption that they might be answered. In other words, Mathieu's desire is fueled by the presupposition that attainment is possible. Nevertheless, *Le quatrième siècle* proves to stage a pursuit that, as Longoué tirelessly reminds Mathieu (and Glissant's readers), is doomed to be frustrated—though not fruitless.

Even for Longoué, who knows better, the search for the past is inevitable. "Because," he chides Mathieu, "you have to go to the beginning" (53). The text's structure steers itself toward a destination in the past as well, following Mathieu and Longoué's families all the way back to their earliest known origins: that is, to the written history of their appearance on the island as slaves, at the plantation Acajou in Martinique. The two families have long been rivals, on war footing since the original battle between each family's patriarch on a slave ship. Extending that binary structure of two families with their two warring ancestors, the text's narrator explains that the two men's bloodlust was appreciated by two *Békés*, or slave-owning whites, who had their own animus and who decided to purchase the two men in order to combat each other by proxy. Their names, not incidentally, are Laroche (the spelling of this surname varies in the text) and Senglis, a phonetic inversion of Glissant's own family name.

Seething with his hatred for the Béluse family, the Longoué primogenitor escapes slavery and lives as a Maroon near the plantation, leaving Béluse to toil in the fields. The two whites descend into Faulknerian ruin and Laroche comes to be killed as he is caught up in a rebellion of soon-to-be slaves. As for Senglis, his enslavement of the Béluse family (recall that Béluse is Mathieu's surname) leads to his downfall. In true Faulknerian fashion, "The birth of Béluse's son was the cause of Senglis's final ruin" (LQ 130)).

Longoué's response to Mathieu's demands for truth is to reframe Mathieu's objectives in terms of a contradictory teleology moving at once toward both absence and presence. Mathieu's desire to make present what is absent—that is, to draw the past in its plenitude into the light of the present—risks becoming dangerous. And the simplicity of the question "what happened?" belies the fact that the historian's task is always already an impossible one. Infuriated with this comingling of absence and presence implicit in Mathieu's line of questioning, Longoué interpellates the void of the night in the language of his Caribbean religious tradition: "—Where is presence, Master-night? Master, with three legs? A little young-one who lives for science. But Lord, oh, who is demanding? Who can run after ghosts? And look. He who leans back will be burned by the southern wind! What is he seeking, this boy?" (LQ 44). What is clear becomes opaque, and questions spawn further questions: where might such a presence even lie, how might its truth be shaped by the one who seeks it? And once again, in an early echo of *Tout-monde*, what is the precise object of Mathieu's quest anyway?

For Deleuze and Guattari, the fact of framing desire as the movement toward an object that is absent is a fundamental misunderstanding. Worse, it constitutes a form of nihilism.

> In a certain way the logic of desire misses its object from its first step: the first step of the platonic division that makes us choose between *production* and *acquisition*. As soon as we put desire on the side of acquisition, we make an idealistic (dialectical, nihilist) conception of desire for ourselves, which determines it in the first place as a lack, a lack of an object, lack of a real object. (*L'Anti-Oedipe* 32)

Glissant, a close friend of Félix Guattari, had dedicated his novel *Tout-monde* to the radical French psychotherapist's memory. And it is perhaps no coincidence that *Le quatrième siècle* parallels closely Deleuze and Guattari's critique of desire. Anne Béluse, an oddly named male ancestor of Mathieu, feels the pain of this construal of desire-as-lack, "Because he suffered . . . from something that he did not possess" (LQ 160). And elsewhere, the first man of the Longoué line, free in the hills surrounding the plantation, was driven mad by his yearning for a woman who was confined in the master's house. In strikingly similar language, Glissant writes that *that* Longoué "suffered from something that he did not possess; and perhaps he thought that kidnapping the girl would get hold of that thing for him" (LQ 164). Framing desire in terms of acquisition, it would seem, is inevitably a cause of suffering in the Glissantian fictional universe.

It was in a whirlwind (*tourbillon*) of the marine sort that the potential object of acquisition that is the past has become absent to Glissant's Caribbean subjects. While the past is inaccessible to varying degrees to all human subjects, descendants of Africans taken as slaves experience that absence differently and yet more powerfully. "And not one of us," Mathieu laments, "knows what happened in the country over there beyond the waters, the sea has rolled over all of us, even you who see history . . ." (LQ 68). The category of the past thus becomes that absence itself, the "whirlwind of death out of which we must draw memory . . ." (LQ 68) As if in answer to his own question, "We call that the past," Mathieu plainly states. And while the past-as-negation is a source of trauma, it also engenders an imperative: to seek out knowledge that cannot be found in the written records, knowledge that does not emanate from and thus belong to someone else, that is not "inherited" (LQ 35).

Lydie Moudileno argues that it is the task of literature to respond to that imperative as it confronts a yawning gap in knowledge. For her, "Just as much as Caribbean History is characterized by the break and the discontinuity of (hi)stories [*histoires*] literature will also suffer from this always-deferred/differed relationship to the origin" ("Retrouver la parole perdue" 85). And yet, seeking out the past through the mediation of language, which is exactly what historical narratives such as *Le quatrième siècle* set out to do, is problematic. "I'm telling you, Mathieu my son," Papa Longoué tries to explain, "luckily you have books in order to forget details . . ." (LQ 141). Books are not tools for memory; quite the contrary. Longoué's underlying belief is that there exists no perfect book, no textual conduit to or encapsulation of the truth of the past. That is no doubt why Dominique Chancé holds that "the writer-historian is the central character in many Caribbean novels, and not history itself. Discourse and method are in effect just as essential as the narrative" (*L'Auteur en souffrance* 9). Mathieu corroborates Chancé's argument, shrugging off what little clarity Longoué can offer him in his recollections of the past, and demanding more artistry, a more novelistic rendering of the story of the past. "Too clean cut. Too simple . . . I can't," he complains to Longoué (LQ39). The text's narrator explains that due to Mathieu's influence, even Longoué has come to frame his quest for the past in terms that are simply too logical. "Not yet knowing that Mathieu had vanquished him, since the young man was forcing him to follow the path of the 'most logical,'" Longoué comes to "'reason in *thats*, in *therefores*, in *afters* and *befores*, with knots of *whys* in his head, drowned in a storm of *becauses* (53).

Mathieu has not gained the upper hand over Longoué, however. For the elder's oral disquisition, which is inevitably transcribed in Glissant's text (without that transcription, there of course *is* no text), makes continued returns to opacity. Language, and spoken language particularly, will always resist. Hence Mathieu's realization that Longoué's language is "altogether mannered and full of repetitions," and Mathieu is disappointed by the fact that Longoué "obviously didn't foresee anything and to tell the truth he let himself be guided by the capricious aftermath of the words" (LQ 17).

Increasingly skeptical with regard to the truth-value of Longoué's words, and increasingly cynical with regard to the content of the category of history itself, Mathieu reattributes absence to the heart of history. Beyond inquiring into nature of the content of that always-unattainable category, Mathieu comes to doubt whether the category itself even exists, protesting to Longoué that "You want to make me believe . . . that there was a history, before? Is that what you are saying?" (LQ 38). In his turn Longoué too will later find Mathieu's skepticism to be infectious, provoking him by asking, "And when you say: 'The past,' how can you know if there even is a past[?]" (LQ 169). In order to explain instances of such radical, and no doubt traumatic doubt, Chancé argues for a conception of Caribbean history in terms of absence-as-presence.

> According to Caribbean writers such as Édouard Glissant, then Patrick Chamoiseau and Raphaël Confiant, it's because it is not possible, in effect, to reconstitute, to tell the History of the Caribbean that the latter is an affair for writers rather than for historians . . . According to them there are no historians

of the Caribbean because there is only 'non-History.'" (*L'Auteur en souffrance* 12–13)

Far from deploring a lack of knowledge or positing an irrationalist opposite of knowledge, Chancé's portrayal of non-History in relation to Caribbean literature can help us understand why it is that in Glissant's work, meditations on the past often become reflections on land and landscape. When you look to the past, *Le quatrième siècle*'s narrator tells us, look to the land. The land, what Glissant frequently calls the "*pays*" (a French term signifying "country" in both the topographic and the political senses), is thus the site of the past, the material context in which it can be pursued. In yet another rehearsal of *Le quatrième siècle*'s enterprise of definition, land and past become one, as time and the land and as time and space come to be interconnected: "The land: a reality torn out of the past, but also, a past dug up out of the real. And from now on Mathieu saw time as being tied up with the earth" (LQ 322). The land is at once the reality that is torn free of the past and the past unearthed from the real: matter drawn from time, and time made matter. Glissant explains his own veneration of the land as a literary device: "These successions of landscapes have plunged me into a primordial awareness that was begging to resurface. I tried to assemble it in the novel *Tout-monde* and my first (hi)story ["*histoire*"], which naively produced a narrative, *La Lézarde*, is fleshed out beginning with the source of the river . . ." (CL 90–91). Land and landscape become, for Glissant, another means of expressing the simultaneous absence-presence of the past.

Far from being a simple game of repetition, Mathieu's repeated inquiries into the nature and content of the category of the past have real political significance in the present. What Longoué calls the "misery" of the Americas, or the lingering legacy of slavery and oppression, has its reverberations today. Returning to the metaphor of landscape but concentrating this time on the island's flora, Mathieu explains the urgency of his quest for the past. Recalling an event where the "forces of order," the *Gendarmes*, opened fire on protestors in Martinique, Mathieu explains that while the island has left slavery behind, an organic continuity nevertheless remains. "That," he says of the episode, "was not the past, but rather the mechanism inherited from the past which, by the sheer strength of monotonous repetition, made the present into a dying branch" (LQ 322). A part of the same plant, the present is a withered, dying leaf on that stalk that is the past (LQ 259). Just as Longoué and Mathieu are skeptical as to whether the past ever had any existence at all, they come to make similar claims with regard to the present. Claims such as "There is no present," or "One never catches up to the present" illustrate that radical doubt amply (LQ 259, 322). Mary Gallagher perceives this profound experience of disintegrated temporality in the Francophone Caribbean in writers from Chamoiseau to Xavier Orville, both of whom share what she calls "this same sense of the French Caribbean being caught in a time warp, of time standing still, or of being stuck in space, as it were" (*Soundings* 79).

Le quatrième siècle's response to this temporal quagmire is to turn from individual anguish to the suffering of the collectivity. Or rather, it is to foreground both the pressing need for that collectivity to exist, and to voice the trauma created by the realization that that collective people remains missing. If it were to exist, such a people would affirm its connection to the land on which it lived, and experience the present in a harmonious relationship with the past. But the novel is pessimistic with regard to such a possibility. Listening once again to Papa Longoué's storytelling, Mathieu believes that he hears the voice of his ancestors. But he also becomes aware of the tenuous grounds that the past offers for the creation of a better present, realizing how the ancestors can be forgotten, never to be found again.

> He was experiencing how people (he wasn't going to go so far as to say: a people) could leave, dry up with no real progeny, without a future fertility, closed up in their death . . . for the simple reason that their words were dead too, stolen. Yes, because the world, of which they were a fierce or passive audience, didn't lend an ear to their absence of voice. (304–5)

Glissant thus adds a third facet to the past-land dyad, and one that recalls the Deleuzo-Guattarian concept referenced by Sartorius: the people that is missing. And that people's absence is a real danger, since it means that they can disappear, with no potential for future creation (what Mathieu thinks of as a "future fertility"). The rest of the world can all too easily become deaf to their voice. Or, more paradoxically put, the world may not listen to the absence of their voice. What Mathieu seeks in his quest for the past, it would seem, is an impossible representation of an absence.

Whereas Mathieu had earlier sought to satiate his desire by making the past present, he comes to learn that his only possible access to the past comes from making an absence present. But that absence undermines the possibility of a new people coming into being, and the people that is missing is excruciatingly absent. "And why not 'long live us'? Mathieu said" (LQ 232). His odd phrasing "long live us" underscores the political unlikelihood of a Martinican people coming into being as a political entity. For even their own understanding of their relationship to the past, in Glissant's portrayal, remains opaque. In yet another attempt to bend language to meet this unlivable situation, Mathieu protests that "But we all, all of us (and not you nor him) we don't even know if the dead have reached out their hand . . ." (LQ 180). Mathieu's experience of the absence-presence of history is one of epistemological failure and consequent torment.

In nearly all of Glissant's theorizations of Caribbean history one argument consistently resurfaces: that composite cultures such as those of the Caribbean and the Caribbean cultural zone (including the US Gulf South and parts of Brazil) could never form a collectivity in the same way that "atavistic" cultures (i.e., those who claim a legitimacy founded on clear genealogical lines and fixed origins) might ("L'Europe et les Antilles"). No unbroken lines of filiation, no unitary origins are available to the collectivities of composite cultures, on account of both the slave trade's obscuring destruction in the past and the unpredictable play of creolization in the present. For that reason, Jacques André has posited that the experience of origins that is possible for Caribbean subjects and those of the African Diaspora in the Americas more broadly is one of an "excessive origin" or an "over-reality of origin" (47, 48). *That* relationship to origins is a paradoxical one, where origins are simultaneously far-too present (in that the past weighs on the present, poisoning it) but also out of reach or obscured. Nearly forty years before the publication of *Faulkner, Mississippi*, the Mathieu of *Le quatrième siècle* foreshadows the later essay's central argument with despair, coming to the agonizing knowledge that in the Caribbean, "we never catch hold of the genealogical line" (LQ 180; cf. FM 87, 110, 135).

And yet, catching hold of that line of filiation is as impossible as it is unavoidable. For, as Glissant insists, the people(s) of the French departments that lie in the Caribbean basin must be able to theorize their relationship to their near-unimaginable past if they are to exist as *a* people. That is perhaps what Glissant had in mind when he referred to a "quest" in his dedication of *Le quatrième siècle* to Paul Niger. Given that both authors were fierce partisans of Martinican independence from France, Glissant's quest can be read both as one for the truth of the past and as one for a future polis—since the two are, for him, inseparable. In H. Adlai Murdoch's words,

> Glissant's accomplishment is thus a remarkable mediation of the theoretical and the practical, an extended analysis of the factors

underlying and determining the construction of the post-colonial Caribbean discursive subject and an elaboration in fictional form of the alienation and dislocation which are the product of the historical trace. Throughout both aspects of his work, emphasis is given to the notion that awareness and acceptance of the past must precede the construction of an independent cultural identity in the present. (Murdoch 10)

The *Discours antillais* tersely voices the swarm of difficulties surrounding that effort to fashion a "cultural identity in the present" with two of the titles of its subsections: "*History as Trap*" and "*The Quarrel with History*" (221, 222). No future without a past, and no past without a future: the Caribbean's relationship to the past is a temporal vector pointing in (at least) two directions simultaneously.

Mycéa, whom Mathieu falls for in *Le quatrième siècle* and whom he marries in 1946 (the year in which, coincidentally, Martinique became an Overseas Department of the French nation-state), urges Mathieu to rethink his approach to the land and to the possibility of a viable Martinican people. Her urgings come as she and Mathieu found their own, new genealogy with the birth of their child. Mycéa yearns to "make Mathieu admit that another thing was born that day, a thing that replaced all of the old ones. Because, with regard to a genealogical line that had begun there (and not in a marvelous, faraway distance), memory had buried its seedling in the new earth . . ." (LQ 329).

Turn away from the past in order to rejoice in the present's fecundity: such is Mycéa's advice to Mathieu. And as Cilas Kemedjio points out, it is also Glissant's critique of anyone who would ache for a now-unattainable, African past (105). The novel *La Lézarde* manifests a similar idea as the character of Raphaël decides to leave his home in the text's concluding pages. His roots will be picked up, transported elsewhere in order to locate a new origin of his choosing ("*réensouchées*") (LQ 331). Glissant's choice of the word "*souche*" is noteworthy here, given the decades-long debates in France surrounding who or what constitutes a *Français de souche*, or an "ethnic," "original," "*true*" French person, as opposed to someone who has immigrated or who is descended from an immigrant background.

Later in *Le quatrième siècle*, yet another reprimand from Longoué pushes Mathieu to undo and reshape his preconceived notions with regard to the past. Returning to the feud that has pitted Papa Longoué's family against Mathieu's for generations, Longoué voices his argument in metaphors grounded in the Martinican landscape.

Did they not think that they first had to learn the land [*pays*] in its lowlands just as much as in its highlands? Longoué used to say: 'he has the son of slavery.' But he's the one who's going to plant his machete in the earth in order to uproot [*dessoucher*] something the root of which was already in him, and that he did not know. Because if he was lacking that thing, if he didn't possess it, it's because he didn't feel it, but it was in him. And you can see that science does not give you the thing in question . . . Because the past is not like a palm tree straight and smooth with a tuft at the end, no, it starts with the first root and goes on budding without stopping all the way up to the clouds. (LQ 170)

The parallels between Longoué's laments and Deleuze and Guattari's critique of what they deem to be arborescent or tree-thought are striking. It is no doubt because of the deleterious nature of tree-thinking, Longoué suggests, that Mathieu "staggers" as he sets out to attain the past (TM 200). There is no end, no ultimate purpose to his search, Longoué tells him; it simply goes on and on, budding and growing infinitely as Mathieu continues his quest.

The last lines of *Le quatrième siècle* amount to a consummate attack on the understanding of teleology that Glissant has worked to undo throughout the text. In a trance of sorts, Mathieu finds himself in front of a group of laborers cutting cane in the scorching heat. With another mystical, stream-of-consciousness narration, readers share Mathieu's subjective experience: "it's fever it's a world the world and the word buries the voice grows the voice burns in the fixed fire and it turns in my head carrying away sweeping away ripening—and has neither an end oh, nor a beginning" (LQ 331). With that erasure of both origins and ends, *Le quatrième siècle* concludes without concluding. For Jacques André, Glissant's work exemplifies the task of all literature in modernity, in that "The possibility of a literature is intimately linked to the faculty of elaborating the category of the past, which is to say, producing from it an original narrative that links, transforms and associates varied elements . . . Writing is thus a task of rewriting, starting with a first narrative" (48). Though the search for origins is inevitable for everyone, the experience of Caribbean subjects is archetypal, for André as for Glissant, of all literary quests for the past in modernity. It is an endless quest, one that can only be recounted through infinite "rewriting." Glissant's vision of the past frames it as the always-deferred object of a search that has no end. Or rather, the search is its own end, in both senses of the term: it is an objective, and it is its own finality. In that way

Le quatrième siècle is not the staging-grounds for a scene of attainment but rather an end-as-process, a quest as an end in itself.

Conclusion: "So That Was It? This Obscure Reason. This Hidden Source." (TM 512)

If *Tout-monde* is in fact, as Glissant has put it, an "exploded novel" (IPD 129), both it and *Le quatrième siècle* can be said to stage an exploration of exploded directionalities. Trajectories that might at first glance appear to be clear and linear—into the past, into the future, turning inward toward the island, or outward to the world—prove to be paradoxical. As Glissant stages these self-contradictory renderings of time and space, we can derive two conclusions from our engagements with these two texts: first, that for Glissant such spatiotemporal paradoxes are key to the Caribbean condition. And second, that what Glissant has to say about Caribbean subjects' lived experience of those paradoxes in time (a turn to the past is a turn to the future) and space (leaving the island is tantamount to returning to it) can be fruitfully extrapolated to our interpretative engagement with Glissant's texts.

As *Le quatrième siècle* shows us, the past, to rephrase Faulkner's dictum, is far from past. Mathieu seeks to find the past just as he lives within it, and as a Caribbean subject he cannot escape it. And yet, the past is always fleeting, and it is perhaps not even one, unitary thing to be obtained anyway. As Papa Longoué tells him, "*ah! There are how many pasts that come all the way down to you, you have to do some gymnastics if you want to catch them . . .*" (LQ 235). In *Tout-monde*, a quest for an unnamed and unclear object proves to be a desire for the world-as-whole, and for being swept up into the world's movement—and that way of being in the world is precisely what the text and its protagonist were already in the process of doing. Richard Watts notes *Tout-monde*'s "use of multiple, disconnected narrators and fragmented, non-linear, *non-teleological* narratives" (121; emphasis added). He argues the point that the narrative form of *Tout-monde*, inasmuch as it is structured by these exploded, rhizomatic directionalities, sets a standard for writing in modernity: "Episodes from the past abut episodes from the present, and although they are linked (through the recurrence of characters and places), the links seem to make the primary point that writing, in the world of *Relation*, must be in all chronotopes simultaneously" (121). Likewise, as past, present, and future are displaced from a linear framework and set into a rhizomatic relation in *Le quatrième siècle*, Mathieu comes to learn that the process of desiring is more productive and creative than any final acquisition of an original object of desire could be.

The inexorable absence-presence of the legacy of slavery in Martinique, which is part and parcel of what Watts calls the "wounds of locality" that still have not closed there, extends well into the neocolonial present: *Le quatrième siècle*'s political message is clear and direct in that regard. But even the ludic, postmodern novel *Tout-monde* maintains that it too has concrete, political aims, albeit of a different sort. As one of the narrative voices of *Tout-monde* contends, invoking the Creole word *drive*, which has its roots in the French *dériver*, meaning "to drift" or "to divert": "And yet the powerful must be taught a new boldness for changing living humanities, that is, they must be taught the *drive* of dreams and the imagined things that cloud the depths of men and women . . . They really must be taught, the powerful" (TM 514; emphasis added). The novel *Tout-monde*, this particular narrative voice proclaims, carries its own political lesson within it. It demonstrates Glissant's fundamental belief that our most basic ways of imagining, even dreaming our world, ought to be shaken up and renewed. And those who hold power over others are in yet greater need of that upheaval on the plane of the imaginary.

Tout-monde and *Le quatrième siècle* abandon a linear teleology that would progress forward toward an attainable goal as they move in multiple, and often contradictory directions. Their narrative impetus resembles a rhizome much more than a tree. Such exploded directionalities help to explain the fact that each narrative is bereft of any conclusion to speak of. Rhizomes within the book intersect with rhizomes beyond the book, as each Glissantian text relays again and again to others, forever deferring the fixity of final interpretation, even of finality of any sort. In Moudileno's words, "Glissant's intertextual practice, by refusing to bring the book to a close, suggests that there is no book, if there are not other books" (*L'écrivain antillais* 115). No present without a past, no Martinique without the rest of the world: all is relationality.

As a result, these two philosophical novels shed light on the question as to whether Glissant's thought can be said to succeed in its lofty ambitions. When asked in an interview whether he was a utopian, Glissant eagerly allowed that he was one, and one of the most unrepentant sort, going on to insist that nothing worthwhile has ever been achieved on earth without utopian goals (IPD 100). Working toward a utopia, in other words, is for Glissant requisite to any considerable accomplishment in this world. Has

Glissant achieved a consummate analysis of the Caribbean relationship to the past, and can he be said to have cleared the path that leads to the utopian *Tout-monde*? In response, I would like to suggest that Glissant's ideas on the Caribbean condition can also function as a paradigm for readers' encounters with his texts and their aims. His strategies for framing teleology in narrative can also speak to the overall objectives of his philosophical work, and whether their purpose is ever achieved.

A desire thwarted proves to be a desire satiated, albeit satiated in an unexpected way. A teleology's end is, in the end, the process of its unfolding. Readers who are in search of, or indeed who are already convinced of, a fundamental clarity and coherence to Glissant's thought, are bound to be displeased by such nonconclusions. But those who would balk at the contradiction and ambiguity of Glissant's paradoxical rewriting of teleology need look no further than Glissant's repeated insistences to the effect that an unstable, a nonsystematic, and most importantly an *ambiguous* way of thinking is the most fitting approach that we have to our world today (cf. IPD 24–25). And what holds for our lived experience of our material world also holds for our experience of the Glissantian textual world since, for Glissant, contradiction and ambiguity are at play in both.

Glissant's essays frame objects of desire as somehow both available in the present and continually deferred into a utopian future: the *Tout-monde* is *ici-là* (read: at once here and yet over there), the works of Faulkner and Glissant simultaneously augur and exemplify a new category of literature. Mathieu's experiences hint that the Caribbean past can only be understood in an ongoing, writerly process. In Glissant's view, what is more, the very process of working through desire can be creative. As with Mathieu's experience, our quest as readers for the things that we might desire as an outcome of Glissant's philosophical efforts and our engagement with them—again, the harmonious relationality of the *Tout-monde*, or radical, worldwide political transformation—remain yet to come, undecided, unpredictable. That fact poses no problem for the author of the *Tout-monde*. Glissant is, as he humbly submits, no more than a "preface-writer," opening doors to future creation, literary and otherwise (Dash, *Glissant* 184). In the next chapter, I argue that the essay *Philosophie de la Relation* carries on this rethinking of desire and teleology. For that text, as we shall see, entices readers to seek out a conclusive, philosophical treatise within its pages, insinuating that it will serve as a zenith of Glissant's philosophical work. But it also continually defers its conclusion, thus shaping our experience of the text. Rather than seeking out a *telos* in Glissant's final and most outspokenly philosophical text, the very nature of that text enjoins us to ask: how might we read it not as a place in which to acquire, to *mine* meaning, but rather as an entreaty to *make* meaning? As in this chapter, my contention there is that Glissant is concerned more with process than with the end result of that process.

Four

Philosophie de la Relation

Making Sense with Glissantian Philosophy

> I have spoken the chaos of writing in the ardor of the poem.
> —Édouard Glissant, *Soleil de la conscience*

> Do I contradict myself?
> Very well then I contradict myself,
> (I am large; I contain multitudes.)
> —Walt Whitman, "Song of Myself"

"Paraphilosophizing around the science of chaos"—thus Édouard Glissant described his efforts in his 1996 *Introduction à une poétique du divers* (*Introduction to a Poetics of the Diverse*) (82). Glissant's choice of the prefix *para* opens onto a world of interpretive possibilities: among the definitions that the *Merriam-Webster's Online Dictionary* offers for this prefix are: "beside," "alongside of," "beyond," "aside from," "closely related to," "faulty," "abnormal," "associated in a subsidiary or accessory capacity," "closely resembling," and "almost." Far from a clarification, Glissant's choice of words is polyvalent to say the least. The title of *Philosophie de la Relation* (2009) takes quite a different tack, however, shedding the prefix *para* and naming itself forthrightly as a text belonging to the philosophical genre, and thereby designating, by extension, its author as a philosopher. The paratext that is the cover page of *Philosophie de la Relation* thus triggers certain expectations on the part of its readers, with regard to elements as diverse as the text's style, its thematic preoccupations, and its intertexts. As such, it would appear to mark a point of rupture with the essays preceding it, and particularly with the *Poétique de la Relation* (*Poetics of Relation*) (1990). The use of the word *Philosophie* names the text's genre as something distinctly different from the earlier series of essays, *Poetics* and *Aesthetics*, and of course from Glissant's output in the various genres of the novel, poetry, theater, manifestoes, interviews, speeches, and other generic experimentations.

I would like to analyze more closely Glissant's *Philosophie de la Relation* (hereafter *Philosophie*), in order to argue that this, his last essay, shows the author at the height of his potential to influence readers' interpretation, as well as their lived experience of reengaging with many of his key ideas. While the text is clearly a continuation of the theoretical work done by previous texts, I will show that it also manifests a certain singularity, both in genre and in argumentation, as *Philosophie* begins dismantling its generic status as soon as the text's title page has been turned. Finally, in light of the solemnity of *Philosophie*'s title as well as its deep concern with History and histories, I will begin to address one of the central questions that the text prompts us to ask: what vantage point, if any, might Glissant's final book-length essay afford us on the body of essays that precede it? *Philosophie*, as we shall see, contradicts itself as soon as it sets out to explain its own aims and methodology. As it does so, it suggests new perspectives on the entirety of Glissant's oeuvre to its readers. It moreover constitutes a test case, overtly sanctioned by its author, of what it might look like to *do* Glissantian philosophy.

Taking the Glissantian corpus, or even a subset of it such as his essays, or perhaps even a single text, as *one* is a problematic gesture. For Glissant is, as it has often been pointed out, an author of *multiplicity, diversity, fragmentation, polyphony*—terms that are not synonymous but nonetheless bear an unambivalent relationship to each other, and in Glissant's work in particular. *Philosophie* displays a great thematic and structural continuity with its predecessors, and most notably with Glissant's essays, amassing and repeating many of Glissant's central theoretical propositions and aphorisms. Taking into account this clear overlap, ought Glissant's readers to think that the author seeks to present himself as one who has *always* produced in the philosophical genre? After all this, his last book is easily identified as a philosophical one. Might this last book's title, in other words, indicate the fundamental nature of Glissant's work throughout his life? *Philosophie* does engage with the long-term preoccupations of Glissant's thought, as it furthers the excursus already discernible in *Une nouvelle région du monde* (2006) into the language and preoccupations of the philosophical genre: the name "Heidegger" is invoked, as are philosophical preoccupations such as the Being/being relationship and the nature of beauty. Numerous subsections undertake a return to key concepts invented or purveyed by Glissant, making clear that they belong to the realm of reflection. Many of them open with the same phrasings, generally italicized as if they were section headings in an introduction to Glissant's thought: *"archipelagic thought"* (45), *"the thought of trembling [la pensée du tremblement]"* (54), *"the thought of creolizations"* (64), and so on.[1]

Much as the *Traité du Tout-Monde* (*Treatise on the Tout-Monde*) (1997) undertook a radical disassembling of the genre of the treatise, however, *Philosophie*'s self-designation as a work of philosophy is subverted as quickly as it is pronounced in a similarly paradoxical fashion. Not unlike Glissant's other essays, its structure is fragmentary and baroque, oscillating between the abstract and the personal, between thorny, dense turns of phrase and frank orality. It opens with a mytho-historical origin of the universe, an origin story that resurfaces periodically in a text mingling commentary on Glissant's own theoretical efforts and autobiographical details, remarks on Aimé Césaire's poetics, and a rather out-of-place "recitation" offered to the Palestinian poet Mahmoud Darwish (153). Somewhat surprisingly, *Philosophie* devotes its last lines to a dithyrambic reference to William Faulkner (156). As *Une nouvelle région du monde* did, *Philosophie* thwarts readers' expectations with regard to the rigor, solemnity, and authoritativeness proper to the rhetoric of the genre that it announces itself as belonging to, in its form and in its content.

Such a gesture will no doubt be familiar to readers of Glissant's essays. As elsewhere, Glissant's thought in his final essay moves in (at least) two, often opposite directions, allowing paradox and ambiguity to unfold throughout. In one sense, the text functions as a sort of inventory of Glissant's ideas since *Soleil de la conscience* of 1956. Concepts and aphorisms that have reappeared in Glissant's work during his half-century of production are no less present here, as the author cites himself with a seasoned ease: "'I change, by exchanging with the other, without losing myself or distorting myself.' We must grant it often, always offer it" (66). Thanks to such repetitions, *Philosophie* often functions as something of an aggregation of many of Glissant's best-known ideas and maxims. More than just a summation, however, we can read *Philosophie* as an apex, the most amplified example of the play of Glissant's thought to date. That is, while the text does serve as a gathering place for many Glissantian tropes, it also pursues the lines of reasoning and critique inherent to these tropes up to their uttermost limits. And yet, while the text's rather grandiose title conveys a certain momentousness, the text dabbles in exegesis only rarely, preferring instead to voice a resistance to structured explication. It neglects to stake out the boundaries of Relation's meaning and, defending the latter term against critique, it foregrounds the themes of un-distinction (*indistinction*), uncertainty, and inexplicability, all the while veering at times into mystical allusions to a primordial and ever-present oneness. While other Glissantian texts may have touched on those themes, *Philosophie* makes them central to its operation.[2]

In doing so, *Philosophie* evidences one of the author's overall preoccupations: it manifests a conflicting need for, and discomfort with, binary oppositions. Such oppositions are inarguably present throughout Glissant's thought. To take a few of the most visible examples, there are globalization and globality, continental and archipelagic thought, root- and rhizome-identity and, need it be said, opposition and apposition. Conversely, Glissant's essays have often staged a contradictory cohabitation of opposite arguments, insisting on a simultaneity of (apparent) antagonists instead of resolving their binary oppositions. They have long foregrounded proclamations that appear to say one thing and its opposite, *at the same time* (*en même temps*), to take up Glissant's cherished phrasing in his reading of Faulkner.

Philosophie perpetuates this tendency to set contradictory elements in cohabitation, taking it yet further as it speaks and repeats a series of motifs that go beyond contradiction while undermining the very process of meaning-making: *unverifiable, un-distinction, inexplicable, uncertain, opaque*, and so on. These moments of saying one thing and its opposite while seeking to undo comprehension are far from meaningless. On the contrary, we might say that they are excessively meaningful. Just as *Philosophie* generates an excess of meaning, however, it also undertakes the opposite operation. Glissant's function as an author proves to limit his text's meaning, channeling interpretation and guiding his readers toward particular lived experiences of his texts. *Philosophie* shows Glissant in a contradictory role, both asserting his presence and staging his absence.

In an essay translated into English as "What Is an Author?" Foucault grants that "criticism and philosophy took note of the disappearance—or death—of the author some time ago" (103). He holds that the notions of the "work" and "writing" (*écriture*) have come to take the author's place, as he posits what he calls an "author function." While Foucault's analysis here is primarily concerned with fiction, it is nonetheless pertinent to our readings of Glissant.

> The author is the principle of thrift in the proliferation of meaning.
> As a result, we must entirely reverse the traditional idea of the

author. We are accustomed, as we have seen earlier, to saying that the author is the genial creator of a work in which he deposits, with infinite wealth and generosity, an inexhaustible world of significations. We are used to thinking that the author is so different from all other men [*sic*], and so transcendent with regard to all languages that, as soon as he speaks, meaning begins to proliferate, to proliferate indefinitely.

The truth is quite the contrary: the author is not an indefinite source of significations which fill a work; the author does not precede the works; he is a certain functional principle by which, in our culture, one limits, excludes, and chooses; in short by which one impedes the free circulation, the free manipulation, the free composition, decomposition, and recomposition of fiction. (118–19)

The author functions, in Foucault's seductive formulation, as "the principle of thrift in the proliferation of meaning." And the narrative of *Philosophie* unfolds at times almost as if its author had this Foucauldian maxim in mind. In both its genre and its argumentation, it seeks to limit the proliferation of meaning produced by Glissant's paradoxical statements, his unification of conceptual opposites, and his fondness for a rhetorical mode that is increasingly tinged with the mystical. The name "Glissant" would thus come to serve as the means by which we readers limit and channel the meaning made by the Glissantian text. Before examining how Glissant-as-author has a limiting function on the potentialities of *Philosophie de la Relation*, however, we must first look closely at the chaotic burgeoning of signification that the text sets in motion.

Making Sense with *Philosophie de la Relation*

Philosophie opens with a curious myth of origins, one with markedly religious, even prophetic overtones.

> There was a sacred word, which arose. And the poem, and so the poem, self-engendered, began to be recognized. (11)

This moment of terse gravity, rendered in stilted language and underscored by the blank space of a paragraph break, is immediately undermined with the line that follows it: "Thus *should have been* pronounced, *perhaps*, in the prehistories of all of the literatures of the world, this very same beginning" (11; emphases added). With this *"should have"* and this *"perhaps,"* the text thus parallels the oscillation that Lydie Moudileno notes in Glissant's manipulation of the novelistic genre. In her reading of Glissant's novel *Mahagony* (1987), she perceives what she calls a coming-and-going ("va-et-vient") that is central to the text's operation (*L'écrivain antillais* 140). In *Philosophie*, these departures and returns take the form of swings from decisive, at times priestly proclamations to frank articulations of a profound lack of certainty.

Intimating that this lack of certainty will be carried yet further in this text within a text, whatever it might be—Glissant refers to this prehistory as "this myth, or this legend or this dream"—are cryptic references to "the fusion of all with all," a "sacred word," and a "sacred stupor" (12). This original and originating poem was the contemporary of "the first blazes of the earth" (12), and as such it serves as a beginning, as *the* beginning of the universal history that the text purports to articulate, and to which it returns periodically. Key in this history is the concept of primal oneness, the notion that differences in the wake of this time before time are merely the shards of a previous whole. This whole partakes of an "unverifiable truth" (12), it represents "this dawn (*avant-jour*), in an abyss (*en gouffre*), and inexplicable" (13). As *Philosophie* takes up the abyss, it reengages with the figure of epistemological failure crucial to the opening pages of *Poétique de la Relation*. In doing so, and in indicating the "obscure" of the poem (13), the "indiscernible" of the poem's fabric (13), *Philosophie* thus opens under the sign of epistemological failure.

In stark contrast to those evocations of myth, the sacred, and the unknowable, at the center of the text lies a deliberate enumeration of a subset of terms from Glissant's theoretical writings: "Trembling" (54), "wandering (*errance*)" (61), the "unpredictables" (67), the "opacity of the world" (70), "Relation" (72) and so on. This listing effort culminates in chapter XIII, which gathers together a set of formulae inevitably familiar to Glissant's readers. Barely a full page, the chapter merits reproduction.

> The thought of the *trace*, at the edge of the fields desolate of memory, which solicits the joined memories of the components of the world-whole (Tout-monde). The thought of languages ("*langues et langages*") where the play of the imaginaries of humanities is decided. I write in the presence of all of the languages of the world.
>
> They ring out to each other with echoes and obscurities and silences. The thought of the *diverse*, our infinite and quantified

rhizome. The thought of *globality*, which we call out to ceaselessly, out of the fear that we shall not know how to distinguish it from the neverending gunfire of our cataclysmic globalizations. The thought of *unique root-identity*, which kills on the spot, or on the contrary of *wending identity* (*l'identité qui chemine*) that does not lead to the unique, [this thought] reinforces ones and others, the here and the elsewhere. The thought of *atavistic cultures*, which mortally founded legitimacy and territory, and of *composite cultures*, those that oppose and mix their digeneses each time, mad primordial births. (80–81)

One by one, each "thought" or "thinking" (*pensée*) appears in a sequence. Their ultimate nature as a list rather than a narrative is highlighted by the relative paucity of verbs in the chapter. As the text's narrative voice, which is presumably Glissant's own, explains shortly thereafter: "*everything must be said all at once*" (82; emphasis in the original). Each mode of thinking thus springs up in its immediacy, its place within the philosophy of Relation clearly demarcated. This facade of theoretical clarity and systematic coherence is rapidly relativized, however, as soon as it is established. Theoretical abstraction is swiftly lashed to geographical particularity, for just as the list ends the narrator intervenes: "But also, off the shores of impenetrable cities, *the drifting hills, the sunken grounds, the sea rocks that no one can go around*" (81; emphasis in original).

Glissant's list of *pensées* is thus supplemented by yet another element, an invocation of Martinican geographical particularity that, at first glance, would have little to do with the theoretical enumeration preceding it. And yet, these geographical figures have been crucial to Glissant's thought since *Soleil de la conscience*, which demonstrated how certain modes of thought manifest an intimate relation to the lived experience of certain landscapes. The philosophy of Relation spelled out here is thus not whole without its supplement in landscapes, which undoes the starkness of its theoretical language. Conversely, its integrity, the terse coherence of this list of modes of thought, is broken both visually in the text's structure by the blank space on the page, and thematically as the "*But also*" abruptly shifts focus.

Philosophie thus catalogs the key concepts and arguments of Glissant's essays, flirting as it progresses with exegesis and candid definitions. "What is it thus, a philosophy of Relation" (82)?, asks the narrator, suggesting that what follows will constitute a clear response (which will not be the case). For crucial to the unfolding of Glissant's sense of relation is the role played by what *Philosophie* calls "uncertains" (*incertains*). In a very Glissantian move of setting apparently similar terms in sharp contrast, Glissant contrasts the "uncertains of Relation" (64) with "incertitude," placing positive valuations on the former and negative valuations on the latter. The uncertain "does not represent failure, if it neither limits nor distorts" (97); it is a fertile and creative lack of certainty. *Incertitude*, on the other hand, is a deleterious lack, contrary to the principles of Relation: "Our most ordinary politics try at times without success to fill in the gap from incertitudes, though without ever drawing authority from the inspirations of the uncertain, which could have tolerated them" (108).

In this discussion of the broadly creative potential of the uncertain, in addition to its potential to bring about more desirable political forms (without, of course, predicting the nature of these), *Philosophie* does not set forth a rigorous elaboration of the terms *Relation* or *the uncertain*. While the text uses the two terms extensively, it asserts that the intellectual enterprise of defining terms cannot be brought to bear on them: "It [the uncertain] is that very thing within relation that posits itself as a boundary between lived experience and thought, without any definition coming along and making a boundary" (97). Similar asseverations to the effect that certain terms may not yield to definition are on display elsewhere in *Philosophie*. Returning to the question of opacity, Glissant's figure of epistemological boundaries par excellence, *Philosophie* declares that the "opacity of the world" is an "opacity that is not to be defined or commented upon" (69). A concept (or rather a nonconcept) that refuses definition might not shock readers of the philosophical genre, but holding that the term *opacity* is not to be commented on altogether is quite another matter. (It goes without saying, of course, that Glissant's own comments on the term, such as the one cited above, are allowed, authorized as they are both in and by Glissant's texts.)

Under the aegis of a philosophy of Relation, the text thus combines the abstract and austere self-designation that is its title with arcane origin myths redolent of mysticism, following both with the undoing of meaning, itself coupled with an argument for the impossibility of defining terms. The book's baroque structure defies any assignation of a unified meaning, making periodic detours into very personal details of the author's life, via a memory of a search for his childhood home (18), or a reference to his mother's death (145). *Philosophie* therefore both makes and unmakes sense, in its form as in its content. It makes clear what will be unclear (opaque). And it delineates what cannot be known, predicted, or defined. The question as to the positivity of Glissant's theoretical work necessarily arises. In other words, what can we as readers *do* with these concepts? what conclusions might we draw, what actions might we undertake, in the wake of our engagement with opacity writ opaquely?

Glissant's Authorial Comings and Goings

The Batoutos of Glissant's *Sartorius: le roman des Batoutos* (1999) appear and disappear, popping up throughout history in the most disparate cultural contexts. They are at once present and absent, and they have an objective that is similarly paradoxical: they "are incubating a hidden project, of showing the invisible, or at least arranging visits with it" (*Sartorius* 243). Like this Batouto nation that is not one, Glissant-as-author both advances and recedes. At times his texts exhibit the strong authorial presence of an embodied and fallible individual, and at times they claim a near-scientific authority, disconnecting themselves from the individual who penned them. Also like the Batoutos, Glissant is thus at once, and paradoxically, visible and invisible, present and absent.

Glissant's essays exhibit a marked oscillation between two contrary assertions of authority. Glissant at times establishes himself as a modern-day avatar of what Foucault has called a "universal intellectual," and at other times undermines his authority by mingling autobiographical details, a casual tone, and affronts to the generic forms he slips into and out of. As Barry Smart has argued in his discussion of Foucault's universal intellectual, "The function of such a 'universal' intellectual has been to uphold reason, to be the 'master of truth and justice,' to represent the universal and to some extent to be the 'consciousness-conscience' of everyone" (67). Glissant would no doubt take issue with many of the descriptors that Smart employs, and first and foremost with the term *universal*, which, for him, was the sine qua non of Western colonial expansion. "Alone among all civilizations," he writes, "the Western one has known this propensity toward generalized expansion, toward conquest, of knowledge and of faith, inextricable, which required the Universal as a guarantor of its legitimacy" (TTM 102–3). Smart's emphasis on reason and mastery as key attributes of the universal intellectual inevitably invokes yet other bugbear of Glissantian critique. Nonetheless, Glissant's self-presentation qua author does share much with Smart's sense of the Foucauldian term. Glissant has incontestably attacked the notion of the "universal" throughout his career ("the generalizing universal, which is always ethnocentric . . . authorized Stalinism's monstrosities" (PR 235). And yet, he has often made claims about ideas and phenomena that "hold for each person and everywhere" ("*valant pour chacun et partout*") (PhR 37), thus veering quite close to the most basic definition of *universality*. Nevertheless, Glissant insists on this point: that the philosophy of Relation must be distinguished from universalizing tendencies.

> We have a premonition that a particular value need not worry about *extending* itself in value (what you call "universalizing itself"), it rises up, on the contrary, to enter into Relation.
>
> ☙
>
> The universal, as it was universally conceived, is first and foremost a propagation, which is founded on likenesses (semblances). It is only afterwards that its values shall affirm themselves. (PhR 38–39)

By changing the axis of analysis from extension to elevation ("it rises up"), and by insinuating that the universal is founded on identification, on making what is different seem to be the same ("semblances"), Glissant sketches out the line of cleavage that separates his Relation from universalization. Yet *Philosophie* nevertheless expands the concept of Relation, holding that "there are no limits to Relation, even though it may be first and foremost a realized (finite) quantity of the different elements of the world" (46–47). In its pages, the "literatures of Relation" represent "what the world experiences . . . But *holding for all*, with anguish and great happiness" (42–43; emphasis added). The "poem" to which *Philosophie* returns repeatedly, "the poem buried in times outside of humanity" ("*le poème enfoui en des temps hors humanité*") is deemed to be universal in everything but the name in a terse aside: "This poem, not universal but *holding* for each person and everywhere" (37).

Glissant has repeatedly made claims to the effect that Relation is increasingly omnipresent, or that "the whole world is becoming-archipelago and becoming-creole (TTM 194). Such assertions similarly flirt with the metaphysical, pronouncing on the nature of the entirety of the world and its human cultures, and predicting where these might be going—even if Glissant's predictions are usually backed by assertions of unpredictability ("*l'imprévisible*"). The inclination to believe that Glissantian thought might yield, per Smart, a sort of "consciousness-conscience" would not be wholly unfounded either: take, for example, the claim in *Introduction à une poétique du Divers* that without embracing the mode of thinking that Glissant calls the "imaginary" ("*imaginaire*") of Relation—the lynchpin, lest we forget, of his theoretical work—humankind is destined to repeat its bloody historical errors (90).

Such claims are bold, to say the least, and as such they inevitably raise the question of Glissant's proprietary relationship to the key terms of his theoretical work. In other words, ought we to perceive the individual author Glissant as the owner or originator of such ideas, or is he rather a vector through which they pass, doing the work of articulation and defense while maintaining, once again, that they "hold for each person and everywhere"? Otherwise put, as Glissant asserts the importance of an increasingly widespread (*pour ne pas dire* "universal") adoption of the thinking of Relation, is he claiming that ideas that are fundamentally and originally his own will be shared by everyone? Taking into account Glissant's solidly critical view of the imposition of one individual's or culture's ideas on others, the answer would appear to be a clear no. Such impositions are, after all, the defining activity of what he identifies as the "West-as-project" (TTM 102–3).

On the other hand, *Philosophie* makes some surprising claims with regard to Glissant's personal relationship to the all-important figure of "creolization," establishing him as a prophetic master of discourse. Under the rubric of "*the thought of creolizations*," Glissant links his own, subjective "I" to the now-omnipresent term *creolization*: "In this way I suggested the word, which was naturally (or by force) gathered up (welcomed) everywhere, as it met up with its reality" (64). Creolization thus departed from dual origins in order to find its singular unity: the ontic (the reality of the increasingly global phenomenon) has come to meet with the ontological (Glissant's expressed idea).

Elsewhere in *Philosophie*, Glissant's language bespeaks something of a prophetic[3] stance: "The infinite diversity is evoked or told or illustrated elsewhere, but it is only spoken to the poem" (83). Borrowing a term from the Judeo-Christian religious lexicon, Glissant continues, stating that this poem "also *announces* totality" (83; emphasis added). The author of *Philosophie* is thus subject to revelation and knowledge of the future, as implied by his use of the word *announces*: it was, lest we forget, to *him* that the annunciation of this totality, which is both present and to come, was made. *Philosophie* thus sets forth a complex conjugation of Glissant's lived individuality as an author with the authority that he arrogates to himself via his access to "the poem . . . beginning anew the gesture of the first times" (83).

The widely ranging subject matter of Glissant's writings also evidences his self-imputation of broad authority. Imbricated into a body of work generally received under the rubric of "Caribbean Studies" are departures into physics and chaos theory (*Introduction à une poétique du divers* [1996]), Medieval Studies (*Les entretiens de Bâton Rouge* [2008]), world history (*Poétique de la Relation* [1990]), and literary criticism (*Faulkner, Mississippi* [1996]), not to mention ethnography and art criticism. And yet, given Glissant's persistent critique of domination, and given moreover his texts' tendency toward narrative experimentation, it follows that he should put in question the authority that is buttressed by his production of such a multifarious and broad body of writing.

Glissant qua author proves to emerge *as* disappearing, presenting himself as an author who dismantles his own authority, losing it among the polyphony of voices that marks so many of his fictional works. Texts weave private, rather puerile jokes into seemingly scholarly forms: the appendices of *Tout-monde*, for example, abruptly reproduce a *contrepétrie*, a vulgar play on words. His texts break with the rigor of scholarly work by citing a source whose attribution the author is not quite sure of, accompanied by the reflection that he ought to verify his sources (TM 609; CL 28).

Glissant's writing also inscribes his presence as an authorial individual as it sheers toward the autobiographical mode, staging, for example, a familial intimacy through its repeated use of the character Mathieu. This oft-appearing character bears a name that is, as Dominique Chancé points out, both Glissant's original first name and the name that the author would later give to his own son (*Les fils de Lear* 145). Furthermore, Glissant hints that his novel *Sartorius: Le roman des Batoutos* was spun out of bedtime stories that he once read to his son Mathieu ("L'Europe et les Antilles"). In another permutation of Glissantian contradiction, shifted onto the plane of family relations, while Glissant's works have often broken with the tradition of the quest for identity (*quête identitaire*) by setting in motion a quest for non-origins, or for origins that are ceaselessly deferred (again, as in *Le quatrième siècle*), they have also showcased the author's dabbling in a search for the origins of his own surname. Senglis, a French slave owner in the Antilles, surfaces from time to time in Glissant's work, fictional and otherwise, personifying the author's musings to the effect that his own name might be a transformation of the surname Senglis (TTM 77–78; 206).

Elsewhere, as Glissant stresses his presence as an author and creator, he inscribes his authority under the sign of absence. The essay *Une nouvelle région du monde*, whose engagement with philosophical discourse is even more pronounced than that of *Philosophie*, dodges an assertion of authority with its approach to the seemingly simple question of whether, or perhaps where, the *Tout-monde* might exist today.

And we are entering into the Tout-monde, which always covers the totality of the world for us, but now this world-whole is also in our times *another region of the world*, a wholly new region, and the world is there, it is here-there [ici-là], it is before us, we who say it without saying it, saying it all the while, again undertaking a new category of literature. (NR 96)

Indeed, as we have seen, the question as to whether the *Tout-monde* is or is not proves to be invalid, unanswerable in Glissantian language. Philosophie's concluding reference to William Faulkner employs a similar, contradictory maneuvering, stating, as in *Faulkner, Mississippi*, that "We are pursuing the prophetic disorder of this man of the South, who said without saying, saying all the while (*qui a dit sans dire tout en disant*)" (156). Glissant's methodology restrains the potential for meaning-making in such phrasings, but avoids prescriptive arguments all the while. In light of such turns of phrase, Buata Malela has argued that Glissant's core concept of Relation is exemplary in that it is defined through negation.

[Glissant] joins through another modality the question of the One and the Many (Multiple) more familiar to ancient and contemporary philosophy . . . Glissant . . . questions the relationship of the oneness (*unicité*) of the world to the multiplicity of that same world. His poetic and philosophical response, conceived through repetition, is also centered upon a modification of imaginaries generated by a contact about which nothing can be said without being beyond thought, as is the case for the One. It can nonetheless be conceived of by means of negation (*apophasis*): that is why Glissant can indicate that the thought of Relation is *not* a system-thought, is *not* the imposition of an absolute upon being. (11–12)

Nothing may be said about this "contact" without entering into a state of being "beyond thought." Glissant, in Malela's reading, proceeds through negation, working to limit an unruly, shifting, ever-proliferating process of meaning-making bordering on the mystical (in Malela's words, "like the One," "beyond thought"). He tells us what Relation is *not*, rather than making exclusively or primarily positive claims. At the same time, direct addresses to his readers such as "What does that mean? You understand it." indicate a mystical mode of communication between reader and text, one that is tacit, perhaps beyond language, perhaps even beyond consciousness (PhR 47). His presence-absence as author lends cogence to his invocations of uncertainty and his admonitions to the effect that certain of his key ideas are not compatible with explication or commentary at all. For Roger Toumson, the very legitimacy of Glissantian discourse is an effect of his self-presentation as author.

> The economy of language, in Glissant's work, is not that of the oral but rather that of the written. It is not oral (*oralitaire*), it is scriptural. Glissant is an ideologue of subjectivity that is thought through (*la subjectivité pensée*). The legitimacy that his discourse claims is proper to the place whence he speaks, to the auctorial place. It is thus by right that he asserts himself as wholly an author. (122)

Such authorial strategies, coupled with his consistent embrace of contradiction, check the unruly production of meaning in the Glissantian text. They also begin the enterprise announced through many such deployments of contradiction: the "creation of a new category of literature" (NR 96

Conclusion

At once present and absent, at once visible and invisible, saying something while not saying it, though saying it all the while: the name "Glissant" would thus designate a tension between opposites, an author whose work is drawn taut, moving in (at least) two different directions at once. It points to an individual author who is multiple, producing multiply. This oscillation, both within dyads and with them, structures, or rather unstructures, many of Glissant's key concepts and claims. Glissant's binary oppositions might lead his readers to think of his work in dialectical terms, whereby the tension produced by two opposites creates another term or terms. But the thinking of Relation, as Glissant insists, calls for a wholly new way of thinking dialectics.

> The dialectic would have no chance of entering into what we refer to as being the real, if it kept to its constitutive bifidities (*bifidités*), for example the pro and the con, the positive and the negative, the master and the slave, Being and nothingness.

Today's humanities call out to the unexpected (wild) dialectics of multiplicity. (67–68)

These unexpected, "wild" (or *sauvage* in the original [68]) dialectics shift from the binary to the multiple, which both includes and adds to the binary form. Once again, latent in this turn to multiplicity is a paradoxical sense of oneness, and Glissant's use of the term *bifidities* is key here. As the Latin root *bifidus* implies, a bifidity is a bipartite entity that was originally a whole; it is a whole that has been split in two. Dialectical opposites, therefore, are no more than the remains of an earlier, undivided whole. Here as elsewhere in Glissant's essays, binary oppositions fade into and out of unification. They partake of multiplicities. In that way, *Philosophie* continually brings its focus to bear on that notion of oneness, of oneness in and through multiplicity.

Rather unexpectedly, one opposition that has appeared throughout the entirety of Glissant's oeuvre becomes a oneness in *Philosophie*: "the time of archipelagoes has become the time of continents, behold the wonder!" (32) The opposition of continental and archipelagic thought is thus undone here—though, contradictorily, it will later resurface elsewhere in the text as a firm contrast. For François Noudelmann, who admires Glissant's ability to marvel unceasingly at the changes and encounters that breathe life into the *Tout-monde*, "[Glissant's] astonishment recalls a primary virtue of philosophy and of a child's wonderment. It suggests an availability, a curiosity, it reminds us of the joy of understanding, the gay science and the anxiety of thought" (42).

Glissant's work in *Philosophie* seems to be just what Noudelmann has in mind, as it rejoices in questioning, in speaking its wonder before the myriad possibilities that the philosophy of Relation has to offer. It showcases a philosophy that seeks to be all-encompassing, undoing old divisions and reinscribing new ones, reveling in its wonder before the constant production of novelty. As we have seen, *Philosophie* deals in the unification of opposites, which it frames more precisely as a *re*unification of opposites. Its fragmentary structure and its playful dismantling of multiple generic categories also point to a oneness, much as its mythical origin-poem does. The text's title, for example, sets it in inevitable dialogue with the *Poetics of Relation*, and thereby alludes to the age-old opposition of poetry and philosophy. As the text unfolds, however, it repeats that poetry and philosophy can become, or rather that they already are, one. Relation, by definition (or rather by nondefinition), "engenders magnetisms between different elements" (73).

Yet the esoteric discursive mode at play in the pages of *Philosophie* undertakes staggering equivalences, staging moments of confluence that are dissolved as quickly as they appear, before reappearing once more. In its pages, philosophy and poetry prove to be both one and yet distinguishable: "What is it then, a philosophy of Relation? An impossible, if it is not a poetics" (82). Or, yet more pointedly: "The poetics of Relation is always a philosophy, and vice versa . . . the language of philosophies is first that of the poem" (87).

The political joins in this joyous combination of philosophy and poetry as well. The poet is inherently the one who understands the relationship of poetics and politics. As Glissant puts it in an article titled "Solitary but in Solidarity" in the collection *Pour une littérature-monde* (2007), "When I say the poet, I don't mean to speak of he [*sic*] who writes poems but rather of he who has a conception of the true relationship between poetics and politics" ("Solidaire et solitaire" 84). In *Philosophie*, particular poetics are, quite simply, politics—the key qualification being their allegiance to the particular over the universal: "The particular politics that have arisen in the world are politics that are realizable everywhere: as poetics, and as non-universal particularities" (85). The triangulation of poetics, politics, and philosophy thus comes to be complete. Philosophy becomes poetics, which in turn becomes politics; in a Glissantian future, as Britton has pointed out, poetics and politics are one ("'Always Changing, while Still Remaining'" 111).

What are we, as readers, to make of this great aggregation? How are we to work, to live with the terse yet far-reaching declarations of Glissant's last essay? The answer, I would like to suggest, lies in *Philosophie*'s engagement with the Glissantian figure of the imaginary and its potential to generate different modes of thought and life. *Philosophie* is turned toward the future; it is revolutionary, and even messianic at times. It heralds the coming of new literary forms, rearticulating the annunciation made in *Faulkner, Mississippi* thirteen years earlier. It trumpets the *Tout-monde*, prophesies limitless Relation. It guides interpretation, channeling readings of Glissantian theory away from certain paths.

Indeed, the sequences of "thoughts" ("*pensées*") in *Philosophie* would at times appear to function like a sort of user's guide, ushering readers through the unpredictable terrain of Glissant's thought. Nonetheless, the *pensées*' primary function is to serve as an act of repetition of aphorisms, thus reinscribing the terms' opacity rather than illuminating them. It bears repeating, in a gesture true to Glissantian method, that the idea of opacity in his work goes undefined (cf. 69). As Glissant reminds his readers: "Opacity is an attribute of Being-as-being, which philosophy takes account of, without illuminating it" (70). *Philosophie* does not articulate what opacity *is*; rather, it explains what opacity *is not* (again, advancing via negation, per Malela). It takes account, rather than illuminating. But *Philosophie* also begins to indicate what opacity *does*. Relation receives a similar treatment, as Glissant focuses on it as a process rather than a product: the idea of Relation must be returned to "at the end of this list, as to all of these splendors, which at the same time relink, relay, and relate [*relient, relaient et relatent*]" (72).

More than this, Relation connotes action and future, creative potential. "[Relation] *creates* poetics and *engenders* magnetisms between different elements" (73; emphases added). Creation, engendering: Glissant's focus on creation in his description of Relation represents one of the many points of confluence linking his thought to the work of Deleuze and Guattari. In a now oft-cited injunction that has come to play a crucial role in the reception of Gilles Deleuze's approach to literature, Deleuze issues a command that can prove fruitful in our encounters with Glissant's work: "experiment, never interpret" ("*expérimentez, n'interprétez jamais*") (60). For Deleuze, when we as readers engage with a text, we mislead ourselves if we perceive the act of reading to be one of interpretation, of mining the text for an isolable meaning that can be fully and finally seized. The functioning of Glissant's *Philosophie* invites readers to attend to Deleuze's directive, frustrating meaning-seeking and obliging us to accommodate contradiction and ambiguity. As we read *Philosophie*, we have no choice but to experiment with different approaches to and interactions with the text.

While English-language translations of this Deleuzian injunction tend to render the word "*expérimenter*" as its cognate, *experiment*, it bears underlining that the French term *expérimenter* has an alternate translation: "to experience." Deleuze's encouragement might invite readers to experiment with texts, but it also encourages a lived experience of the text, an experience of living otherwise. Glissant's *Philosophie* performs some its key concepts, and as a result it invites its readers to think otherwise. Through writing opacity opaquely, through defining terms by holding that they are incompatible with definition, and through concluding inconclusively, it invites an alternative lived experience of reading a text.

Philosophie thus becomes one of the new literary forms whose coming it announces. Moreover, alongside these new forms of literary creation come, once again, new forms of political life: Glissant thus traces a line from thought to action, as new ways of reading call for new actions in the imaginary. *Philosophie* thus enjoins us to read differently, and thereby to think and act differently in the world. The very act of experimenting with and experiencing Glissant's theoretical work amounts to living Relation. Or rather, to experiencing/experimenting with its imaginary ("*imaginaire*"), as we experience philosophy as a continuous unknowing, a repeated call to imagine anew.

We must recall that for Glissant, it is the "imaginary of Relation" that is key to changing our human mentalities. That imaginary is, for him, more important than any economic, military or political intervention if we seek to bring about change in the world (PR 90). This term *imaginary*, which Glissant contrasts with the French word *imagination*, and which resists so opaquely translation into English, is the driving force behind the last Glissantian pronouncement that we will hear now as we close this particular experimentation with and experience of *Philosophie de la Relation*, though never finally.

> That was the imagination of the world, which is so beautifully or crudely of continental inspiration.
>
> The imaginary of the world would be entirely different. The imaginary foresees, divines, finds, it predicts nothing in terms of relationships, it accompanies neither possession nor knowledge. It in no way concludes. It supposes in an archipelago (*en archipel*). (109)

Conclusion

How to Think Like an Archipelago

Archipelagoes, need it be recalled, are themselves quite incapable of thought. What Édouard Glissant means when he refers to the "thought" or "thinking" of archipelagoes, then, requires something of a suspension of disbelief. His sense of "archipelagic thought," by which he has in mind the thought that emanates from the Caribbean archipelago and that somehow resembles it, is perhaps best summed up in the eponymous chapter of *Philosophie de la Relation*. There, it becomes clear that the way of thinking and knowing the world that has its grounds in the archipelago form is first and foremost a means of resistance to what Glissant frames as the moribund fixity of the Western intellectual tradition. Glissant writes,

> *Archipelagic thought*, the thought of the attempt, of the intuitive temptation, which could be apposed to continental thoughts, which would first be system-thoughts. With continental thought the mind sprints with audacity, but that fact makes us think that we see the world as a bloc, taken wholesale, all-at-once, as a sort of imposing synthesis, just as we can see, through the window of an airplane, the configurations of landscapes or mountainous surfaces. With archipelagic thought, we know the rivers' rocks, without a doubt even the smallest ones . . . (PhR 45)

For Glissant, archipelagic thought is aligned with particularity (the rivers' rocks in the above citation), and above all with focusing on and preserving the infinite quantity of all particularities. Continental (read: Western) thought, on the other hand, has devolved into a reductive and homogenizing synthesis. That much is clear. As Aliocha Wald Lasowski has laconically put it in his reading of *Philosophie de la Relation*: "Caribbean thinking, land of archipelagoes: every philosophy is a geography" (977). The archipelagoes of the Caribbean generate, for Glissant, a model of thought that can, and indeed ought to, be transposed onto the entirety of the rest of the world (TTM 226–7). They are accordingly "superbly common places (*lieux-communs*)" (TTM 227).

Glissant's website (*edouardglissant.fr*), at once personal and institutional (since Glissant himself has become something of a living institution, alongside the *Institut du Tout-monde* that he founded), offers a tab linking to a "Glissantian glossary." The latter appears as a spiraling mass of the late thinker's best-known ideas: creolization, opacity, utopia, and so on. An image marked "ideas in archipelagoes" figures conspicuously at the center of the page, a page that is in essence a flowchart remarkable at first glance for its preference for curved arrows and its striving to depict flux, despite its necessarily still arrangement of interconnected ideas. This body of work and this way of thinking are, the layout suggests, anything but linear or teleological, as ideas relay incessantly to one another, in a series of interconnecting loops. The page is also noteworthy for the place that it accords to the idea of the archipelago: it lies at the center, whereas archipelagoes themselves of course have no center. That decentered and decentering center is paradigmatic of Glissant's thought, since any attempt to pin down a center within it immediately points outward to a host of surrounding key terms. The archipelagic center is composed of, or perhaps rather decomposed by, all that surrounds it. The site explains its unique glossary format parenthetically as the "elements of a process." And it does so quite appropriately, for while some of the links relay yet further to other, exegetical pages featuring quotations, commentary, and recorded presentations by Glissant, others remain incomplete, yet to be developed.

In addition to its emphasis on the particular and its multiple and decentered nature, another feature of archipelagic thought in Glissant's work stands out. It is a timely way of thinking; its temporality is that of the *now*, of modernity as what Glissant has termed *globality* (*pour ne pas dire* globalization). Whereas continental thought, with its "thoughts of systems that have until today reigned over the History of humanities . . . is no longer adequate for our burstings, our histories, nor for our no less sumptuous wanderings," the thinking inspired by the archipelago form "fits the speed of our worlds" (TTM 31). In light of these, "our" histories today, as Glissant writes in one of his many critiques of systematicity and system-thinking, neither "systems of thought" nor "thoughts of systems" have any meaningful hold on the real; they can offer "neither the comprehension nor the measure" of what happens in historical conflicts and contacts (IPD 87). For system-thinking, and for these specters of humankind's violent past, Glissant substitutes what he calls the "erratic" dimension. In French as in English, the world connotes both changeability and, significantly for Glissant's purposes, mobility, and wandering. This erratic dimension, which Glissant holds to be "the dimension of deterministic systems with multiple variables," has become "the dimension of the Tout-monde" (IPD 87). Hence the vitalist orientation of Glissant's use of the archipelago form: archipelagoes come to indicate motion, mutability, and openness to difference and change, in stark opposition to what he portrays as the deathly inflexibility of the closed system.

Archipelagic thought does more than pose a viable alternative to the deleterious system-thinking that has haunted the Western intellectual tradition. More than that, it strikes at the very roots of rationalism. Critics most sympathetic to Glissant will perhaps be disappointed by the contours of a syllogism that emerges smoothly out of Glissant's various descriptions of archipelagic thought. Put succinctly, and in Glissant's own words, "archipelagic thinking" is "the thinking of the ambiguous" (cf. TTM 31, IPD 89, et passim). It follows, then, that if "the world is archipelago-izing" (*'le monde entier s'archipélise'*) then it is the case that the world is becoming more ambiguous. It follows, in other words, that for Glissant, ambiguity would be increasingly the case everywhere. If that is so, then the ambiguity that at times characterizes Glissant's argumentation implies that his rhetoric is a reflection of the real. When his ideas, or his expression thereof, are ambiguous, then, they are therefore, and paradoxically, a clear analysis and extension of the truth of the world. Again, in Glissant's words, "I believe that we will have to come closer . . . to a non-system of thought that will be neither dominating nor systematic, nor imposing, but that will be perhaps a non-system of intuitive, fragile, *ambiguous* thought, one that will be the most appropriate to . . . the world in which we live" (IPD 24–25; emphasis added).

The notion of chaos plays a parallel role in Glissant's understanding of archipelagic thought. He explains his notion of the "chaos-world" as "the shock, the entanglement [*l'intrication*], the repulsions, the attractions, the collusions, the oppositions, the conflicts between cultures and peoples in the contemporary totality-world" (IPD 82). "The same thinking of ambiguity that the specialists in the sciences of chaos emphasize at the very basis of their discipline" controls the imaginary of Relation and of today's chaos-world (IPD 89). "The wager," as Glissant puts it in language that strains to avoid the temptation of final and finalizing mastery that is the goal of the metaphysical proposition, "is that Chaos is order and disorder, excess [*démesure*] without an absolute, destiny and becoming" (PR 207).

The critic Mary Gallagher's conception of the Caribbean dovetails with Glissant's vitalist, chaotic vision. "The Caribbean is held to be unthinkable, then," she writes, "as a static, demarcated area. Part of the Atlantic continuum, it is first and foremost fluid and, as such, comprises currents, flow, passage, and displacement" (*Soundings* 2). Caribbean creolization, for Glissant as for Gallagher, epitomizes that fluidity and unpredictability, and for that reason Glissant is emphatic in insisting that it is not equivalent to *métissage* (the term, usually translated as *hybridity*, connotes mixing, particularly of a racial sort). In Glissant's understanding of the term, hybridity implies the convergence of specifically two terms in order to produce a third term. As Huddart explains, for Homi Bhabha, the critic with whom the theorization of hybridity has increasingly come to be associated, the hybridity of cultures refers to their 'impurity,' except that no culture (or identity) is ever pure (6–7); in other words, cultures "are always in contact with one another, and this contact leads to cultural mixed-ness" (7). Hybridization for Bhabha is thus an "ongoing process" (Huddart 7). Glissant shares Bhabha's emphasis on the processual but takes a narrower view of hybridity, holding that the outcome of hybridity can be foreseen, whereas "Creolization is the unpredictable" (IPD 89). That predicate of unpredictability also explains Glissant's fondness for (his understanding of) chaos theory. In a passage that strives to sketch an ontology alongside an ethics of intersubjectivity, Glissant seeks to indicate why it is that his thought requires a particular sort of articulation. Poetics, and poetics writ ambiguously, he asserts, generate a sort of language that cannot be reduced to the clarity of the concept. "[T]he poetic vision makes it possible to live with the idea of the unpredictable because it makes it possible to conceive of unpredictability not as a negative but as a positive" (IPD 103).

In his thoughts on chaos lies what we might call the Glissantian theory of everything: in other words, the truth of all reality, past and present, is chaos. Rapidly, however, Glissant's work leaves the realm of ontology in order to apply this concept of chaos to interests that are at once principally politico-cultural and aesthetic. It is the *history of the world's peoples*, Glissant insists, that has led to the dynamics of his vision of chaos (PR 45). In this vision of history-as-chaos, each detail is as complex as the ensemble of all particulars; each part exhibits a movement that is implicated in the movement of all the other parts (PR 45). Surprisingly, and perhaps in order to temper his privileging of chaos, Glissant explains that the beauty of chaos lies not in its exploded, unyielding excess, not in its unpredictability, but rather in its patterns, its constants: "Chaos is beautiful on the condition that we try, via the imaginary, to track, to trace in it not the laws but the constants. A bit like physicists" (IPD 134).

The entire world is creolizing and becoming an archipelago, and the same can be said of the peculiar configuration of Glissant's many texts. They too adhere to a pattern: they are a reflection of the archipelago form. The body of Glissant's work is an archipelago in that "Each text-island," in Joubert's apt formulation, "is the neighbor of its sisters [*sic*], close to them, and at the same time irreducible in its singularity" (Joubert 318). A turning-inward, as Glissant has argued of the Caribbean conception of totality that he grounds in the archipelago form, is also a turning-outward. Archipelagic thought has its reflection in both the form and the content of what Joubert identifies as "the paradox of this corpus, which is organized in the continuity of a cycle by the permanence of return (of characters, themes, images, words) and that is broken up into the abruptness of discontinuities" (Joubert 318). Individual texts likewise reflect the formal structure of the archipelagic Glissantian corpus taken as a whole: multiple, fragmented, interrelated, and decentered. The Glissantian oeuvre, like the world, is also creolizing, in Glissant's sense of creolization as itself the unpredictable (cf. CL 229). For while Glissant has defended his decades-long repetition of aphorisms by maintaining tersely that "one must repeat oneself," and furthermore, that his "propositions . . . must be repeated, as long as they are not being understood," he has also argued for the "uncertainties" of his philosophy of Relation, or for a representation of the world that frames unresolvable contradiction and tension as integral of the fabric of the world's reality (TTM 37, 39).

Beyond chaos, uncertainty, and ambiguity, archipelagic thought is also the thought of the *essai*, of the try or attempt (PhR 45). And again, as Glissant puts it in his final book-length essay, the imaginary that best conforms to the ultimate reality of the world "*concludes nothing*," "it *supposes* in an archipelago" (PhR 109; emphases added). As we read Glissant's novels alongside his essays, following Glissant in his confounding of genres, it becomes clear that his work simultaneously calls for, and performs, just such experiments and attempts. Lydie Moudileno has skillfully analyzed Glissant's deconstruction of the novel form in his *Mahagony*

(1987), calling his oscillation toward and away from the traditional form a "going-and-coming," neither a definitive departure from, nor an embrace of, established forms (*L'écrivain antillais* 140). That novelistic strategy constitutes, for her, an infinite series of what she calls "essais," or "attempts," referring to the original meaning of the French word *essai* before it came to describe the genre that Montaigne launched. "These attempts," she argues, "end up at something other than the imagined renunciation. . . . This something other is thus Glissantian Relation, a relation of attempts that are only meaningful in the network of convergences and differences that they trace in the book" (*L'écrivain antillais* 139). In their far-reaching scope, flexible structure, and playfulness, his essays recall those of Montaigne more than the conclusive, rigorous and clear form that readers might expect in the early twenty-first century. The Glissantian text, like the Glissantian corpus as a whole, is thus an archipelagic series of comings-and-goings, or of attempts, all of which unfold against the backdrop of a long-term rejection of stability and final conclusions. Glissant's essays are, in this sense, unfinished, and deliberately so. And much the same is true of the overall, near sixty-year arc of his thought.

The concluding words of a notable number of studies of Glissant reflect that lack of completion. Concluding a systematic analysis of a "nonsystem" such as Glissant's, and moreover of one that resoundingly rejects conclusion, is a delicate matter (IPD 91). Jean-Pol Madou's final chapter in his monograph on Glissant, titled "By Way of Non-Conclusion," speaks to that dilemma. Similarly, the first monograph on Glissant in English, J. Michael Dash's landmark *Édouard Glissant* (1995), closes with the following lines, themselves a gloss of the final pages of Glissant's *Poétique de la Relation*: "Reality remains a sea of indeterminate flux, resisting total explanation. As in the final words of Walcott's *Ormeros*, 'When he left the beach the sea was still going on'" (Dash, *Glissant* 182). One of Dash's qualifications is key, however, particularly in light of the centrality of paradox and unpredictability in Glissant's thought: the world may very well exist in a state of indeterminacy and in flux, but it is not as a result inexplicable, a raw, befuddling, chaotic mess. To the contrary, reality as envisaged by Glissant resists, in Dash's words, "*total* explanation." Through his characterization of his own philosophizing as an enterprise of paradox, ambiguity, and uncertainty, Glissant would seem to be indicating that a final, totalizing understanding of his work—or of reality itself—may very well be impossible. Understanding Glissant, or understanding the world, thus demands a different sort of explicative approach.

The Author and/of the World

Taking those core facets of archipelagic thinking into account, and faced with the tension manifested in Glissant's thought as it is drawn between its militantly activist point of departure and its utopian ends, Glissant's self-representation as an author merits closer analysis. Glissant advances as he recedes: he acts as an authoritative commentator on a dizzying array of subjects, but also presents himself at times as an individual who has merely one set of values among many. As we have seen, Glissant takes on the role of a critic of various forms of art (painting, poetry, sculpture), or of a philosopher of science, a philosopher of being and ethics, a utopian thinker, a novelist, a poet, an essayist, a playwright, and an activist, not to mention a political and economic commentator and public intellectual.

Glissant's self-presentation qua author corroborates Foucault's sense of the modern category of "the author." First, like the Foucauldian framing of the modern author, Glissant strives to be consistent with himself. His rhetoric of self-presentation is thus faithful to Foucault's description of the author as a fixed subject who is taken to exist in a stable state throughout time until the moment of his/her death, an event that confers yet greater legitimacy on the author's intellectual and stylistic constancy (Foucault 101–20). One of the more striking instances of Glissant's self-consistency can be found in his prolonged reading of Faulkner in *Faulkner, Mississippi* (1996), after its near-identical articulation almost thirty years earlier in *L'intention poétique* (1969). Glissant's comments on Faulkner in *L'intention poétique* not only foreshadow his later monograph on the Southern author, but seem even to summarize it in its near-entirety (cf. IP 176–82). And any reader of Glissant's oeuvre will note his steady recapitulation of a set of aphorisms throughout his productive decades. "I can change, while exchanging with the other, nevertheless without losing myself or distorting myself"; "The entire world is archipelago-izing and creolizing"; and so on (CL 25; TTM 194). The author, much like the phrasings he repeats, would thus seem to remain constant over time. Indeed, Glissant has often repeated that he feels the need to repeat himself (IPD 82).

Readers of Glissant often tend to submit to this imperative of repetition themselves, reproducing Glissant's aphorisms near-verbatim. Patrick Chamoiseau, Glissant's longtime collaborator and a brilliant author in his own right, often provides noteworthy examples of that mimetic impulse on the part of Glissant's admirers. Chamoiseau has used language that is clearly a reflection of Glissant's own in order to describe his authorial preoccupations: "My problematic is a problematic of countries connected [*reliés*] to the Tout-monde and of peoples connected to the totality of the world, who must lay their foundations and live the exchange that changes. That's it, my problematic, and it's a problematic of the future" (727). Such unerringly faithful reproductions of Glissant's rhetoric testify to its remarkable powers of seduction.

Glissant's entire corpus can be read, in one sense, as a long-term exegesis of, and apology for, his own literary-critical practice. His work explains and defends key terms such as Relation, creolization, the rhizome, or the *Tout-monde*, just as much as it performs them. Other writers are often lauded in his literary-critical work insofar as they represent, or corroborate in spirit if *avant la lettre*, these ideas (cf. FM 215). Despite its overall emphasis on openness and interrelation, Glissant's rhetoric often closes itself within a hermetically sealed discourse, one whose truth-value depends on its structural integrity and on reference to other terms within it. If ideas cannot be drawn into Glissantian discourse, they will, in his thought, remain untouched by its assignation of truth-value.

In fact, that move of drawing nearly anything into his own rhetoric often proves irresistible to Glissant. In the novel *Tout-monde*, one narrator recalls his tour of an Egyptian temple, where he struggled to decipher an inscription with the aid of a guide. Together, they arrived at "I weave the truth in the sun's light." Once alone, however, Glissant, or a narrative voice that presents itself as Glissant's, proposes another translation: "Perhaps this: '*I shed light on the truth as I show its basic outline. The rhizome, Relation*'" (TM 538). That translation of a millennia-old text into Glissantian language is also notable for its shift in authorial positioning. Rather than the direct declaration "I weave the truth," Glissant's rendering prefers a basic outline, partial illumination, to an unveiled truth laid bare in the stark light of day.

As it repeats the trope of revelation as nonrevelation, his thought accommodates its seeming weaknesses, going so far as to brandish them as strengths. On closer analysis and when taken as a whole, Glissant's oeuvre proves to account for what would appear to be the cracks in its structural integrity. For him, if ideas such as Relation, creolization and what he frames as their corollaries in ambiguity, unpredictability, and contradiction are increasingly the case everywhere and for everyone, the presence of ambiguity or contradiction in Glissant's writing only serves to prove that it reflects the truth of the world. In the end, Glissant can be said to be consistent even in his inconsistency. In other words, when Glissant's thought shows itself to be in contradiction with itself, it provides for such discrepancies, such unpredictability, by reveling in that very contradiction. In that sense, Glissant can reclaim the contradictions that might at first glance appear to be authorial blunders, framing them instead as evidence of the ultimate authority: that of infallibility.

Another way in which Glissant's argumentation accords authority to itself lies in its periodic retreats onto the terrain of the irreproachable. His forays into the contested field of globalization studies, through his increasingly prominent concepts of the *Tout-monde* and later globality, are exemplary in that regard. There, Glissant's treatment of the *Tout-monde* all too often confines its analysis to the compelling. That is, it advances arguments about the state of the world (a state that is either actual, or imminent, or somehow both) that could inspire virtually no dissent. Assuming that readers share his values with regard to what constitutes the positive and the negative aspects of globality/globalization, and confining his critique primarily to an assault on overly powerful multinational companies, woeful cultural homogenization, and "savage ultra-(economic) liberalism," Glissant makes his readers an offer they cannot refuse (CL 15). Who among Glissant's readers, we are led to wonder, would argue against his call for the preservation of all languages, or take issue with his concern with bringing the multiplicity of the world's cultures into respectful and enriching contact? That drift into near-indisputable claims is crystallized in Glissant's rather dismissive clarification to the effect that his theory of "globality" is quite simply the positive, flip side of all that is negative about globalization (CL 15). In the most basic sense, who could disagree with Glissant as he campaigns for all that is not-negative about the world? Glissant's engagement with globality is thus exemplary of his rhetorical efforts to proclaim the incontestable.

In a parallel vein, the *Tout-monde* represents what we might call a happy globalization. Glissant's model of totality seeks to remain conscious of history's weight and the many dangers of globalization, all the while rejoicing in the ever-increasing interconnection and mobility of humankind. The *Tout-monde* often looks very much like a defanged globalization, modernity without the menace—or, more troublingly, a modernity whose dangers have been shuttled out of the foreground.

Glissant also favors the innocuous over the contentious in his attacks on the trope of universality. For Glissant, "[W]e must abandon the idea of the universal. The universal is a lure, a deceptive dream" (IPD 136). In its stead, as we have seen, Glissant proposes totality, and explains this move in a later text through a contrasting of *quantity* and *quality*, privileging the former over the latter.[1] Rather than the hierarchical structure that quality as a factor of differentiation would necessitate, Glissant suggests that we think through a model of the world-as-quantity. "We must conceive of the totality-world as a totality, which is to say as a realized *quantity* and not as a sublimated value drawn from particular values. That is fundamental, and that changes without our knowing it the majority of facts about world literature today" (IPD 136; emphasis added). Here as elsewhere, Glissant warns against the sublimation of a particular value or set of values to the rank of universality, or of what he terms the *One*. Generalizing particular values is a hegemonic tendency, Glissant warns. It was best exemplified by colonialism, which erected the values of the West, or even of particular Western nation-states, as universals. In a key formulation, Glissant hints at why it is that he has come to privilege quantity over quality. His alternative to the sublimation of particular values to the rank of the universal is a harmonious cohabitation of a multitude of values. "One can quantify all sorts of particular values," he writes—not, of course, in order to universalize them, but rather in order "to make of them a rhizome, a fabric, a framework of values that are different but that *touch one another* and *interlace* all the time" (IPD 136; my emphases).

While it is certainly the case that, as he puts it, one *can* portray the totality of the world's values and value-systems as a field, a weave wherein values inoffensively touch one another [*s'entretouchent*] and interlace [*s'entrecroisent*], in doing so one would overlook the (very Nietzschean) point that values often conflict, seek to eliminate or assimilate one another, and fuel rifts and divisions in the world. The above model of a nonhierarchical totality of values, what is more, does not even itself escape the tendency of privileging certain values over others. For there is a hierarchy of values, even in Glissant's vision of a flattened totality of values that would avoid hierarchy. As we have seen, the *Tout-monde* is characterized by terms such as *sharing*, *exchange*, and *solidarity*. And the above injunction to quantify rather than qualify values is colored by a certain ethical stance significant for its positive valuation of nonviolence, respect, equality-in-difference, communication and dialogue, and so forth. In a very Glissantian contradiction, those values are privileged over others in the context of his urgings to avoid any hierarchization of values whatsoever.

Despite Glissant's claims that he has no pretensions of founding or defending a school of thought and that he would rather remain "solitary and in solidarity" (IPD 143), he does place positive value-judgments on his own values, and encourages others to share them. In fact, some of the value judgments Glissant makes sound, *pace* Glissant, much like moral judgments. For example, he esteems that "Thinking that one's own value enters into an interlacing of the values of the totality of the world, that is in my opinion a much *grander, nobler* and *more generous* project" (IPD 136; emphases added). To hold that one way of thinking is *more* "grand" or "noble" in comparison others is of course itself a reinscription of hierarchy. While his invocations of "interlacing" strive to appear harmless in their positivity, they nonetheless portray other values (others' values?) as inferior. We may very well agree with Glissant's enthusiasm, but even his relativism has its limits.

Glissant's purportedly noncoercive utopian vision also strays on occasion into the domain of the prescriptive. His optimism extends itself to his sense of the profound importance of literature, and particularly its potential effects on the imaginary, in bringing about and maintaining the state of affairs that is the *Tout-monde*. And it is in this treatment of the imaginary that Glissant, despite his claim to do away with moral injunction altogether, comes to argue that certain ways of thinking and certain (which is not to say, *particular*) ways of conceiving of and using the imaginary *must* be adopted by everyone (CL 25). At times, Glissant's tone borders on the coercive, or at the very least the injunctive: "We *must*, in *all* domains of our activities, fill ourselves with the idea of globalization [*sic*]"; "We *must* abandon the idea of the universal"; "We *must* think of the totality-world as a totality," and so on (IPD 103; IPD 136; ibid.; emphases added). Once again, such injunctions stand in troubling contradiction to Glissant's manifest distaste for coercion and the promoting of particular values over others. One wonders whether there is something of the gloriously impossible Glissant's theorization of value in the *Tout-monde*. As it reinstates hierarchies and issues injunctions, Glissant's own articulation of his vision serves to demonstrate the impossibility, or at the very least the paradox, of making it tenable.

If we take the reasons for Glissant's indictment of the West-as-project into account, his approach to the Caribbean may prove problematic as well. Again, for Glissant, the West's mission is one of elevating particular cultures, their ways of thinking and their value systems, over others. In holding that the entire world is creolizing, or in holding that the Caribbean holds a special place in the origination or the grounding of the imaginary of Relation, is Glissant not maintaining, despite his insistences to the contrary, that the world is becoming, indeed that it *ought* to become, increasingly like one culture—that is, his own? That question is troubling, given his emphasis on the "intervalorization" that lies at the heart of creolization (TTM 194), as well as his claims in *Poétique de la Relation* that the historical period in which one culture could value itself over others is finally drawing to a close. Nonetheless, creole societies and creole individuals, Glissant tells us, maintain a special purchase on what is increasingly becoming a worldwide reality. They are archetypes of that reality, and for that reason creole peoples—with Glissant himself presumably providing the consummate example—would appear to be capable of a clearer and truer grasp of reality.

In the opening pages of the novel *Tout-monde*, for example, readers are informed that places such as Martinique offer a special perspective on, and thus a superior knowledge of, the world; it is from places like Martinique that "one can *truly* see and imagine the world" (18; emphasis added). Another example of the privileged position Glissant grants to creole cultures is furnished by the character Mathieu, who comes the closest to serving as a protagonist among the multitude of characters who populate the novel *Tout-monde*'s pages. In one of the many scenes of Mathieu's travels throughout the world, he finds himself in an idyllic Italian village with a group of local friends. The latter advance the now-familiar argument that no language is truly pure, that what can be said of creole languages is true to varying degrees of all languages. Mathieu agrees grudgingly, then objects. Laughingly granting them their point, Mathieu cannot help but explain to them that there is nevertheless something special about creole languages, that "creole languages are even more creole than the others" (TM 58).

While the world as a whole is moving toward creolization and archipelagoization, it would seem that some places are doing so more quickly, or rather that they have already accomplished it, and in a more intense form. Creole cultures are those nodes of creolization's intensity. Such places are no doubt what Glissant had in mind when he allowed that "I think that probably we are all going towards the Tout-monde, but there are different speeds, different moments" (IPD 140). There nonetheless remains that certain *something* about creole cultures that lends them exemplarity for Glissant. In Glissant's eyes, for example, while mixing and migration have always occurred more or less everywhere, albeit to varying degrees, what happened in the Caribbean stands apart. And, lest we forget, Glissant maintains that the now markedly popular trope of creolization was *his* idea. To cite the "Thought of creolizations" chapter of *Philosophie de la Relation*, "*I* thus proposed the word [creolization], which was naturally (or by force) taken up (welcomed) everywhere, joining up with its reality" (64; emphasis added).

Glissant's profound belief in the Caribbean-as-paradigm has indeed proven convincing to many writing in his wake. Recent scholarly books have located creolization in far-flung and at times surprising contexts: a nonexhaustive list would include Gordon's *Creolizing Political Theory* (2014), Gordon and Roberts's *Creolizing Rousseau* (2014), Patel's *Creolizing Europe* (2015), or Lionnet and Shih's *The Creolization of Theory* (2011). Academic article titles such as Ferrier and Ménard's "Creole Japan; or, the Vagaries of Creolization" (2010), or Jane Webster's "Creolizing the Roman Provinces" (2001) displace creolization yet further. The figure of creolization may have had its origins in the Americas, and in the Caribbean cultural zone more precisely, but it has proven to be remarkably exportable today.

That fact can perhaps be chalked up to the positive valuations Glissant places on sharing and exchange, on interconnection, on the world-as-one, or on maintaining the integrity of diverse, multiple places. That vision of creolization is open and unobjectionable enough to appeal to the majority of his readers. Likewise, his repeated appeal, "I demand for everyone the right to opacity, which is not the same as withdrawing into oneself," which has appeared in various forms, and which calls for a knowledge of and contact with the other that would not be reducible to violence or mastery, borders on the unassailable (cf. TTM 29, et passim). Yet his seductive vision of the creolized *Tout-monde* as a happy, vivacious admixture of everyone and everything exists in a problematic relationship to the Caribbean. Whether the Caribbean is to be understood as origin, exemplar, or avant-garde of the truth-of-the-world today, Glissant's persistent privileging of his own home and culture is troubling in light of his calls for incessant relativization, or for a recognition of the equality-in-difference of all cultures.

The role of primacy that Glissant accords to the Caribbean also helps to account for some notable historical errors in his arguments. By casting himself as a Foucauldian universal intellectual, Glissant authorizes himself to make large-scale historical generalizations. Two of them represent, I would submit, generous applications of his preconceived notions to the historical record. Both claims emanate out of a pairing of his more strongly held beliefs: namely, in the (undesirable) exceptionality of the West-as-project, and the (desirable) exceptionality of the Caribbean as a template for the future of the world.

Glissant holds that the world has never known such an aggressive, violent project of military and economic domination coupled with a robust belief in oneness as that which was evidenced in the colonial period. He argues that "Alone among all civilizations, the Western one has known this propensity to generalized expansion, to expansion of conquest, of knowledge and faith, which are inextricable, and which required the Universal as a guarantor of their legitimacy" (TTM 102–3). In making such claims, however Glissant ignores at least one other historical episode about which many of the same comments might be made: that is, the Arab conquests beginning in the seventh century, which were characterized by the robust, monotheistic message of Islam and the imposition of monolingual religious practice, not to mention the patterns of state formation that the invaders brought with them.

Second, I would like to take issue with Glissant's argument that composite, and particularly Caribbean cultures, preclude the specters of genocide or ethnic cleansing. As Glissant has it, "In the Caribbean, for example, it is obvious that there is no possibility of ethnic massacres or ethnic cleansing on account of the very notion of ethnicity that is found there. There are other problems, but not that one" ("L'Europe et les Antilles"). Here, Glissant accords a special status to the Caribbean. Unceasingly, Glissant has argued that the world stands to learn from Caribbean cultures if it to create a more peaceful future, one notable for its emphasis on relation over antagonism (in Glissant's vocabulary, a preference for *a*pposition over *o*pposition). Aside from the ever-present forms of racism and color-based oppression extant in the Caribbean in the postcolonial era, Glissant overlooks with his hyperbolic assertions ("there is *no possibility* of ethnic massacres or ethnic cleansing") the 1937 massacres of thousands of Haitian immigrants (and others who were perceived to be such) in the Dominican Republic under Trujillo. Glissant would no doubt attribute such decidedly un-Caribbean behavior to a backslide into what he calls an "atavistic" cultural form, but the fact remains that the shift from composite to atavistic culture is clearly possible in the Caribbean, and that what would later be called "ethnic cleansing" did happen there.

As he grants himself a mastery of the historical record, Glissant's personal investment in pitting the Caribbean against the West, as well as in arguing for the Caribbean-as-paradigm, takes precedence over historical accuracy. Attention to these oversights highlights the authoredness of his all-encompassing claims. Every system, as Deleuze would have it, is vulnerable to leaks (*fuites*). Glissant's (non-)system is no exception. For each of the apparent flaws in Glissant's thought, however, there are also moves to address the corpus's own deficiencies. For example, if Glissant's thought overlooks important issues, if it contains gaps or inaccuracies, that is because Glissant is an antisystematic thinker. If his ideas seem to remain unclear or ambiguous, that fact can be attributed to his veneration of the figure of opacity. If his thought is incomplete or marked by contradiction, it is all the more faithful to itself insofar as the world shares those traits as well: the presence of contradiction in reality extends into the Glissantian text.

What Glissant offers us, then, is a well-wrought, self-defending nonsystem. The capstone of Glissant's wall of defense against criticism is the fact that his thought claims to be coextensive with the world, both to speak of the world and to be, per his vitalist cosmology, a conduit through which the world expresses itself. Glissant is an author of the world, in both senses of the expression: he has authored a world, breathing life into a specific conception of the world (i.e., the *Tout-monde*). He is also *of* the world, in that he seeks to belong to the world, to become its mouthpiece, one among many avenues of the expression of its realities: to speak of it and to speak it. Glissant's thought contains contradictions, inconsistencies, gaps—and it is for this reason seamless, true to its aims. Simply put, the text resembles the world: it is chaotic, but it has its patterns. It is always changing, and full of life. In Britton's words, Glissant's work crosses "the boundary that in a more classical conception of art separates a representation from that which it represents. There is no difference in principle between the forces internal to the work and those in the world outside it" (*Language and Literary Form* 161).

Glissant's rhetoric concludes by holding that it cannot itself be final. If it is the breath of the world that gives life to the multitudes teeming within Glissant's thought, then the rules that govern his literary and paraphilosophical production are those of the world, and decidedly not the rules governing the genres that his texts rethink. For Glissant, any book that would seek to take the measure of the world will be marked by the ambiguity and mutable nature that are the lifeblood of its object. In his *Essay on a Measure of the World in the Twentieth Century: Édouard Glissant* (*Essai sur une mesure du monde au XXème siècle: Édouard Glissant*), Romuald Fonkoua has argued of Glissant's writings that

> The book, like writing, is only a rough draft of the world because the measure of the world can only be taken in rough drafts. For [Glissant], in effect, the book is only a *vagary* of literary communication . . . Not a unity in itself, but rather the place where the construction of a certain unity of the diversities of the world operates. (301)

If Glissant's thought lacks finality or completion, if it manifests contradiction or paradox, all the better. After all, as Glissant insists, "All possibles, all contradictions are in the world's diversity" (IPD 25). Glissant's oeuvre, re-imagined from that perspective, looks very much like the fulfillment of a fantasy that the youthful Glissant pondered in his first essay. *Soleil de la conscience*'s last page asked,

> Who has not dreamed of the poem that explains everything, of the philosophy whose last word illuminates the universe, of the novel that organizes *all* truths, all passions, steering them and shedding light on them? A work that would begin with the tranquil northern nights, unveiling each fjord, setting the Tropics alight, in order to calm itself in the white fogs of the South, a Novel that would offer the connections, the tangles, the synthesis, the ONE? (84)

Thinking the Other of Thought

That hyperbolically positive dream of a book that would simultaneously encompass and mirror all reality scintillates behind the scenes of the negative work that Glissant's thought undertakes. His abiding preoccupation with paradox and contradiction are, for that reason among others, irreducible to mystification or obscurantism. In Eric Prieto's explanation, Glissant's concern with totality, on full display in his oft-criticized shift in focus from "the homeland" to "the big picture," has a concrete, political objective: it "provides just the kind of reconceptualization or reframing of the postcolonial condition that will make possible new solutions to the old intractable problems" ("Littérature-monde" 120). In a riposte to those among Glissant's critics who perceive a neglect of the political dimension in Glissant's post-1990 works, Prieto adds, "the fact that these solutions may seem frustratingly indirect or conciliatory to the militants among us is no sign of their inferiority. On the contrary." ("Littérature-monde" 120).

Philosophie de la Relation has mused that in the wake of decolonization, "we no longer know exactly where meaning is and where meaninglessness is, neither do we know whether meaningless has become the master of meaning" (44). Such provocative assertions take on new meaning when placed in the context of the peculiarly *vitalist* current of Glissant's thought—in other words, in its overall push to bring novelty into the world, to encourage new ways of living and thinking, in order to engender creative solutions to Prieto's "old intractable problems" (44). Moreover, Glissant's work is remarkable for its promulgation of what I call an aesthetic vitalism. That is, it portrays artistic production as playing a central, if not *the* central, role in fostering Life itself. *Poétique de la Relation* had already intimated those concerns with its allusions to "The poetic force (the energy) of the world, kept alive within us . . ." (173). But Glissant's later alliances of Life and art connect his vitalism to his use of paradox, and thus to each of the thematic concerns of the preceding pages.

To begin, the literature of the *Tout-monde*, just as rooted in the particularity of Place as it is afloat in the totality, is drawn taught between the poles of Place and totality. It is therefore fecund, unpredictable. For Glissant, knowing the other as unknowable both protects the other's life and enhances the life of the knowing self. Teleologies without an end in narrative show that process holds more creative potential than any finally attainable product ever could. And finally, Glissant's peculiar philosophical method, which refuses to conclude and takes pleasure in illuminating the world as opaque, constitutes, in his view, the clearest vision of the world to date. To put it in yet more starkly vitalist terms: Glissant's rethinking of totality-in-Relation is grounded in a sense of the fundamental oneness and interconnectedness of all beings, of a force traversing everything that breathes life both into embodied beings and into artistic creation; his literary-critical framing of alterity takes as its foremost concern the protection of the life of the other; his staging of teleology frames it as a proliferating, ever-augmenting and creative vivacity, and his own philosophical methodology as exemplified in *Philosophie de la Relation*, calls for an inconclusive, ever-active lived experience of meaning-making on the part of his readers.

Glissant is not alone in recognizing an affinity between vitalist thinking and Caribbean cultural contexts. In her *Cultural Conundrums: Gender, Race, Nation and the Makings of Caribbean Cultural Politics* (2006), Natasha Barnes draws a similar connection between elements of vitalist discourse and Caribbean cultures of all languages. Barnes explains that her methodology is based on "the protean, frenetic, and improvisatory character of Caribbean cultural productivity—its capacity to shape itself from disparate sources and its refusal to be straightjacketed by any single set of meanings" (12). Likewise, in her *L'écrivain antillais au miroir de son écriture*, Lydie Moudileno shows that Glissant's response to what Barnes has called the "conundrum" of the Caribbean writer can be seen in the "going-and-coming of the correspondences and opacities of a writing that at once mixes up and embraces the past and the future, the subject and the object, authors and readers, the book and the dream of the book, in what becomes a meditation on conjunction and separation" (140). As Moudileno shows, Glissant's vision of a Caribbean philosophical and literary practice is one of a vitalist, paradoxical intermingling of customarily opposed terms (past and future, conjunction and separation, etc.), a great coming-together of disparate and at times contradictory ideas that breathes new life into all of them.

That grand coalescence is on full display at the center of *Poétique de la Relation*. As the title of Vincent Descombes's history of French philosophy *Le même et l'autre* (*The Same and the Other* [1979])[2] suggests, the philosophical tradition in France since World War II has long taken the question of otherness, or what Glissant calls the "thought of the Other," as one of its central concerns. It is, moreover, no surprise that much the same can be said today of the discipline of Postcolonial Studies, given the enormous influence of "French Theory" on the triumvirate of Spivak, Bhabha, and Said. While he acknowledges his own deep preoccupation with the thought of the O/other, however, Glissant invites us to think instead of something different, what he calls the "Other of thought."

> The thought of the Other is the moral generosity that would lead me to accept the principle of alterity, to conceive that the world is not all of one piece and that there is not only one truth, my own. But the thought of the other can live in me without moving me from my path, without "diverting" me, without changing me within myself. It is an ethical principle, one which it would be sufficient not to break.
>
> The Other of thought is that very movement. At that point, I have to act. It's the moment where I change my thinking, without giving up its contributions. I change, and I exchange. It's a question of an aesthetics of turbulence, whose corresponding ethics is not given in advance.
>
> If we are therefore to grant that an aesthetics is an art of conceiving, of imagining, of acting, the Other of thought is the aesthetics that is put into action by me, by you, in order to join, to take part in a dynamic. It is my share of the aesthetics of chaos, the work to be done, the road to travel . . . The Other of thought is always set in motion by the whole of confluences, where each is changed by the other and changes the other. (PR 169)

Exactly what Glissant might have meant by "the Other of thought" is far from clear. We can discern, however, that this notion gathers together a surprisingly wide array of ideas: movement, action, change, exchange, ethics, aesthetics, chaos and so on. What is more, the fact of engaging with this "Other of thought" would also appear to be transformative, eliciting change in the world (*"I have to act"*), in the self (*"I change"*), and of course in thought.

The ideas with which Glissant surrounds his formula of the Other of thought (action, thought, aesthetics, change, exchange, etc.) are themselves spread out in an archipelago. They are multiple, and they cohere only insofar as they fall under the rubric of one, fragmented category: that of the Other of thought. But that category is of course itself paradoxical: how, after all, might one go about thinking that which is other to thought? Thought's Other by definition lies beyond the boundaries of thinking's grasp; the Other of thought is, at bottom, that which cannot be enveloped or subsumed by thought, and thinking it would be by definition impossible. How, then, are we go about making sense of this very Glissantian formulation?

The title of Gary Gutting's history of the last five decades of French philosophy, *Thinking the Impossible* (2011), is altogether pertinent to Glissant's Other of thought. It is worthy of note, however, that although the always-incisive Gutting weaves together a remarkable synthesis of a diverse intellectual tradition, his history ends on a note of ambivalence. Gutting begins his conclusion by conceding that "There is much to admire in the work of recent French philosophers," that their work "suggests potentially fruitful lines of thought about . . . the limits of conceptualization, the uniqueness of ethical obligation . . . the possibility of radical metaphysical innovation, and counter-conventional readings of the history of philosophy" (202). And while Glissant grounds his radical philosophical enterprise in what he frames as the natural and cultural realities of the Caribbean rather than continental France, those appraisals by Gutting show to what extent Glissant's work is conversant with that of his contemporaries in Paris. One can imagine, however, what Glissant might have thought of Gutting's closing lines (Gutting's book was published in 2011, the year of Glissant's death), which read as something of an indictment of that half century of French philosophy.

> But the riches of recent French thought typically require patient excavation, refinement, and development before they will meet the (legitimate) standards of analytic philosophizing. They adumbrate achievements of thought that the humdrum analytic mind

is not likely to envisage on its own. But, without the analytic insistence on doggedly thinking through the mundane details, these achievements will unnecessarily remain—to use Derridean language—in a state of the perpetually-to-come. (202–3)

Gutting's tone throughout his conclusion suggests that recent French thought has promised a product that it has been unable or unwilling to deliver. It *"suggests potentially* fruitful lines of thought"; it *"adumbrates,"* and for that reason it is, as Chancé has said of the Caribbean author, *en souffrance*. In other words, it is, lamentably, yet to arrive (Chancé, *L'Auteur en souffrance* 5). And yet, Glissant's utopianism and his general optimism with regard to the unpredictability of the future beg the question: why not the to-come? Glissant's Other of thought is not a state, something that one arrives at, but rather, as he puts it, a "movement," a "turbulence," an "action" (PR 169). And the ethics that it would generate are decidedly not "given in advance" (PR 169). Some ideas, for Glissant, can only be approached (read: neither grasped nor pinned down) through a chaotic, and perhaps impossible, literary melding of poetics and philosophy. Returning to the title of his 1969 essay *L'intention poétique*, Glissant insists that "a poetic intention can allow me to conceive that in my relation to the other, to others, to all others, to the totality-world, I change myself while exchanging, while remaining myself . . . one needs a whole poetics to conceive of those impossibles" (IPD 103).

Glissant's speaking paradoxically, his asking us to think the impossible (*"Nothing is True, all is living"*), both represent a means of bringing about experimental change in readers, through shaking up and reformulating fundamental categories of thought. Such experiments seek to bring something new into the world—and the nature of that something new is, by necessity, unknown in the present. It does not fall to Glissant, who has proclaimed himself to be "solitary but in solidarity," to prescribe particular interpretations or actions (IPD 143). Rather, Glissant's texts encourage us to rethink our ideas, to rethink even the way we think or what thought might be capable of doing—in other words, to engage with what Glissant calls the Other of thought. In his efforts to gloss that Glissantian enigma, Drabinski shows that Glissant thinks of thought in terms of process over product, thereby fusing thought with becoming. The Other of thought shows, for Drabinski, that "Glissant's vision of the Caribbean is that of a form of knowing as irreducibly becoming, moving across the dynamic space of thinking and its other without cessation" (*Levinas* 152).

Glissant's essays foreground paradox in their constant returns to the Caribbean as a creative locus even at their moments of highest abstraction. The problems they isolate as they do so can be grouped together in broad strokes by a turn to the correlation in Glissant's work (and particularly in his figure of the Other of thought) between *being* and *thought*. Anjali Prabhu explains the being-thought relationship in Hegelian language in her clarification of Glissant's "Other of thought." Prabhu deciphers Glissant's riddle by holding that it "explodes the cognitive into a social act" (87). The mere fact of attempting to think through Glissantian ideas, of engaging with thought's other, would thus constitute the beginnings of a social activity. Glissant himself, as we have seen, posits a causal relationship between thought and being, where a change in thought must precede a change in lived experience. For Glissant, only by changing "the imaginary, the mentality and the drives of today's humanities" can the reality of the totality-world be preserved and protected (IPD 134). Spelling out exactly what sort of social change he has in mind, Glissant insists that scenes of slaughter such as those of Rwanda or the former Yugoslavia will be repeated if the imaginary that he advocates is not taken up (IPD 90–91). It is the task of art and of the artist, the calling of the philosopher-poet, to change our imaginaries. And concrete change in the world will be the result (cf. IPD 56–57).

Our task as readers of Glissant is a different one, however. Glissant's paradoxical philosophizing calls for continuous *experimentation and experience* rather than fixed and final comprehension (PR 206). It prompts readers to reread and rethink Glissant's own work, while the Glissantian corpus experiments in its turn with thinking through contradiction and ambiguity, ad infinitum. If we are to persist today in taking philosophy to be the love of wisdom, then Glissantian philosophy is a love whose ardor builds as it recognizes its object as at once present and forever fleeing, and as an object that is for that reason all the more vivacious and worthy of wonder. What Dash says of the first four decades of Glissant's career would therefore hold for the last two as well—for the late as for the early Glissant, in other words: "This oeuvre," in Dash's view, "is still very much a work in progress. This will always be the case because of its innate restlessness and circularity, as each theoretical construct is undone or extended by a deconstructing poetic energy. In a sense, there has always been a creative chaos to Glissant's thought" (*Glissant* 182). That oscillation between robust, theoretical argumentation and its subsequent contradiction or deconstruction does indeed operate at the heart of Glissantian methodology. It is always unsettled and at times unsettling, resistant to conclusion and unwilling to cease creation. Glissant's vision of the future is traversed by his injunction to "change our imaginaries," to read, to think, and then to live otherwise (CL 34). And therein lies its transformative potential in the barest sense, as Glissant points us in the direction of further creation, of new and other forms of being and thought. He works to trigger ways of thinking and writing that will reflect his vision of the world, just as they offer glimpses of the future literature whose advent they herald. That literature to come would be, in Glissant's words, "the obscure and the too-vast, the too-luminous"; it would be "fragile, ambiguous, ephemeral, but it would shine with all of the world's contradictory radiances" (IL 116–17; FM 140).

Notes

Introduction

1. All translations from the French or Spanish, be they citations or the titles of other texts, are hereafter my own unless otherwise specified.
2. My use of this process-product distinction owes much to the thought of Professor Helene Meyers of Southwestern University.
3. The website edouardglissant.fr, launched during the author's lifetime and still in a state of growth and flux, features a recording of that talk, in addition to a remarkable wealth of information on Glissant's life, including videos, photos, and autobiographical notes.
4. See, for example: Carminella Biondi and Elena Pessini, *Rêver le monde, Ecrire le monde: Théorie et narrations d'Édouard Glissant* (2004); Dominique Chancé, *Édouard Glissant: un 'traité du déparler'* (2002); Katell Colin, *Le Roman-monde d'Édouard Glissant: Totalisation et tautologie* (2008); Georges Desportes, *La Paraphilosophie d'Édouard Glissant* (2008); Romuald Fonkoua, *Essai sur une mesure du monde au XXème siècle: Édouard Glissant* (2004); Samia Kassab-Charfi, *Et L'Une et l'autre face des choses: La déconstruction poétique de l'Histoire dans* Les Indes *et* Le Sel noir *d'Édouard Glissant* (2011); Jean-Pol Madou, *Édouard Glissant: De mémoire d'arbres* (2004); Alain Ménil, *Les Voies de la créolisation: essai sur Édouard Glissant* (2011); Manuel Norvat, *Le Chant du Divers: la 'philopoétique' d'Édouard Glissant* (2015); Aliocha Wald Lasowski, *Édouard Glissant, penseur des archipels* (2015).
5. Cf. *Mémoires des esclavages: La fondation d'un centre national pour la mémoire des esclavages et de leurs abolitions, Préface de Dominique de Villepin* (2007); *Quand les murs tombent: L'identité nationale*

hors-la-loi? avec Patrick Chamoiseau (2007); *L'intraitable beauté du monde: Adresse à Barack Obama, avec Patrick Chamoiseau* (2009); *Manifeste pour les 'produit' de haute nécessité, avec Patrick Chamoiseau, Ernest Breleur, Serge Domi, Gérard Delver, Guillaume Pigeard de Gurbert, Olivier Portecop, Olivier Pulvar, Jean-Claude William* (2009); or *10 mai: Mémoires de la traite négrière, de l'esclavage et de leurs abolitions* (2010).
6. Valérie Loichot's *Orphan Narratives* (2007) skillfully analyzes the various permutations of authority and influence among Glissant, his fellow writers, and even his fictional characters.

Chapter One

1. Catriona Cunningham raises doubts as to whether Glissant's emphasis on *terre* over *territoire* succeeds in leaving behind the logic of private property. Hers is an important question, given the privileged status Glissant accords to Martinique as an ideal vantage point from which to see and know the world-as-whole. For Cunningham, "It is somewhat paradoxical that despite Glissant's emphasis on the rhizomatic 'lieu' rather than the more rooted 'territoire,' the sense of personal outrage that pervades his description of this violation [of Martinican territory] implies that there is a strong attachment to the land itself" (290).
2. This title is inspired by Romuald Fonkoua's *Essai sur une nouvelle mesure du monde au XXème siècle: Édouard Glissant* (*Essay on a New Measure of the World in the Twentieth Century: Édouard Glissant*), Paris: Honoré Champion, 2002.
3. For an in-depth discussion of Glissant's points of convergence and divergence with Deleuze and Hegel, particularly with regard to the questions of dialectics and difference, as well as the relationship of difference to landscape in Glissant's works, see Britton's *Language and Literary Form in French Caribbean Writing*, pp. 159–61 and 164–66.
4. Glissant is not always consistent with his use of capitalization (R/relation) or hyphens ("totality-world" vs. "totality world"). My English translations of his French carry over Glissant's uses of capitalization or hyphens as they appear in the original.
5. Unless otherwise indicated, all citations of this text are drawn from the original, one-page version of the "Pour une littérature-monde en

français" newspaper article, and will hereafter go without parenthetical documentation for that reason. Citations drawn from Le Bris's chapter with the same title, in the collection also bearing the same title, are cited by use of their author's name.

Chapter Two

1. Here as elsewhere, Glissant plays on the distinction in French between *langage* and *langue*, both of which are customarily rendered as *language* in English. The two terms and the distinction between them have meant different things for different thinkers throughout history. For Glissant's purposes, *langage* refers principally to the general code or sign system through which the subject frames his or her world. *Langue*, on the other hand, represents a particular, concrete linguistic instantiation of *langage*. In French more generally, *langage* signifies "word choice" or "diction" (as in "a rather Shakespearian language"). *Langue*, however, corresponds to the English word *tongue*, in terms of both the anatomical feature and the language spoken by a person (as in "the English language"). This contrast allowed Glissant to argue in 2005 that authors writing in the various languages (*langues*) of the Caribbean speak a common language (*langage*).
2. Mary Gallagher sketches some points of connection between Glissant and that other thinker of alterity, Emmanuel Levinas, in her "La poétique de la diversité dans les essais d'Édouard Glissant" ("The Poetics of Diversity in the Essays of Édouard Glissant").
3. *Faulkner, Mississippi* betrays a fascination with Faulkner's choice of the word *endure* to describe the suffering of his black characters (cf. 87, et passim).
4. For a discussion of this name, its history, and its meanings in relation to opacity, see Celia Britton's *Édouard Glissant and Postcolonial Theory* (160–63).
5. Glissant's revaluation of this "bastard complex" recalls Deleuze's people that is invented by literature—a bastard, minor people—which Deleuze opposes to the aspirations to racial purity on the part of other, major peoples that would seek to dominate the minor people: "Maybe it only exists in the writer's atoms, a bastard, inferior, dominated people, always in a state of becoming (*en devenir*), always incomplete. Bastard no longer designates a family status, but rather the process

or the drift of races" (*Critique* 14). This "drift [*dérive*] of races," like Glissant's creolization, grants a privileged position for political action.

> Literature is delirium, but the delirium is not a matter of mommy-daddy . . . Delirium is a sickness, sickness *par excellence*, each time it elevates a race pretended to be pure and dominant, but it is the measure of health when it invokes this bastard, oppressed race that never ceases to writhe beneath dominations, to resist everything that crushes and imprisons, and to appear implicitly in literature when it is taken as a process. (*Critique* 15)

6. This written, Batouto language even begins to infect Glissant's French, as the adjective *batouto* comes to agree with the French noun it modifies: for example, "sa nature batoutoo" (*Sartorius* 215).
7. Glissant's emphasis on Faulkner could, I would submit, be seen as vulnerable to J. Michael Dash's critique of the all-too-common assignation of what amounts to a single origin to Francophone Caribbean writing: that is, the Surrealist contact ("Caraïbe Fantôme: The Play of Difference in the Francophone Caribbean").
8. While Glissant's definition of the epic turns around concepts such as "source" and "roots," the *Concise Oxford Dictionary of Literary Terms* does not accord primary importance to them, defining the epic as "a long narrative poem celebrating the great deeds of one or more legendary heroes, in a grand ceremonious style. The hero, usually protected by or even descended from gods, performs superhuman exploits in battle or in marvellous voyages, often saving or founding a nation . . ."
9. With Patrick Chamoiseau in *Quand les murs tombent: l'identité nationale hors-la-loi?*, Glissant writes that "The same skin can clothe different imaginaries [*imaginaires*] . . . Madam Condoleezza Rice draws on the same imaginary as Mr. George W. Bush, and has nothing to do with Mr. Mandela or with Martin Luther King."

Chapter Three

1. Not incidentally, as Cilas Kemedjio notes, *Tout-monde* is also "the novel in which the presence of contemporary Africa is most concrete, unlike the earlier novels where Africa is above all linked with that which is impossible to extricate from the obscurity of the Africa that it was" (108).

2. In other words, if the speaker claims that he or she "Does not control the emission of speech" (IPD 131), how are readers to evaluate the authority, the truth-value, of that particular statement, made by the selfsame speaker?
3. Again, for Glissant this distinction is rather moot, given that for him the novelistic and the artistic modes of creation are, in his words, "two sides of the same dimension" (cf. "L'Europe et les Antilles").

Chapter Four

1. All citations in this chapter are from *Philosophie de la Relation* unless otherwise specified.
2. In his "Late Glissant: History, 'World Literature,' and the Persistence of the Political" (2010), Charles Forsdick draws inspiration from a late work of Edward Said, published posthumously, as he approaches Glissant's end-of-life production.

   > Said's thesis is that the final works of many great artists are characterized by a "late style" that is to be understood "not as harmony and resolution, but as intransigence, difficulty and unresolved contradiction." The book thus contradicts the received wisdom that late works customarily "crown a lifetime of aesthetic endeavour," positing instead that for certain artists and writers—Said's principal examples include figures such as Beethoven and Ibsen—late works may instead provide "an occasion to stir up more anxiety, tamper irrevocably with the possibility of closure, and leave the audience more perplexed and unsettled than before." The notion of *lateness* is thus to be associated with a series of other critical positions explored in Said's work, most notably the *exilic*, the *liminal*, and the *contrapuntal*, with the third of these in particular reflected in the idea that "late style" is "in, but oddly *apart* from the present." (122)

3. In a subsection titled "The Caribbean Writer as Prophet and Shaman?" Antoinette Tidjani Alou holds that Glissant is especially inclined toward this discursive stance.

   > Many Caribbean writers seem to be mythically engaged at several levels. At least, this appears to be true in the case of

many of the earlier writers, and it is certainly true of Glissant. But what do we mean by this? Writers seem to believe that they have a Godgiven or self-appointed duty to do something about the Caribbean situation evoked above. They seem to set themselves the task of rediscovering origin, exploring chthonic realms, of reconstructing the deleted past, inventing foundations myths and ancestors. Self-appointed questers or elected intermediaries, they invent meaningful symbols meant to heal the traumatized, to revive enthusiasm, to lead the lost home. To repair ruptured relationships, to "know and to teach," to open the universe, to erect monuments of landscape, to bring into the world. They seem to cast themselves as redeemers, elects, prophet or shamanic types, if we take their "manifests" or "intentions" at face value. (169)

Conclusion

1. Glissant's reasoning here exhibits remarkable parallels with Deleuze's treatment of the quantity-quality distinction for Nietzsche in his *Nietzsche et la philosophie* (pp. 48–53). In Deleuze's reading,

   > [E]ach time that [Nietzsche] critiques quality, we must understand: qualities are nothing, if not the difference in quantity to which they correspond . . . In short, what interests Nietzsche is never the irreducibility of quantity to quality; or rather that only interests him secondarily, or as a symptom. What primarily interests him is, from the point of view of quantity itself, the irreducibility of the difference in quantity to equality. Quality is different from quantity, but only because it is that which is un-equalizable in quantity, that which is un-cancelable in the difference of quantity. The difference of quantity is therefore in one sense the irreducible element *of* quantity, and it is in another sense the element that is irreducible *to* quantity itself. Quality is nothing else than the difference of quantity, and corresponds to it in each force that is in relation. (49–50)

2. Translated by L. Scott-Fox and J. M. Harding as *Modern French Philosophy* (Cambridge UP, 1980).

Works Cited

Alou, Antoinette Tidjani. "Myths of a New World in Édouard Glissant's Novels *La Lézarde* and *Le quatrième siècle*." *Tydskrif vir Letterkunde* 44.2 (2007): 163–78.

André, Jacques. "Le renversement de Senglis: Histoires et filiations." Paris: *Centre Antillais de Recherches et d'Etudes*, N. 10, 1983. 32–51.

Aranjo, Daniel. "L'opacité chez Édouard Glissant ou la poétique de la souche." *Horizons d'Édouard Glissant: actes du colloque international*. Eds. Yves-Alain Favre and Antonio Ferreira de Brito. N.p.: J & D Éditions, 1992. 93–112.

Barnes, Natasha. *Cultural Conundrums: Gender, Race, Nation and the Makings of Caribbean Cultural Politics*. Ann Arbor: U of Michigan P, 2006.

Barthes, Roland. *Image, Music, Text*. Trans. Stephen Heath. New York: Hill and Wang, 1977.

Baugh, Bruce. *French Hegel: From Surrealism to Postmodernism*. New York: Routledge, 2003.

Benítez Rojo, Antonio. *La isla que se repite*. [1989] Barcelona: Editorial Casiopea, 1998.

Bernabé, Jean, Patrick Chamoiseau, and Raphaël Confiant. *Eloge de la créolité*. Paris: Gallimard, 1989.

Bhabha, Homi. *The Location of Culture*. New York: Routledge, 2004.

Biondi, Carminella, and Elena Pessini. *Rêver le monde, Ecrire le monde. Théorie et narrations d'Édouard Glissant*, Bologne, CLUEB, 2004.

Bloom, Harold. *The Anxiety of Influence: A Theory of Poetry*. New York: Oxford UP, 1973.

Bongie, Chris. *Islands and Exiles: The Creole Identities of Post/Colonial Literature*. Stanford: Stanford UP, 1998.

———. "Resisting Memories: The Creole Identities of Lafcadio Hearn and Édouard Glissant." *Substance* 26.3.84 (1997): 153–78.

Britton, Celia. "'Always Changing, while Still Remaining': A Tribute to Édouard Glissant." *Small Axe* 15.3 (2011): 108–14.

———. *Édouard Glissant and Postcolonial Theory: Strategies of Language and Resistance*. Ed. James A. Arnold. New World Studies. Charlottesville: UP of Virginia, 1999.

———. *Language and Literary Form in French Caribbean Writing*. Liverpool: Liverpool UP, 2014.

Cailler, Bernadette. "*Sartorius. Le roman des Batoutos*, ou la brisure de l'o/eau." *Migrances, Diasporas et Transculturalités Francophones: Littératures et cultures d'Afrique, des Caraïbes, d'Europe et du Québec*. Eds. Hafid Gafaïti, Patricia M. E. Lorcin, and David G. Troyansky. Paris: L'Harmattan, 2005. 257–76.

Césaire, Aimé. "Entretien avec Aimé Césaire, Paris, 1975, à l'occasion de la réédition de *Tropiques* (Paris: Editions Jean-Michel Place, 1978). 5–38." *Aimé Césaire: le terreau primordial*. Ed. Jacqueline Leiner. Tübingen: Narr, 1993. 111–27.

Chamoiseau, Patrick. "De la problématique du territoire à la problématique du lieu: Entretien avec Patrick Chamoiseau." *JSTOR* 73.4 (2000): 724633.

Chancé, Dominique. *Édouard Glissant: un «traité du déparler*. Paris: Karthala, 2002.

———. *L'auteur en souffrance. Essai sur la position et la représentation de l'auteur dans le roman antillais contemporain (1981–1992)*. Paris: Presses Universitaires de France, 2000.

———. *Les fils de Lear: É. Glissant, V.S. Naipaul, J. E. Wideman*. Paris: Editions Karthala, 2003.

Colin, Katell: *Le Roman-monde d'Édouard Glissant: Totalisation et tautologie*. Québec: Presses Universitaires de Laval, 2008.

Cornette, Jérôme. "The *Recherche* as 'Tout-monde': Toward a Francophone Proust." *Contemporary French and Francophone Studies* 9.1 (2005): 87–95.

Coursil, Jacques. "La Catégorie de la Relation dans les essais d'Édouard Glissant: Philosophie d'une poétique." *Poétiques d'Édouard Glissant: Actes du colloque international, Paris-Sorbonne, 11–13 mars 1998*. Ed. Jacques Chevrier. Paris: Presses de l'Université de Paris-Sorbonne, 1999. 86–112.

Crosta, Susan. "Des poétiques de relation et de globalisation dans la Caraïbe francophone." *Convergences and Interferences: Newness in Intercultural Practices*. Eds. Kathleen Gyssels, Isabel Hoving, and Maggie Ann Bowers. New York: Rodopi, 2001. 29–42.

Crowley, Patrick. "Édouard Glissant: Resistance and *Opacité*." *Romance Studies* 24.2 (2006): 105–115.

Cunningham, Catriona. "Reclaiming 'Paradise Lost' in the Writings of Patrick Chamoiseau and Édouard Glissant." *French Cultural Studies* 18.3 (2007): 277–91.

Dash, J. Michael. "Caraïbe Fantôme: The Play of Difference in the Francophone Caribbean." *Yale French Studies* 103 (2006): 93–105.

———. *Édouard Glissant*. Cambridge Studies in African and Caribbean Literature. Cambridge: Cambridge UP, 1995.

Deleuze, Gilles. *Critique et clinique*. Paris: Editions de Minuit, 1993.

———. *Nietzsche et la philosophie*. 1962. Paris: Quadrige/PUF, 2003.

———, and Félix Guattari. *Kafka: Pour une littérature mineure*. Paris: Les Editions de Minuit, 1975.

———, and Félix Guattari. *L'Anti-Oedipe. Capitalisme et Schizophrénie 1*. Paris: Les Editions de Minuit, 1980.

———, and Félix Guattari. *Mille plateaux. Capitalisme et Schizophrénie 2*. Paris: Les Editions de Minuit, 1980.

———, and Claire Parnet. *Dialogues*. 1977. Paris: Flammarion, 1996.

Desportes, Georges. *La Paraphilosophie d'Édouard Glissant*. Paris: L'Harmattan, 2008.

Drabinski, John E. *Levinas and the Postcolonial: Race, Nation, Other*. Edinburgh: Edinburgh UP, 2013.

———. "What Is Trauma to the Future? On Glissant's Poetics." *Critical Humanities and Social Sciences* 18.2 (2010): 291–307.

"Epic." *The Concise Oxford Dictionary of Literary Terms*. Ed. Christopher Baldick. Oxford UP, 1996. *Oxford Reference Online*. Oxford UP. U of P. 1 October 2007. http://www.oxfordreference.com/views/ENTRY.html?subview=Main&entry=t56.e320.

Fanon, Frantz. *Peau noire, masques blancs*. Paris: Editions du Seuil, 1952.

Faulkner, William. *Sartoris*. 1929. New York: The New American Library of World Literature, 1964.

Ferrier, Michaël F. "Creole Japan; or, The Vagaries of Creolization." *Small Axe* 14.3 33 (2010): 33–44.

Fonkoua, Romuald. *Essai sur une nouvelle mesure du monde au XXème siècle*: *Édouard Glissant*. Paris: Honoré Champion, 2002.

Forsdick, Charles. "Late Glissant: History, "World Literature," and the Persistence of the Political." *Small Axe* 14. 3 33 (2010): 121–34.

Foucault, Michel. "What Is an Author?" *The Foucault Reader*. Ed. Paul Rabinow. New York: Pantheon Books, 1984. 101–20.

Gallagher, Mary. "La poétique de la diversité dans les essais d'Édouard Glissant." *Horizons d'Édouard Glissant*: *actes du colloque international*. Eds. Yves-Alain Favre and Antonio Ferreira de Brito. N.p.: J & D Éditions, 1992. 27–35.

———. *Soundings in French Caribbean Writing Since 1950*: *The Shock of Space and Time*. New York: Oxford UP, 2002.

———, ed. *Ici-Là*: *Place and Displacement in Caribbean Writing in French*. Amsterdam: Editions Rodopi, 2003.

Garraway, Doris. L. "Toward a Creole Myth of Origin: Narrative, Foundations and Eschatology in Patrick Chamoiseau's *L'esclave vieil homme et le molosse*." *Callaloo* 29.1 (2006): 151–67.

Glissant, Édouard. "Au fond du miroir." *Le quinzaine littéraire* n. 437. 1—15 April 1985, p. 7.

———. *Faulkner, Mississippi*. Paris: Editions Stock, 1996.

———. *Introduction à une poétique du Divers*. Paris: Gallimard, 1996.

———. *La cohée du Lamentin*. Paris: Gallimard, 2005.

———. *La case du commandeur*. Paris: Gallimard, 1981.

———. "La 'créolisation' culturelle du monde, entretien avec Édouard Glissant." By Tirthankar Chanda. *France diplomatie*. 27 Oct. 2005. Ministère des Affaires Etrangères et Européennes. 1 Oct. 2007. http://www.diplomatie.gouv.fr/fr/.

———. *La Lézarde*. Paris: Editions du Seuil, 1958.

———. *Le discours antillais*. 1981. Paris: Gallimard, 1997.

———. "Le monde entier se créolise." *Outre-mers, notre monde*: *entretiens d'Oudinot*. Paris: Éditions Autrement, 2002. 210–13.

———. *Le quatrième siècle*. Paris: Editions Gallimard, 1964.

———. *Le traité du Tout-Monde*. Paris: Gallimard, 1997.

———. "L'Europe et les Antilles: Une interview d'Édouard Glissant." *Mots Pluriels*. May 1998, Jan. 2008. motspluriels.arts.uwa.edu.au.

———. *L'intention poétique*. Paris: Editions du Seuil, 1969.

———. *Mahagony*. Paris: Editions du Seuil, 1987.

———. *Mémoires des esclavages. La fondation d'un centre national pour la*

mémoire des esclavages et de leurs abolitions. Paris: Gallimard, 2007.
———. *Ormerod*. Paris: Gallimard, 2003.
———. *Poetics of Relation*. Trans. Betsy Wing. Ann Arbor: U of Michigan P, 1997.
———. *Poétique de la Relation*. Poétique III. Paris: Gallimard, 1990.
———. *Sartorius: le roman des Batoutos*. Paris: Gallimard, 1999.
———. *Soleil de la conscience*. Paris: Éditions du Seuil, 1956.
———. "Solitaire et Solidaire." *Pour une littérature-monde*. Eds. Michel Le Bris and Jean Rouaud. Paris, Gallimard 2007. 77–86.
———. "'Supposez le vol de milliers d'oiseaux sur un lac africain' . . ." *Outre-mers, notre monde: entretiens d'Oudinot*. Paris: Éditions Autrement, 2002. 14–21.
———. *Tout-Monde*. Paris: Gallimard, 1993.
———. *Une nouvelle région du monde*. Paris: Gallimard, 2006.
———. "Un peuple invisible pour sauver le monde reel." Interview with Héric Libong et Boniface Mongo-Mboussa. *Africultures*. www.africultures.com. Nov. 1999, 24 Aug. 2016.
———. *Visite à Édouard Glissant: entretiens réunis par Gérard Cléry*. By Claude Couffon. Paris: Editions Caractères, 2001.
———, and Ernest Breleur, Patrick Chamoiseau, Serge Domi, Gérard Delver, Guillaume Pigeard de Gurbert, Olivier Portecop, Olivier Pulvar, Jean-Claude William. *Manifeste pour les 'produits' de haute nécessité*. Paris: Galaade, 2009.
———, and Patrick Chamoiseau. *Quand les murs tombent: l'identité nationale hors-la-loi?* Paris: Galaade Éditions, 2007.
———, and Patrick Chamoiseau. *L'intraitable beauté du monde. Adresse à Barack Obama*. Paris: Galaade, 2009.
———, and Lise Gauvin. *L'Imaginaire des langues: Entretiens avec Lise Gauvin (1991–2009)*. Paris: Gallimard, 2010.
———, and the Institut du Tout-monde. *10 Mai: Mémoires de la traite négrière, de l'esclavage et de leurs abolitions*. Paris: Galaade, 2010.
Gordon, Ann Jane, and Neil Roberts, eds. *Creolizing Rousseau*. New York: Rowan and Littlefield, 2015.
Gourgouris, Stathis. *Does Literature Think? Literature as Theory for an Antimythical Era*. Stanford: Stanford UP, 2003.
Hallward, Peter. "Édouard Glissant Between the Singular and the Specific." *Yale Journal of Criticism* 11.2 (1998). 441–64.
———. *Out of This World: Deleuze and the Philosophy of Creation*. New York: Verso, 2006.

Henry, Paget. *Caliban's Reason: Introducing Afro-Caribbean Philosophy.* London: Routledge, 2002.

Hess, Deborah M. *La poétique de renversement chez Maryse Condé, Massa Makan Diabaté et Édouard Glissant.* Paris: L'Harmattan, 2006.

Hocine, Hamid, and Brigitte Marin. "Les identités blessées: onomastique, mal-être et quête de soi dans la littérature d'expression française." *Synergies Algérie* 16 (2012): 13–25.

Huddart, David. *Homi K. Bhabha.* London: Routledge, 2006.

Irigaray, Luce. *Ethique de la différence sexuelle.* Paris: Editions de Minuit, 1984.

Joubert, Jean-Louis. "L'Archipel Glissant." *Poétiques d'Édouard Glissant: Actes du colloque international, Paris-Sorbonne, 11–13 mars 1998.* Ed. Jacques Chevrier. Paris: Presses de l'Université de Paris-Sorbonne, 1999. 317–322.

Kassab-Charfi, Samia. *Et L'Une et l'autre face des choses: La déconstruction poétique de l'Histoire dans* Les Indes *et* Le Sel noir *d'Édouard Glissant.* Paris: Honoré Champion, 2011.

Kemedjio, Cilas. "Founding-Ancestors and Intertextuality in Francophone Caribbean Literature and Criticism." *Research in African Literatures* 33.2 (2002): 210–29.

Lambert, Gregg. "On the Uses and Abuses of Literature for Life: Gilles Deleuze and the Literary Clinic." *Postmodern Culture* 8.3 (1998). *Project Muse.* 23 Aug. 2005. www.library.upenn.edu.

Le Bris, Michel. "Pour une littérature monde." *Pour une littérature-monde.* Eds. Michel Le Bris and Jean Rouaud. Paris, Gallimard, 2007.

Le Bris, Michel, Jean Rouaud, and Nathalie Skowronek, eds. *Je est un autre: pour une identité-monde.* Paris: Gallimard, 2012.

Leupin, Alexandre. "The Slave's *Jouissance.*" *Callaloo* 36.4 (2013): 891–901.

Lionnet, Françoise. *Autobiographical Voices: Race, Gender, Self-Portraiture.* Ithaca: Cornell UP, 1989.

Lionnet, Françoise, and Shu-mei Shih, eds. *The Creolization of Theory.* Durham: Duke UP, 2011.

Loichot, Valérie. *Orphan Narratives: The Postplantation Literature of Faulkner, Glissant, Morrison, and Saint-John Perse.* Charlotte: U of Virginia P, 2007.

Madou, Jean-Pol. *Édouard Glissant: De mémoire d'arbres.* Amsterdam/Atlanta: Rodopi, 1996.

Malela, Buata. "La mondialisation culturelle dans la pratique littéraire afro-antillaise: l'exemple d'Édouard Glissant. *French Studies Bulletin: a Quarterly Supplement* 110 (2009): 1–12.

Mengue, Philippe. *Gilles Deleuze ou le système du multiple*. Paris: Editions Kimé, 1994.

Ménil, Alain. *Les Voies de la créolisation: essai sur Édouard Glissant*. Paris: De l'Incendie éditeur, 2011.

Miller, Christopher. *Theories of Africans: Francophone Literature and Anthropology in Africa*. Chicago: U of Chicago P, 1990.

Moudileno, Lydie. "Positioning the 'French' 'Caribbean' 'Woman' Writer." *Feasting on Words: Maryse Condé, Cannibalism, and the Caribbean Text*. Eds. Vera Broichhagen, Kathryn Lachman, and Nicole Simek. Princeton, NJ: PLAS Cuadernos 8, 2006. 123–45.

———. *L'écrivain antillais au miroir de sa littérature*. Paris: Karthala, 1997.

———. "Retrouver la parole perdue. Le récit d'esclave reconstitué (Édouard Glissant)." *Romanic Review* 90.1 (1999): 83–91.

Murdoch, Adlai. *Creole Identity in the French Caribbean Novel*. Gainesville: UP of Florida, 2001.

———. "(Re)Figuring Colonialism: Narratological and Ideological Resistance." *Callaloo* 15.1 (1992): 2–11.

"Mystical." *Merriam-Webster's Online Dictionary*. 2006–2007.

"Nation." *Merriam-Webster's Online Dictionary*. 2006–2007.

Nesbitt, Nick. *Caribbean Critique: Antillean Critical Theory from Toussaint to Glissant*. Liverpool: Liverpool UP, 2013.

———. "The Postcolonial Event: Deleuze, Glissant and the Problem of the Political." *Deleuze and the Postcolonial*. Eds. Simone Bignall and Paul Patton. Edinburgh UP, 2010. 103–18.

Norvat, Manuel. *Le Chant du Divers: la "philopoétique" d'Édouard Glissant*. Paris: L'Harmattan, 2015

Noudelmann, François. "Glissant le déchiffreur." *Litterature* 154 (2009): 36–42.

N'Zengou-Tayo, Marie-José. "Can Language Free us from Subordination?" *Callaloo* 23.4. (2000): 1514–15.

"Panoply." *Merriam-Webster's Online Dictionary*. 2006–2007.

"Para." *Merriam-Webster's Online Dictionary*. 2006–2007.

Patel, Alpesh Kantilal, Encarnación Gutiérrez Rodríguez, and Shirley Anne Tate, eds. *Creolizing Europe: Legacies and Transformations* (*Migrations and Identities*). Liverpool: Liverpool UP, 2015.

Porra, Véronique. "'Pour une littérature-monde en français: Les limites d'un discours utopique." *Intercâmbio*. 2nd Ser., 1. (2008): 33–54.

Prabhu, Anjali. "Interrogating Hybridity: Subaltern Agency and Totality in Postcolonial Theory." *Diacritics* 35.2 (2005) 76–92.

Salmon, Christian. *Tombeau de la fiction: essai*. Paris: Denoël, 1999.
Santí, Enrico Mario. "El paradigma, o paradoja, del Caribe." *El Caribe como paradigma: Convivencias y coincidencias históricas, culturales y estéticas. Un simposio transareal*. Eds. Ottmar Ette, Anne Kraume, Werner Mackenbach, and Gesine Müller. Berlin: Edition Tranvía, Verlag Walter Frey, 2012. 58–68.
Smart, Barry. *Michel Foucault*. New York: Routledge, 2002.
Suk, Jeannie. *Postcolonial Paradoxes in French Caribbean Writing: Césaire, Glissant, Condé*. New York: Oxford UP, 2001.
Toledo, Camille de. *Visiter le Flurkistan ou les illusions de la littérature-monde*. Paris: PUF, 2008.
Toumson, Roger. "Les polylogues d'Édouard Glissant." *Small Axe* 15.3 (2011): 115–23.
Van Haesendonck, Kristian, and Theo D'Haen, eds. *Caribbeing: Comparing Caribbean Literatures and Cultures*. Amsterdam: Editions Rodopi, 2014.
Wald Lasowski, Aliocha. "La Philosophie d'Édouard Glissant.' *Critique* 750 (2009): 971–80.
——. *Édouard Glissant, penseur des archipels*. Paris: 12–21, 2015.
Watts, Richard. "The 'Wounds of Locality': Living and Writing the Local in Patrick Chamoiseau's *Ecrire en pays dominé*." *French Forum* 28.1 (2003): 111–29.
Webster, Jane. "Creolizing the Roman Provinces." *American Journal of Archaeology* 105. 2 (2001): 209–225.
Weinstein, Philip M. *Becoming Faulkner: The Art and Life of William Faulkner*. New York: Oxford UP, 2010.

Index

absence/presence, 72, 103, 106–8
abyss(es), 11–12, 39, 100
Acoma (journal), xxxi
Afrocentrism, 62
Alou, Antoinette Tidjani, 139n3
alterity, xvii, 8, 97, 130–33; ethics of, xxvi, 37; opacity of, 39–42, 54, 57, 66; as philosophical category, xxxvii; Western humanism and, 38–39
American Indians, 40
André, Jacques, 88, 90
Aranjo, Daniel, 51
archipelagic thinking, xxii, xxviii, 21, 97–98, 109, 113–19; definitions of, 97, 113; system-thinking versus, 8–9, 114–15
archipelagoes, 11, 20–21, 112, 131; creolization and, 3–9, 104; as paradigm, 125–26, 133
"archipelago-izing," 3–9, 104, 115, 117, 119, 124
atavistic cultures, 11, 47, 48, 101, 126

Barnes, Natasha K., xix, 129

Barthes, Roland, 57
"bastard complex," 47, 137n5
Baudot, Alain, 71
Benítez Rojo, Antonio, xxiii, xxiv
Bernabé, Jean, xx–xxi
Béville, Albert, 71, 80, 81, 88
Bhabha, Homi, 20, 116, 130
bifidities, 108–9
Bildungsroman, 49, 68
Bloom, Harold, 58
Bongie, Chris, xiv–xv, xxxii–xxxiii, 45–46
Braidotti, Rosi, xxxviii
Britton, Celia, 9, 31, 127; on Glissant's early/late works, xxxii–xxxvi; on Glissant's language, 37; on opacity, 41, 47, 53
Bush, George W., 138n9

Cailler, Bernadette, 59–60
Camus, Albert, 57–58
Caribbean Studies, 105–6
Carpentier, Alejo, 36, 58
Césaire, Aimé, xxx, 50, 97; Hegel and, 18; language of, 58; Toledo on, 27

Chamoiseau, Patrick, xxxv, 81, 119–20; Chancé on, 85–86; Gallagher on, 87
Chamoiseau, Patrick, works of: *Eloge de la créolité*, xx–xxi; *Quand les murs tombent*, xxix, 138n9
Chancé, Dominique, xix–xx, 84–86, 106, 132
chaos, 75, 115–17, 130–33; poetics of, 70; sciences of, 95, 115–16; of *Tout-monde*, 15, 28–29, 31
chaos theory, xxxiii, xxxviii, 106, 116–17
"chaos-world" (*chaos-monde*), xxxiii, 34, 55, 115–16
Chirac, Jacques, xxix
Civil War (US), 39
colonialism, 8, 103, 122, 125; "hidden truth" of, 41; *mission civilisatrice* of, xviii, 18, 25; slavery and, xviii, 80, 92. See also postcolonialism
"community-world" (*communauté-monde*), 23–24
Confiant, Raphaël, xx–xxi, 85–86
"consciousness of consciousness," 6, 38–39
"consciousness-conscience," 103–5
continental thought, 8, 20, 98, 109, 112–15. See also archipelagic thinking
contradiction(s), 106, 120–21; ambiguity and, 126–27; Chancé on, xix; paradox and, xvi–xxviii, 127–28; in *Philosophie de la Relation*, xxviii, 98; of *Tout-monde*, xxv
contrepétrie ("play on words"), 106

Cornette, Jérôme, 70
counterpoetics, 37
Coursil, Jacques, xxxvii
creolization(s), xxii, 124–25; archipelagoes and, 3–9, 104; characteristics of, 6; creoleness versus, xx–xxi; definitions of, 5–6; Faulkner on, 39, 56; hybridity and, xxiv, 6, 39, 45–46, 59; modernity and, xli, 45, 50; origin myths and, 11; slave trade and, 11, 23, 88; "thought" of, 97, 105; unpredictability of, 3–7, 39, 104, 116, 120–21. See also hybridity
"creolizing," 3–6, 117, 119, 123, 125
Crosta, Susan, 59
Crowley, Patrick, 37
Cunningham, Catriona, 136n1

Darwish, Mahmoud, 97
Dash, J. Michael, xiii, 118, 138n7; on diversity, 21; on Glissant's early/late works, xxxii, 133; on opacity, 42, 53; on Relation, 9
Deleuze, Gilles, 76, 111; Faulkner and, 36, 56–59; on Nietzsche, 140n1; on opacity, 43, 58–59; on "a people that is missing," 35, 43, 46, 63–64, 87, 103, 137n5; on relationality, xxxix; on systems, 126
Deleuze/Guattari, xxxix–xl; on the arborescent, 90; on *expérimenter*, xxviii, 111, 133; Mengue on, 76; "nomadology" of, xxxiii; rhizome of, xxxviii, xl, 10; *Sartorius* and, xxvi; *Tout-monde* and, 69;

on vector of becoming, 49
Deleuze/Guattari, works of: *Anti-Oedipus*, 83; *Kafka: Toward a Minor Literature*, 35–36; *A Thousand Plateaus*, 69
dépassement, 15, 32
Derrida, Jacques, 43, 57, 84, 132
Descombes, Vincent, 130
Desportes, Georges, xxxviii
D'Haen, Theo, xvi
"dialectical consummation," 15, 21
dialectics, 108–9
différance, 43, 57, 84
digenèse ("digenesis"), 11, 63
Dominican Republic, 126
Drabinski, John E., xxxiv, 132

ek-stasis, 27
Eloge de la créolité (Bernabé et al.), xx–xxi
enthousiasme-monde, 28
epic, 62–63, 65, 72, 138n8
equality-in-difference, 122, 125, 140n1
"erratic dimension," 18, 115
essai, 117–18
ethnicities, 11, 13; ethnic cleansing and, 126, 133; Le Bris on, 26; origin myths of, 48–49, 89
experience/experimentation, xxviii, 111, 133

Fanon, Frantz, xxx, 2
Faulkner, William, 35–66, 98, 119; black characters in, xvii, xxvi, 40, 43; on Camus, 57–58; Deleuze and, 36, 56–59; "hidden truth" in, 41; language of, 40–41; *Philosophie de la Relation* on, xxvii; racism of, xxv–xxvi, 39–41, 56
Fonkoua, Romuald, 127
forgetting/memory, xxix, 12, 81–82, 84, 89
Forsdick, Charles, xiii, 139n2
Foucault, Michel: on authorship, 98–99, 119; "universal intellectual" of, xxviii, 103, 125
Francophonie, 24–27

Gallagher, Mary, xxii, 87, 116, 137n2
Garraway, Doris L., 62, 72
Gauvin, Lise, 31–32
genealogies, 60–63, 82, 88–89. *See also* origins
genetically modified organisms (GMOs), xxxv
genocide, 126, 133
Glissant, Édouard, xiii, xxvi–xxvii; birth name of, xxx; early/late works of, xiv–xv, xxxi–xxxvi, 133–34; self-representation of, 56–57, 119–28; teaching career of, xxxi, 56–57; websites of, xxviii, 114, 135n3
Glissant, Édouard, works of: *Faulkner, Mississippi*, xxxi, 12, 34–43, 53, 56–58, 61–65, 98, 107; *Introduction à une poétique du Divers*, 13, 55, 70, 72, 95, 104–5; *La case du commandeur*, 46; *La cohée du Lamentin*, xxxvii, 10, 63–64; *La Lézarde*, xxi, xxx, 71, 79, 89; *Le monde incréé*, 33; *L'intention poétique*, xxxi, 68, 119; *Mahagony*, 100, 117–18;

Glissant, Édouard (*continued*)
Malemort, xxxi; *Mémoires des esclavages*, xxix; *Ormerod*, 60–61; *Pour une littérature-monde*, 110; *Quand les murs tombent*, xxix, 138n9; "*Rien n'est Vrai, tout est vivant*", xiii, xxxi, 132; *Traité du Tout-monde*, xxxiii, 1, 5, 30, 67, 97; *Une nouvelle région du monde*, 1, 16–17, 30, 31, 96, 97, 106–7. *See also individual works*
"globality," 14–15, 28, 69, 101, 114, 121
globalization, xviii, 121, 123; "cataclysmic," 101; *Tout-monde* and, xxv, 1, 14, 121
Gourgouris, Stathis, 65
griots, xli, 17
Guattari, Félix, 59, 71. *See also* Deleuze/Guattari
Gutting, Gary, 131–32

Haiti, 126
Hallward, Peter, xxxii, xxxviii, 16, 32, 69
Harris, Wilson, 36, 58
Hegel, Georg Wilhelm Friedrich, xxx; Glissant and, xxi, xxi, xxxvii–xxxviii, xli, 15–17, 32–33, 133
Heidegger, Martin, 22, 96
Henry, Paget, xiv
Hess, Deborah, 53
"hidden source," 91–94
Huddart, David, 116
humanities, 38–39, 133; History of, 114; imaginary of, xxxiii–xxxiv, 100

hybridity, 6, 45–46, 116; Faulkner on, 39, 56; Santí on, xxiv. *See also* creolization

ici-là ("here-there"), 20–21, 32, 93
identity: cultural, 89; "ministry" of, xxix; quest for, 106; rhizome, xxxix, 10; root-, 10, 41, 101; "wending," 101
imaginary, xxxiv–xxxv, 3; of humanities, xxxiii–xxxiv, 100; "insurrection" of, xv, xxxv; of Relation, 12, 34, 105, 112, 123
"inextricable," 5, 13, 15, 56, 103, 125–26
Institut du Tout-Monde, xxxi, 1, 114; literary prize of, xxix
Institute Martiniquais d'Etudes, xxxi
interlacing, 52, 122–23
Irigaray, Luce, xxxiv, 38
Islam, 126

Joubert, Jean-Louis, 33, 117
jus soli, 49

Kafka, Franz, 35–36
Kemedjio, Cilas, 8, 64, 138n1
King, Martin Luther, Jr., 138n9

Lacan, Jacques, xxxiv
"language-world" (*langue-monde*), 27
langues/langages, xxxv, 58, 100, 137n1
Le Bris, Michel, 24–26, 137n5
Le discours antillais (Glissant), xv, xxix, xxxi, 37, 55; on cultural identity, 89; on *Tout-monde*, 75; on the "West," xviii
Le quatrième siècle (Glissant), xxvii,

67, 68, 80–91; Chamoiseau on, 81; Prix Charles Veillon for, xxi, xxxi; *Tout-monde* and, 70, 71, 75–76, 91–93
Leiner, Jacqueline, 18–19
Leupin, Alexandre, 16, 32
Levinas, Emmanuel, 137n2
Lévi-Strauss, Claude, 75
"liar's paradox," xiii, 72
Libong, Héric, 44–45
Lionnet, Françoise, xiii, 45, 46
literature, "new," xv, xxv, 33–34, 59–66, 93
littérature-monde movement, 2, 24–28, 110. *See also* World Literature
Loichot, Valérie, 136n6
Longoué, Papa = character
Lorde, Audre, xviii
lucidité, 40

Madou, Jean-Pol, 118
Malela, Buata, 107, 111
Mandela, Nelson, 138n9
Marley, Bob, 49
memory, xxix, 12, 17, 81–82, 84, 89
Mengue, Philippe, 76
Meyers, Helene, 135n2
Miller, Christopher, 25–26
Minh-ha, Trinh T., 45
mission civilisatrice, xviii, 18, 25. *See also* colonialism
mondalité. *See* "globality"
Mongo-Mboussa, Boniface, 45
Montaigne, Michel de, 118
Moudileno, Lydie, 8, 55, 58, 84, 100, 117–18, 129–30
Murdoch, H. Adlai, 88–89

Negritude movement, 10, 18, 47–48, 62, 80
neocolonialism, xviii, 18, 25; slavery and, 80, 92. *See also* postcolonialism
neoliberalism, 121. *See also* globalization
Nesbitt, Nick, xiv
Nietzsche, Friedrich, 19, 65, 122; Deleuze on, 140n1; revaluation of all values by, 6
Niger, Paul. *See* Béville, Albert
nihilism, 29, 83
Norvat, Manuel, xxxvii
Noudelmann, François, 109
N'Zengou-Tayo, Marie-José, 37

opacity, 35–43, 51–66, 72, 83, 110–11, 126–29; of alterity, 39–42, 54, 57, 66; Britton on, 47; definition of, 42; ethics of, 40; hidden source of, 91–94; influence of, xxvi; paradox and, 35, 36; Prabhu on, 43–44; right to, 35, 37, 41–42, 65, 125; solidarity and, 66; of totality, 54; transparency and, 38, 44, 66; of world, 100, 102
origin(s), 44–49, 52, 106; absence of, 72; creolization and, 11; genealogies of, 60–63, 82, 88–89; in *Philosophie de la Relation*, 97, 99–100
Ormerod, Beverly, 61–62
Orville, Xavier, 87
"O/other," xvii, xxxvii, 8; of thought, 130–33. *See also* alterity

pacotilleuses, 74, 75

paradox(es), 118; contradiction and, xvi–xxviii, 127–28; of directionality, 70; etymology of, xvi; of locution, 37–43; opacity and, 35, 36; paradigm and, xxiv, xli, 124–25; poetics of, 35; of *Tout-monde*, 28–34; of vision, 43–53; vitalism and, 130

paraphilosophie, xxxviii, 81, 95, 127

Perse, Saint-John, 59

Philosophie de la Relation (Glissant), xvii, xxvii–xxviii, 27, 93–114, 113, 128–29; contradiction in, xxviii, 98; development of, xxxix; opacity in, 110–11, 128

place-totality relationship, 17–24, 129; archipelagoes and, 20–21; sense of belonging and, 33

Plato, xli, 17, 83

poetics, 116; of chaos, 70; counter-, 37; of paradox, 35; philosophy and, xxxvii–xxxix, 133; politics and, xxxv; of Relation, 9–10, 16, 21–24, 42–43, 73; "utopian," xxxii

Poétique de la Relation (Glissant), xxix, xxxi, 23, 53–54, 73, 95–96, 109, 123–24; Britton on, xxiii; development of, xxxix; opening of, 100; vitalism and, 129; world history and, 106

Postcolonial Studies, 10, 20, 26, 130

postcolonialism, xix–xxviii, 126, 128; Bongie on, 45–46; literature of, 26, 130; Murdoch on, 89; Suk on, xl; Toledo on, 27. *See also* colonialism

poststructuralism, xl, 19–20

"Pour une littérature-monde en français," 2, 24, 136n5; Toledo on, 26–28

Prabhu, Anjali, 43–44, 133

Prieto, Eric, 26, 28, 30–31, 128

Prix Carbet de la Caraïbe et du Tout-monde, xxix, 1

Prix Charles Veillon, xxi, xxxi

Prix Goncourt, 25

Prix Renaudot, xxi, xxx, 25

quantity versus quality, 121–22, 140n1

quimboiseur (shaman), xxvii, 67, 71, 81–82

"racial mixing," 39, 56. *See also* hybridity

Rastafarians, 49

Relation, xxvi–xxvii, 4, 9–12, 104–5, 111, 120; Britton on, xxxiii; definitions of, 3, 10, 110; Deleuzian relationality and, xxxix; etymology of, 9; imaginary of, 12, 34, 105, 112, 123; Moudileno on, 118; philosophy of, 9, 22–23, 101–2; poetics of, 9–10, 16, 21–24, 42–43, 73; politics of, 45; totality in, 129; *Tout-monde* and, 10, 12–13, 27; "uncertains" of, 101–2; universalization and, 104

Relation-identity, 9, 11

renversement ("overthrowing"), 53, 65

rhizome(s), xxxviii, xl, 2, 35, 92, 120; identity and, xxxix, 10; quantification and, 122; *Tout-monde* and, 69

Rice, Condoleezza, 138n9

Rimbaud, Arthur, 29, 32
"root-identity," 10, 41, 101

Said, Edward, 20, 130, 139n2
Santí, Enrico Mario, xxiii–xxiv, xli
Sarkozy, Nicolas, xxix
Sartorius: le roman des Batoutos (Glissant), xxvi, 34–36, 44–53, 58–64, 103; Cailler on, 59–60; origin of, 106; *Tout-monde* and, 71
Senghor, Léopold, 18–19
slave trade, xvi, 46–47, 68; creolization and, 11, 23, 88
slavery, 7; colonialism and, xviii, 80, 92; Faulkner on, xxvi, 41; legacy of, 11; museum of, xxix; Watts on, 92
"slime" (*limon*), 38–39
Smart, Barry, 103
Soleil de la conscience (Glissant), xxx, 70, 95, 97; on chaos, 95; on "dialectical consummation," 21; on oneness, 128; on Relation, 10, 101; on universality/particularity, 19
Southern University (Baton Rouge), 56–57
Spivak, Gayatri Chakravorty, 20, 41, 130
Stalin, Joseph, 18, 104
Suk, Jeannie, xix, xl
system-thinking, 18, 126–27; archipelagic thinking versus, 8–9, 114–15; "hidden truth" of, 41

teleology, 67–68, 82, 92–94, 114; of *Tout-monde*, 69–80, 129
theory of everything, 116–17

time travel, 80–91
"time-world" (*temps-monde*), 25, 31
Toledo, Camille de, 26–28
totalitarianism, 10, 17–18, 104
totality-world, 17, 22, 54
Toumson, Roger, 108
Toussaint Louverture, xiv, xv
Tout-monde ("Whole-world"), xxii, 1–34, 107, 123, 129; aesthetics and, 21–24; Chamoiseau on, 119; definitions of, 1–3, 13; erratic dimension of, 115; globalization and, xxv, 1, 14, 121; Hegelian philosophy and, 15–17; *ici-là* and, 93; *langages/langues* and, xxxv; opacity and, 42, 66; paradoxes of, 28–34; Prieto on, 30–31; Relation *and*, 10, 12–13, 27; rhizome and, 69; translations of, 2; universality and, 121–23; utopian, 67, 92–93
Tout-monde (Glissant's novel), xxvii, 7–8, 21, 31, 59, 67–80, 106, 120; creole culture in, 124; as "exploded novel," 71, 91; Kemedjio on, 138n1; *Le quatrième siècle* and, 70, 71, 75–76, 91–93; teleology of, 69–80
Towa, Marcien, xxxvii
tragedy, 62–63, 65
transparency, 38, 44, 66. See also opacity
Trujillo Molina, Rafael Leónidas, 126

"uncertains" (*incertains*), 101–2
"uncreated world," 33
"universal intellectual" (Foucault), xxviii, 103, 125

universal-particular relationship, 3, 18, 19, 33, 104, 110, 123
unpredictability, of creolization, 3–7, 39, 104, 116, 120–21
"utopian poetics," xxxii
utopianism, xv, xxxv, 63–64, 132; *Tout-monde* and, 67, 92–93

Valéry, Paul, 15
Van Haesendonck, Kristian, xvi
Villepin, Dominique de, xxix
vitalism, xxxix, 54, 116, 127, 129–30

Wahl, Jean, xxx

Walcott, Derek, 118
Wald Lasowski, Aliocha, 114
Watts, Richard, 41, 91–92
West, xviii, 113; atavistic cultures of, 11, 47, 48, 101, 126; continental thought of, 8, 20, 98, 109, 112–15; humanism of, 38–39; as project, 105, 123, 125–26
Whitman, Walt, 95
Wing, Betsy, 53–54
World Literature, xxv, 25. *See also littérature-monde* movement

Yugoslavia, breakup of, 12, 133